TRIADIC MYSTICISM

The Mystical Theology of the Śaivism of Kashmir

TRIADIC MYSTICISM

The Mystical Theology of the Śaivism of Kashmir

PAUL E. MURPHY

MOTILAL BANARSIDASS
Delhi Varanasi Patna Madras

Head Office: Bungalow Road, Delhi 110 007
Branches: Chowk, Varanasi 221 001
Ashok Rajpath, Patna 800 004
6 Appar Swamy Koil Street, Mylapore,
Madras 600 004

First Published : 1986

ISBN: 81-208-0010-9

Printed in India by Jainendra Prakash Jain at Shri Jainendra Press, A-45 Naraina, Phase I, New Delhi 110 028 and published by Narendra Prakash Jain for Motilal Banarsidass, Delhi 110 007.

To my wife

JOAN

PREFACE

The monistic Śaivism of Kashmir with its threefold composition—the Gradation School, the Family School, and the Vibration School—is theologically the most impressive of the many Śaiva systems. Principally because of its triadic structure, the literature often refers to Kashmir Śaivism by the term *Trika*, which may be translated as Triadism. The system can be traced through its literature back to the ninth century; how much earlier may have been its origins, it is not easy to determine. However, we know that the earliest evidence of Śaivism is the description by Patañjali (second century, B.C.) of its austere practices. But despite its ancient foundations, it is rather surprising that due recognition has not been accorded to the teachings of this great Indic faith. In the West, Triadism, Śaivism's outstanding system of theology, remains virtually unknown to student and layman alike. Especially Catholic theologians are somewhat in the dark as to its fundamentals. Therefore, it is a virgin field for scholarly research, and it is to help rectify this problem that the following study of Triadic Mysticism is undertaken.

Although each of the three schools has its own chief exponent, transmitters, and literary works, they all emphasize different aspects of the same metaphysical foundation—the concept of Thirty-six Manifestations or Categories. The Supreme Śiva as ultimate Principle, pure undifferentiated Consciousness, transcendent beyond the Categories, through a sequence of emanations, including His Mirific Power, gradually evolves through its wall of Illusion into the phenomenal world of multiplicity and thus becomes differentiated.

Triadism follows the traditional tripartite structure of theology: (1) the Supreme Śiva or God in Himself; (2) the emanation of the multiplicity of creation from Himself; and (3) a return or reabsorption of that creation into Himself, following a sequence that exactly reverses the order of manifestation and completes the cycle.

The goal of the yogī is to seek the means of liberation which is best suited to him in accordance with the intensity of grace he has received. It is precisely in the ways of deliverance that one

Triadic school is distinguished from another. Although the three schools are in general agreement as to the nature and role of the ultimate Reality, they differ in the Ways that It is to be realized.

The Ways are four: the Individual, the Energic, the Divine (or of Śiva), and the Null. The first two are grouped under the Inferior Path, consisting of ascending degrees of mystical progression, and the latter two form the Superior Path of no degrees or of instantaneous deliverance. The main purpose of this treatise is to examine and compare the major characteristics of each of these methods.

More specifically, the format consists of four chapters: Chapter I, *History and Metaphysics*, offers an historical sketch of the rise of Triadic Śaivism, together with a review of the historical development of the principal schools. Particular emphasis will be placed on the teachings and literary accomplishments of Triadism's principal theologians and propagators; for, it is from these primary sources that the metaphysics and philosophy of the system developed. The most renowned of all the theologians of Triadism is Abhinavagupta (cir. 950-1015). His life and major literary works shall be discussed somewhat in detail, for Abhinava wrote extensively in all areas of Triadic philosophy. He, more than any other, has had profound influence on the system's development and on the leading theologians who succeeded him. Indeed, without such treatment this book would be incomplete. The original works of these theologians—especially those of Abhinava and the devotional poets of Kashmir—are the primary sources for this work. The efforts of various modern authors comprise the secondary sources.

The second half of the chapter proposes a summary of the Triadic metaphysics of the thirty-six categories of cosmic manifestation which results in man's being held in the bondage of ignorance concerning his true nature. Only through the grace of Śiva, the Energic Fulmination, which descends upon man in varying intensities, can the latter be liberated and return to oneness in the divine.

Chapter II, *Gnostic Triadism: The Ways to Liberation*, is the principal chapter; it explores the four Ways, the very foundation of the three Triadic Schools, of delivering the soul from the bondage of ignorance. The Śaiva yogī chooses, as we stated above, the Way best suited to himself; hence, from the Inferior Path, inspired by little to moderate grace, the yogī advances to the Superior Path, achieved through the reception of intense grace.

Chapter III, *Devotional Triadism,* presents a change from the gnostic theology of the various schools. All major religious disciplines experience some sort of conflict between knowledge (gnosis) and love (devotion). Some theologies begin gnostically and confront devotional tendencies at a later period, while others find the process reversed. Hindu theology is representative of the former trend, being predominantly gnostic prior to the tenth century—up to the time of Abhinavagupta, Triadism's last great gnostic theologian.

This chapter is concerned with the new trend toward devotionalism—evidenced in the chief writings of Kashmir Śaivism's three most influential and inspirational poets. The authors are studied together under topical headings. Historically, the first poet is Bhaṭṭa Nārāyaṇa (ninth century), whose poem, *The Wishing-Jewel of Praise* (*Stavacintāmaṇi*) is perhaps the earliest example of Triadic devotionalism. He is followed by Utpaladeva (ninth-tenth centuries) who is also of great prominence in the historical development of Triadism; his poem *The Series of Hymns to Śiva* (*Śivastotrāvalī*) is reported to be the most beautiful of the Śaiva love songs. Finally, The Sayings of Lallā, the fourteenth century poetess, are comparatively examined.

In order to show the influence of Ṣūfī mysticism in the poetry of Lallā, I draw several parallels from the mystical poems of Rūmī, the thirteenth century Persian poet of great renown.

Chapter IV, the final chapter, *Triadic and Catholic Parallels,* attempts to compare the Gnostic and Devotional Triadism previously treated with the writings of various Catholic mystics which incorporate both speculative and mystic tendencies. The chapter is organized under four archetypes, each with a contrasting pair of concepts: (1) *Breaking through the Energy of Śiva and the Return to Light*: the obscuring quality of the Mirific Power in Triadic metaphysics and the obscuration of faith in the writings of the great seventeenth century Thomist, John of St. Thomas. (2) *Sacrificial Self-Annihilation:* the concepts of theocentrism, self-abasement, and sacrifice in their Triadic gnostic form, and in their theist interpretation in the seventeenth century writings of the French School of Bérulle, Condren, and Olier. (3) *The Dark Night of Mystical Awakening:* The Dark Night of Śiva as depicted in Devotional Triadism, and the *Dark Night of the Soul*, by the mystical Doctor of the Church, St. John of the Cross. (4) *The Impassible State of Deification:* the Triadic concepts of impassibility or passionlessness and deification, and their Christian parallels in the *Miscellanies* (*Stromata*), the major work of Clement of Alexandria, the second century Greek Father, on the subject of Christian Gnosticism.

The archetypes distinguish the phenomenal from the transcendental or the manifested universe from the unmanifested Absolute. The first three deal with this relationship as a gnostic experience, employing the metaphors of light (both from radiance and fire) and darkness; the fourth experiences this relationship from the contemplative state of mystical repose resulting from the attainment of gnosis. This comparative method of study is essentially important, not only to the understanding of the common categories but to the deeper knowledge of the specific interpretations given to them by both Triadic and Catholic theologies. Furthermore, it is my contention that in no other major religious tradition can these comparisons be found as qualitatively and quantitatively as they are found in Catholicism.

I conclude this work with a Catholic reflection on what is perhaps the most profound level of comparison between Triadism and Catholicism, namely (in Catholic terminology), the Beatific Vision. I contrast various elements of two fundamental models, representative of the two theological disciplines, drawing, for the Catholic model, upon the insights of the great Baroque theologians, Suárez and John of St. Thomas. After comparing these models, it is my opinion that the two traditions are recipients of the same divine revelation, which is recognizable as basically identical, although it is conceptually articulated in diverse metaphysical models.

What seems to emerge from this overall study, therefore, is that Triadism touches on the most profound problems of mysticism; the conclusions reached after careful analyses are at times remarkably similar to those of Catholicism—more so than any other major religion—and at other times the interpretations are strikingly divergent. These mystical intuitions touch the very core of mystical experience—the unitive experience of God.

As a general rule throughout this literary effort, the original Sanskrit terms are placed in parenthesis (printed in lower case, except for the capitalized titles of primary sources and for certain proper nouns) after the English equivalent only in its initial usage; thereafter, with rare exceptions, just the English terminology is employed. An extensive glossary of Sanskrit terms peculiar to Triadism is included at the end of this study for ready reference. However, the primary source material cited in the footnotes is identified by Sanskrit abbreviations of their original titles. A list for this purpose, as well as other abbreviations utilized for convenience, is inserted immediately preceding the bibliography. The Index of Subjects is in English. It is assumed the reader will first encounter the Sanskrit term in the text proper; after referring to its English equivalent in the glossary, a search of the index for the equivalent term or concept may then be conducted.

And now, to the most pleasurable task of all—a word or two of indebtedness.

There are many persons, some of whom I have never met personally, who have assisted me, directly and indirectly, in researching and writing the doctoral dissertation upon which this volume is based. It would be presumptuous of me to attempt to name them all, and rather than offend through omission, my appreciation, for the most part, I willingly extend to them generally and anonymously; nevertheless, it is genuine and sincere.

To all my past teachers at Fordham University, including those who have since left or are now deceased, who have guided me in course work and consultation, I tender my heartfelt gratitude.

To teachers and staff at other universities and libraries with whom I have consulted, and for their aid in obtaining books and manuscripts that were otherwise unavailable to me, I am deeply appreciative.

To my peers and friends, both inside and outside academe, who have encouraged me over the twelve years of graduate studies to "hang in there," my personal thanks.

Although I feel it necessary to acknowledge my gratitude to so many in this rather "impersonal" way, it would indeed be inexcusable for me not to specifically mention those whose help in this endeavor has been most felt.

To my former mentor, Dr. José Pereira, I owe a debt difficult to describe and virtually impossible to repay. His assistance, encouragement, and friendship, shown in countless ways, have been a sustaining inspiration to me; for, without his support and expertise—never unwillingly or reservedly offered—this task, I am convinced, would never have been accomplished.

To my typist, Mrs. Lena Giordano, who did such an excellent job in so short a time, amid the pressures of family responsibilities, I am also indebted.

And finally, "saving the best wine for last," I owe eternal gratitude to my wife, Joan, and to our eight children. In assuming the role of full-time student, while simultaneously taking on the variegated activities of husband, father, police officer, and teacher, my efforts were shamefully dissipated and neglectful in all these categories. Yet, my wife bore this burden for two-thirds of our married life with a strength and patience that I am only now beginning to appreciate but will never fully understand.

PAUL E. MURPHY

CONTENTS

CHAPTER 1

HISTORY AND METAPHYSICS

A. History

Triadism is the consummate theology of the religion of Śiva, a divinity in whom the contraries of the ascetic, the amorous, the terrible, and the tranquil coincide. His origins can be traced to the first known Indian civilization, that of the Indus Valley, contemporary with, but more extensive than the Mesopotamian and the Egyptian. Purity and virile potency were its ideals, and one of its prominent gods was an ascetic with erect penis, surrounded by powerful beasts—a god obviously identical with the Śiva of classical Hinduism. Yet, Śaivism, as we know it, did not emerge until the concept of an impersonal God arose during the age of the Upaniṣads;[1] it was not until the formation of the six great philosophical systems (ca. 400-200 B.C.)[2] that Śaivism developed into a complete theistic system within the orthodox fold.[3]

1. *Rise of Triadism*

However, I shall not concern myself with the uncertain origins and immemorial history of the Śaiva religion, except as related to

[1]R.C. Majumdar, "Evolution of Religio-Philosophic Culture in India," in *The Cultural Heritage of India*, vol. 4: *The Religions* (Calcutta: The Ramakrishna Mission Institute of Culture, 1956), pp. 35-36. Hereafter abbreviated *CHI* We first meet the God, Rudra (in later portions of the *Veda* He is described as Śiva), in the *Śvetāśvatara Upaniṣad*, III. 2. Here the Highest Reality is identified with Rudra who is responsible for the three functions of creation, protection or maintenance, and destruction. The thrust is unmistakably monistic: "Truly Rudra is one, there is no place for a second..." See *The Principal Upaniṣads*, edited with introduction, text, translation and notes by S. Radhakrishnan (London: George Allen & Unwin Ltd., New York: Humanities Press Inc., (1953), pp. 725.

[2]Only the era designation B.C. will be used; in references to the Christian era, the A.D. abbreviation will be omitted.

[3]Majumdar, pp. 39-40.

Triadism and its theology. I shall begin with the mythological account of its scriptures or "Sacred Traditions" (the *āgamas*).[1]

Śaivas have always believed that their *āgamas* (*tantras*) have, like the *Vedas*, enjoyed eternal existence since they are divine speech or supreme Word.[2] Originally consisting of billions of verses, they gradually diminished as they were handed down along the hierarchy of divine beings. During our own corrupt age (the *kali yuga*), those sages in possession of the remnant *āgamas* disappeard to hidden places, and the Tantric tradition also vanished, leaving a void of spiritual darkness.[3] Then Śiva, moved to compassion for man who was deprived of the *āgamas*, revived the tradition and directed that it be divided into three categories—monist (*advaita*), dualist (*dvaita*), and dualist-monist (*dvaitādvaita*). He entrusted each to the care of his three mind-born sons, Tryambaka, Amardaka, and Śrīnātha, respectively.[4] Thus, towards the end of the fourth century, the different philosophical schools of Śaivism arose.[5] Tryambaka was the first man to propagate Śaiva monism and is therefore recognized as the founder of the Advaita Tantric School.

Traditional Tantric lore seems to have entered Kashmir via various immigrant families around the middle of the eighth century A.D.; we have historical evidence of at least two such families. King Lalitāditya of Kashmir (ca. 725-61), in one of his expeditions, arrived in Kānyakubja, which, in the seventh century, was the most prestigious of Indian imperial capitals and former metropolis of Harṣa (606-97), an outstanding monarch and poet of ancient India. There he met Atrigupta, the earliest known of Abhinava's ancestors, and was so impressed by his great learning that he induced the scholar to migrate to Kashmir with his entire family

[1]When texts are written (especially those that trace a particular tradition) for religious purposes, unfortunately, we often find mythical material mixed in with the historical. Researchers have always been confronted with the difficult problem of trying to separate the two materials.

[2]K.C. Pandey, *Abhinavagupta: An Historical and Philosophical Study*, 2nd ed., rev. and enl. (Varanasi: Chowkhamba Sanskrit Series Office, 1963), p. 132.

[3]Ibid., pp. 133-35.

[4]Ibid., p. 135.

[5]Pandey arrives at this approximate date because Somānanda (ca. 850) speaks of himself as the nineteenth descendent of Tryambaka. Allowing for the usual twenty-five years per generation, we arrive at the fourth century, for Tryambaka (see pp. 137-38).

(ca. 740) and settle there permanently.[1] About the same time, Saṅgamāditya, great, great grandfather of the renowned Somānanda (systematizer of the Self-Awareness or *pratyabhijñā* school of Triadism) ceased his wanderings by settling down in Kashmir.[2] Some time after the separate arrivals of these two families, the ancestors of Vasugupta, author of the *Aphorisms on Śiva* (*Śiva Sūtra*) and founder of the Self-Awareness school, also settled in Kashmir. Thus, the soil was prepared for planting the seeds of Triadism, the harvest of which was to be gathered a century later by Vasugupta and Somānanda.

Other conditions also aided the advent and growth of Triadism. We know that the ancient faith of Kashmir was polytheistic with a leaning toward ritualistic Śaivism. Among the Hindus, Śiva was the most popular divinity; but in the century preceding Atrigupta's, the Buddha received the greater honors. Buddhism had entered Kashmir during the reign of Aśoka (237-32 B.C.) and had influenced the local faith for over nine centuries. It was there that Buddhism had witnessed the florescence of some of its greatest theological schools—Omnirealism (*sarvāstivāda*) and Critical Idealism (*prāmāṇyavāda*). However by the mid-eighth century it was in decline—a process hastened by the advent of Hindu Tantrism.[3] Triadism soon came into being and spread rapidly; it substituted monism for the dualism of early āgamic teaching,[4] combining Tantrism's mystical fervor with Buddhist Idealism's philosophical sophistication. About a century later (ca. 950), Triadism's greatest theologian, Abhinavagupta, was born.

Before we discuss the life and works of Abhinava, let us first direct our attention to these early propagators of Triadism in Kashmir and to their literary efforts upon which the three major schools or systems of monistic Śaivism were built.

[1] Ibid., pp. 5-6.

[2] Ibid., pp. 135-36.

[3] It is customary to link Hinduism's triumph over Buddhism with Śaṅkara (see Pandey, p. 151; Majumdar, p. 51), and that in any place where this triumph occurred it was due to his presence. However, there is more myth than reality to this belief. Śaṅkara was not the reviver of Hinduism, for, if this were so, the Triadists of Kashmir show no sign of it. In fact, he was not an accomplished dialectician—he did not demonstrate a profound knowledge of Buddhism, which was more than a match for his logic.

[4] Majumdar, p. 51.

2. *Schools and Early Propagators of Triadism*

There is some confusion when referring to one or more of the Triadic schools due to the ambiguous use of terms; for instance, *Trika* (Triadism) has been used for each school, both individually and collectively. Similarly, the terms *spanda* (Vibration or Vibrancy) and *pratyabhijñā* (Self-Awareness) have been at times more narrowly understood, referring to only one school; at other times they have been interpreted more broadly, encompassing all of Triadism. Moreover, it is not always clear from the context just what meaning is to be assigned to these terms.

Pandey rightly says that it is just as wrong to call the entire monistic Śaiva thought of Kashmir, *pratyabhijñā* or *spanda*, as it would be to refer to India as "Calcutta" or "Bombay"; they are parts of a whole.[1] He enumerates the various meanings of *Trika*; chief among these are the following:

(1) Self-Awareness or "Recognition," a term which Abhinava also uses when referring to the entire Śaiva thought as presented in his *Light on the Tantras* (*Tantrāloka*);[2]

(2) the triad of monist *āgamas*, which are held to be the chief authority in Triadism—of the *Sorceress* (*Siddhā*), the *Name* (*Nāmaka*) and the *Engarlanded Goddess* (*Mālinī*). The latter is Triadism's principal scripture; the first two are seldom referred to, if at all.

(3) the three triads or powers: Supreme or *parā* (Śiva, His Energy, and Their union), Non-Supreme or *aparā* (Śiva, His Energy, and Man), and the Supreme-Non-Supreme or *parāparā* (the three powers together);

(4) the three aspects of the relationship between the transcendent and the phenomenal—Identity (*abheda*), Difference-in-Identity (*bhedābheda*), and Difference (*bheda*);

(5) the *kula* or Family school, since it acknowledges the three powers referred to above and which are represented by the short vowels: A, I, and U.[3]

Actually, there is no contradiction in terms if one realizes that it was the Vibration or Self-Awareness school that produced the speculative and systematic theologians, while the other schools were composed of, generally, unspeculative practitioners. There-

[1]Pandey, pp. 294-95.
[2]*TA*, I, 28-30.
[3]Pandey, pp. 294-97; see also, pp. 597-603 for additional meanings.

fore, since the Vibration school possessed both speculation and practice, it was able to absorb the other schools.

I will now give a brief sketch of the historical development of the Triadic schools, limiting myself to origins and chief exponents. The major tenets of each school will be discussed in the next chapter.

(a) *Family (of Energies) School*

It has already been stated that the three Tantric schools of Śaivism (monist, dualist, and dualist-monist) arose toward the end of the fourth century. It is believed that a fourth school was founded at this time by Ardha Tryambaka ("half" Tryambaka), a descendant of the daughter of Tryambaka—the first propagator of Śaiva monism. It was called the School of the Family (*kula*), because its ultimate principle was an undifferenced totality of the group or "family" of Categories emanant from itself, particularly of the *two* principles, masculine and feminine (Śiva the Energizer and His Energy), of this family. In Jayaratha's words,

> the plenary Light, intolerant of the specifications of Śiva, Energy and the other categories, the ineffable, supreme Recollection, in essence, the unexcelled—this Light is the ultimate Reality. And only He, desirous through His liberty of irradiating the universe, manifests the natures of Śiva and Energy in His interior being.[1]

It was also called *kaula* ("pertaining to the Family") or Familial school. Mythically, Familism is traced back through different eons or ages until, in our own *kali* age, King Macchanda (also known as Mīna), was recognized as the founder and great sage who passed the tradition on to his sons.[2]

We know little of the successive teachers of the Family school for the next four or five centuries, but we are able to approximate the earliest time that it can be associated with Kashmir. *The Trigesimal on the Supreme Goddess* (*Parātriṃśikā*) is a Tantric work which deals with the *Non-Family* (*akula*), *Family* (*kula*), and *Familial Energy* (*kaulikīśakti*) and, therefore, plainly a work on the Family system. Somānanda (ca. 855) wrote a commentary on its teachings, as did Abhinavagupta and many others.[3] However, it

[1]Commentary on *TA*, II. 75 as quoted in Pandey, p. 842.
[2]Pandey, pp. 546-48.
[3]Ibid., pp. 488-89.

seems that the Family tradition received little attention in Kashmir after Somānanda—to the extent that Abhinava felt it necessary to leave Kashmir and travel to Jālandhara to receive instruction in its teachings from Śambhunātha, pupil of Somadeva.[1] Consequently, since we have no evidence of its existence in Kashmir prior to Somānanda, we cannot date its origin there before 850.

Unfortunately, most of the Tantric literature upon which the Family tradition is based has not come down to us; we learn of it through reference only.[2] The *Kālī Family* (*Kālīkula*) is an important semi-āgamic work of unknown authorship which delineates the line of teachers from very early times, lists the days for the performances of the Family rituals, and recognizes Familism to be the essence of all the *āgamas*.[3] It is considered an important work because in Familism the teacher is the primary bestower of grace, and, as such, he is highly revered by his devotees.[4]

There were at least five authors in addition to Somānanda who lived in ninth-century Kashmir and wrote on the Family system;[5] most important for our purposes, however, is Kallaṭa (850). We mention him in particular, because he not only wrote at least one work on Familism, according to Abhinava,[6] but he also wrote on the Self-Awareness system, as I will soon indicate. Abhinava often refers to him as a thinker of this latter tradition. There are other authors besides Abhinava and Kallaṭa who belong to several traditions—for example, Somānanda, Utpaladeva, and Lakṣmaṇagupta. This versatility makes them all the more important to Triadic studies. Śambhunātha (tenth century), Abhinava's teacher, as I have mentioned, was greatly revered among the successors of

[1]Ibid., p. 144.

[2]Pandey lists and summarizes the eight original *āgamas* of this school, see pp. 550-76.

[3]Abhinava refers to this work often in his *TA*; see Chap. XXVIII. 7, and Chap. XXIX. 23.

[4]Included in this category of teacher is his *dūtī* (wife or female consort).

[5]Pandey lists the following: Īśvara Śiva, who wrote a commentary on the *Vāmakeśvara Tantra* which stressed *kula* philosophy; Śaṅkararāśi and Viśvārarta, contemporaries of Īśvara Śiva; and Dīpikānātha, who, according to Pandey, Jayaratha says wrote the first commentary on the *Vāmakeśvara* (see pp. 587-81).

[6]*TA*, Chap. XXIX. 88. This work treats the importance of the *dūtī* in imparting instructions to the initiated.

Tryambaka. He wrote the *Teaching on the True Import of the Tantras* (*Tantrasadbhāvaśāsana*), a work which deals with formulas (*mantras*) to be used by Familists seeking different occult powers (*siddhis*).[1]

Familism follows two paths to liberation: the Individual or Inferior Way (*āṇavopāya*), and the Divine or Śiva Way (*śāmbhavopāya*) which concentrates on Śiva's infinity and freedom.[2]

(b) *Gradation School*

The Gradation (or *krama*) School was founded by Śivānandanātha in Kashmir toward the end of the seventh and the beginning of the eighth centuries of our era.[3] It is distinct from the other two schools, although Abhinava points out that it is akin to Familism, especially in the concept of the twelve Consuming Energies (*kālīs*).[4] The school receives its name because it holds that the Ultimate is realizable only through successive stages. These are three of its other names: the *kālī* System or *kālīnaya* (because the Ultimate Reality is *kālī*); the Great System or *mahānaya*; and, as Maheśvarānanda calls it, The System of Great Meaning or "Absolute Sense" (*mahārtha darśana*).[5]

Unfortunately, the works of the early teachers—such as Śivānanda, Eraka, and Somarāja—have been lost. The vast amount of literature on the Gradation School is known to us by reference only.

The following are among the more important works on this school by unknown authors:

(1) *The Aphorisms on Gradation* (*Krama Sūtra*), a work in aphoristic style and commented on by Kṣemarāja;

(2) *The Five Hundred Verses* (*Pañcaśatikā*), which presented the idea of twelve *kālīs*; and

(3) *The Gradation Hymn* (*Krama Stotra*), written prior to Abhinava, on which he wrote his famous commentary, *The Gradation Frolic* (*Kramakeli*).[6] Śivānanda (mid-ninth century) was one of the

[1]Ibid., Chap. XXX. 24.

[2]José Pereira, *Hindu Theology: A Reader*, edited with an introduction and notes by Jose Pereira (New York: Image Book, 1976), p. 360.

[3]Ibid.

[4]*TA*, III, 157; see also, *MVV*, 20.

[5]Pandey, pp. 462-63.

[6]Ibid., pp. 471-76.

known early teachers; he, like Abhinava and others, wrote on all three schools. From Abhinava and his successors, we have these works:

(1) *The Gradation Frolic* just mentioned;

(2) Abhinava's *Gradation Hymn*, different from but in close accord with the one cited above;

(3) *Hymn to the Circle of Deities Abiding in the Body* (*Dehastha-devatācakra Stotra*) by Abhinava, which extols the various deities associated with different parts of the body; and

(4) Maheśvarānanda's *Bouquet of Great Meaning* (*Mahārtha-mañjarī*) which is basically a work on the Gradation System, although, as an example of the integrated school, it treats the other Triadic schools as well.

The Gradation School, therefore, can be traced in an unbroken line from the end of the seventh century in Kashmir right up to Abhinavagupta, who received instructions in it from Lakṣmaṇagupta.[1] Based on the Energic Way (*śāktopāya*), it stresses the Goddess, the Wheel of Energies, and, like Familism, ritual sex.[2]

(c) *Self-Awareness or Vibration School*

Theologically, the most important of all the Triadic schools is the Self-Awareness or Vibration School, which is based on the Null Way (*anupāya*) and stresses Śiva's non-duality.

Vasugupta (ca. 825-50 scholastic generation) is credited as having founded the school in Kashmir,[3] although he did not take up the system as a whole, nor is he responsible for its name. In his *Aphorisms on Śiva*, he gave a systematic form to the philosophical ideas of the monistic Tantras. Vasu's *Memorial Verses on Vibration* (*Spanda Kārikā*), also called *Aphorisms on Vibration* (*Spanda Sūtra*) is an amplification of the fundamental principles of Śaivism as given in the *Aphorisms on Śiva*. Bhaṭṭa Kallaṭa, a pupil of Vasugupta, also wrote an *Aphorisms on Vibration* and commentaries on the two works of his master which were mentioned above.[4]

Somānanda, a contemporary of Kallaṭa (ca. 850-75 scholastic generation), gave Triadism its first systematic form in his *Vision of* Śiva (*Śivadṛṣṭi*). He also wrote a commentary on this treatise

[1]Ibid., pp. 482-89.
[2]Pereira, p. 360.
[3]Ibid.
[4]Pandey, pp. 154-56.

and one on the *Trigesimal on the Supreme Goddess.* Abhinava claimed he followed Somānanda's commentary when he wrote his own on the same tantric text.[1]

Utpaladeva (end of the ninth and first half of the tenth centuries) was the son and pupil of Somānanda. Of his eleven known works, three are famous:

(1) *The Memorial Verses on the Supreme Lord's Self-Awareness* (*Īśvarapratyabhijñā Kārikā*) was the first work on the Self-Awareness School as such and, supposedly, gave the school its name. It is also important because of Abhinava's two commentaries, the *Examination* (*Vimarśinī*), and the *Examination of the Gloss* (*Vivṛti Vimarśinī*)—his last two known works, as I will again mention in the next section.

(2) *The Gloss on the Memorial Verses on the Supreme Lord's Self-Awareness* (*Īśvarapratyabhijñā Vṛtti*) is a brief commentary to clarify certain portions of the *Memorial Verses.*

(3) *The Commentary on the Memorial Verses of the Supreme Lord's Self-Awareness* (*Īśvarapratyabhijñā Ṭīkā*) was a detailed commentary on his *Memorial Verses* and one of the few books of accepted authority on the Self-Awareness philosophy. Unfortunately, it seems to be forever lost; it was on this work that Abhinava wrote his famous commentary, *The Great Examination* (*Bṛhatī Vimarśinī*).[2]

Lakṣmaṇagupta (literary period ca. 950-75) was son and pupil of Utpaladeva. Although no works of his have been discovered, he is somewhat famous because he was Abhinava's teacher in the Gradation and Self-Awareness systems.[3]

Before I treat the life and works of Abhinavagupta, there is yet another school that merits our attention—the Integrated School, established by Abhinava himself.

(d) *Integrated School*

Abhinava greatly influenced the literary careers of many theologians in Kashmir in the centuries that followed his own lifetime;

[1]Ibid., pp. 161-62. Pandey claims that the Self-Awareness School "originated in Kashmir from the pen of Somānanda..." (p. 489). However, whether he or Vasugupta was actually the founder of this school is a moot point and of no real consequence to our study.

[2]Ibid., pp. 162-64.

[3]Ibid., pp. 164-65.

two of the most famous of his successors who carried on his work, especially in the integrated area of Triadism, were Kṣemarāja and Maheśvarānanda.

(1) Kṣemarāja (second quarter of the eleventh century) was Abhinava's cousin and foremost among his pupils and commentator-theologians. Like his great teacher, he wrote on all three schools and on the subjects of *tantra*, poetics, and Śaiva philosophy. Perhaps most often cited from among his eighteen known works, as listed by Pandey,[1] are the following:

(i) *Flash on the Tantra of Self-Will* (*Svacchandoddyota*), a commentary on the *Tantra of Self-Will* (*or Freedom: Svacchanda Tantra*);

(ii) *Ascertainment of Vibrancy* (*Spanda Nirṇaya*), a commentary on the whole of Vasugupta's *Memorial Verses on Vibrancy*;

(iii) *The Heart of Self-Awareness* or *The Secret of Recognition* (*Pratyabhijñāhṛdayam*)[2] and a commentary on it; and

(iv) a gloss (*Vivṛti*) on *The Wishing Jewel of Praise* of Bhaṭṭa Nārāyaṇa; the latter was mentioned in the Introduction and shall be treated in Chapter III.

(2) Maheśvarānanda (twelfth century) "He whose joy is the Great Lord (Śiva)," was the surname given to Gorakṣa by his guru, Mahāprakāśa (the "Great Light"), at the moment of the disciple's initiation. He was born around the twelfth century in South India, in the Tamil country or the Coḷa region (so called because it was the land of the Coḷa emperors). He is the greatest of the non-Kashmiri Triadists known to us. Although he received instructions in all three philosophical systems of Triadism, he claimed that he owed his illumination to the Self-Awareness system. However, he belonged to the Great Meaning (*mahārtha*) or Great School (*mahānaya*) mystical tradition, identical to the Northern Tradition, and more particularly to the Yoginī Union (*yoginīmelāpa*) sect whose tradition differs very little from that of the Family school.[3]

[1]Ibid., pp. 254-57.

[2]*Pratyabhijñāhṛdayam* (*The Secret of Recognition*), trans. with notes by K.F. Leidecker (Madras: The Adyar Library, 1938); see also trans.by Jaideva Singh: Motilal Banarsidass, 1963.

[3]Maheśvarānanda, *La Mahārthamañjarī de Maheśvarānanda, avec des Extraits du Parimala*, traduction et introduction par Lilian Silburn, Fasc. 29 (Paris: Publications de Institut de Civilisation Indienne, 1968), p. 9.

Maheśvarānanda wrote eleven known works; but only two—*The Bouquet of Great Meaning*, and his own commentary, *The Fragrance of the Bouquet of Great Meaning* (*Parimala*)—have come down to us. Although the work is basically from the Family school, it is actually a synthesis of all three schools. Gorakṣa was a very ardent follower of Abhinava and quotes him often; he also frequently cites Kṣemarāja's *The Heart of Self-Awareness.*[1]

If we look at a breakdown of the seventy verses of *The Bouquet*, we will realize how, like the *Light on the Tantras*, it is a synthesis of Triadic teaching.[2]

Almost all of the first half of his work is devoted to the Self-Awareness philosophy dealing with the thirty-seven categories (*tattvas*) of reality. He insists on the spontaneous Way of Self-Awareness (*vimarśopāya*,[3] also called *anupāya*, the Immediate or Null Way):

(1) The Primordial Unity of Light and Self-Awareness (vv. 1-11);

(2) Separation of Light from Self-Awareness: The Emanation of the Principles (vv. 12-25); and

(3) Return to Primordial Unity (vv. 26-33).

The author discovers, however, that in order to return to the Absolute, certain exercises become necessary. At this point, then, he turns to the Gradation School and its ascending stages—the progressive Way of Energy:

(4) The Energic Way (vv. 34-48).

Gorakṣa next deals with the Family system of liberation which culminates in the Divine Way, for the Gradation system finds its realization in the Family system. He concludes his poem by returning to the Self-Awareness concept of "Recognition"—that which is beyond all ways:

(5) Divine Way (vv. 49-63); and

(6) Null Way (vv. 64-70).

This brings us to the founder of the Integrated School, "Hinduism's greatest theologian, Abhinavagupta, the emperor of Indic speculation."[4]

[1]Pandey, pp. 272-73.

[2]We will follow Pereira's scheme, pp. 381-88.

[3]*MM* (Silburn), p. 71.

[4]Pereira, p. 42.

3. *Life and Works of Abhinavagupta*

As we have seen, Atrigupta was Abhinava's earliest known ancestor, who settled in Kashmir around 740. However, we know virtually nothing of his progenitors for the next hundred and fifty years until Abhinava mentions his grandfather, Varāhagupta, whom we can place at the beginning of the tenth century. His father was Narasiṁhagupta, alias Cukhulaka, a great scholar and devotee of Śiva; his mother was Vimalā, a devout woman greatly loved by her son. We are able to fix the literary activity of Abhinava from his dated works (from around 990-1015); and due to the vast amount of knowledge and maturity of style evidenced in his works, it would be quite logical to suppose he was in his thirties when he began to write. Thus, Abhinava was probably born between 950-60.[1]

He had an unquenchable thirst for learning, and he soon absorbed the knowledge that his father and other teachers in and around Kashmir had to impart. Still unsatisfied, he travelled outside his native province to learn the secrets of other religions, such as Buddhism and Jainism; all knowledge from whatever source, he felt, was worth the learning. Abhinava's mother died while he was yet a child, which caused his father to renounce the world and become an ascetic. It was also a turning point for Abhinava, for he too shunned worldly pleasures, vowed never to marry, and devoted his life to scholarship and Śiva worship.

Although he seems to have begun his literary career at a mature age, he wrote extensively on all three systems of Triadism—first on Gradation, which he probably learned initially. Although he praises it in his *Gradation Frolic*, he seems to have been unsatisfied with it. Then he turned successively to the Self-Awareness and Family systems.[2] His masterpiece was the *Light on the Tantras*, which we will refer to often. At the time of his death, some time after 1015, the date of his last known work, he had attained the state of the Liberated-in-Life (*jīvanmukta*). Little is known of his actual death; tradition has it that one day, as he finished work, he, along with 1,200 disciples, while reciting the *Paean on the Tremendous God* (*Bhairavastava*), walked into the Bhairava Cave for his

[1]Pandey, pp. 5-9.
[2]Ibid., pp. 11-16.

last trance and was never seen or heard from again. The cave exists to this day.[1]

It is not my intention here to treat all the works[2] of Abhinava, but only those that accentuate the mystical nature of Triadism. Therefore, it is sufficient for my purposes to follow, at least in content, the scheme of Pandey[3] and divide Abhinava's literary activities into three periods.[4]

(a) *Initial or First Theological Period*

We know that Abhinava's first literary efforts dealt with the Gradation system because of the early dates of the *Gradation Hymn* and the *Gradation Frolic*. The latter was a commentary, now lost, on an earlier Gradation Hymn of unknown authorship; it was his first work on the Gradation School. Abhinava treated certain *tantras* from a monistic (Triadic) viewpoint. During this period he also wrote the *Antecedent Pentad* (*Pūrva Pañcikā*), which, most unfortunately, has also been lost. It was a lengthy and detailed exposition on the *Tantra on the Triumph of the Engarlanded*

[1]Ibid., p. 23.

[2]Pandey lists forty-four known works of Abhinava (pp. 27-28), gives the general idea of twenty-four of his available works (pp. 43-77), and an extensive treatment of two enigmatic works—Abhinava's summary of Familism, *The Fifty Limit Verses* (*Paryantapañcāśika*) and his non-theological work, the *Gloss on the Verses of the Poet Ghaṭakarpara* (*Ghaṭakarparakulakavṛtti*).

[3]Pandey classifies Abhinava's literary activities under three chronological headings: *Tāntrika* (*Tantric*) Period, *Ālaṅkārika* (Poetic) Period, and Philosophical Period (pp. 41-43). Although I use the author's three periods, I do so only as a convenient way of referring to Abhinava's important chronological works; for, I consider the divisions of doubtful value. Stressing a Philosophical Period in contradistinction to a *Tantric* Period seems to lack validity, since there is much philosophy in the so-called *Tantric* Period. And the last, or so-called Philosophical Period is, except for the *Gītā*, all *Tantric*. Hence, while retaining the content of Pandey's classifications, I have retitled them, omitting reference to the terms, *Tantric* and Philosophical.

[4]Lilian Silburn adopts Pandey's periodic division in the *Le Paramārthasāra*, Texte Sanskrit Édité et Traduit par Lilian Silburn, Fasc. 5 (Paris: Institut de Civilisation Indienne, 1957), pp. 9-19.

N.B.: Original works such as the *PS* and *PHṛ* have been translated with commentary into various languages by different authors. To avoid confusion, when reference is made in the footnotes of this book to the translated or commented portion of one of these works, the modern author's name shall appear in parenthesis after the abbreviated title of the original source. When, however, the original source is quoted directly, no name shall appear in parenthesis.

Goddess (*Mālinīvijaya Tantra*), Triadism's most authoritative scripture.

Abhinava also contributed to Familist literature with his *Paean on the Tremendous God*, and the *Examination of the Trigesimal on the Supreme Goddess* (*Parātriṃśikāvivṛti*); the latter is a commentary on the *Trigesimal on the Supreme Goddess*, which is the conclusion to the *Tantra on Rudra's Coupling* (*Rudrayāmala Tantra*) and a work of great importance.[1]

The *Fifteen Verses on Enlightenment* (*Bodha Pañcadaśikā*) is the first of his dated works. A short composition on the basic principles of monistic Śaivism, it was supposedly written to help his less intelligent students grasp the fundamental tenets of his philosophy.[2]

The great genius of Abhinavagupta is best seen in his masterpiece, the *Light on the Tantras*, a voluminous work of thirty-seven chapters which, with the commentary of Jayaratha, fills twelve volumes. This work presents a detailed treatment of all the Triadic schools; it was the basis of his Integrated School, which was further developed by Kṣemarāja and Maheśvarānanda. Abhinava's three summaries of the *Light on the Tantras* soon followed—the *Essence of the Tantras* (*Tantrasāra*), the *Gathering of the Tantras* (*Tantroccaya*), and the *Seed of the Tantra Banyan* (*Tantravaṭadhānikā*).[3]

(b) *Intermediate or Poetic Period*

Toward the end of the *Light on the Tantras*, Abhinava's style and mood seem to become more poetic or aesthetic. Among the few known works of this transitional period were the following: the *New Eloquence* (*Abhinava Bhāratī*), a commentary on the *Treatise on the Dance* (*Nāṭya Śāstra*) of Bharata; the *Illumination of the Light of Suggestion* (*Dhvanyāloka Locana*), a commentary on Ānandavardhana's epoch making *Light of Suggestion* (*Dhvanyāloka*) and a lost work, *Exposition of the Wonder of Poetry* (*Kāvyakautuka Vivaraṇa*), a commentary on the work of his teacher, Bhaṭṭa Totā, in the area of dramatic art or aesthetic pleasure—

It is to be understood in the latter case that the cited section has been translated by my former mentor, Dr. Pereira, specifically for this publication; exceptions shall be appropriately noted.

[1] *PS* (Silburn), p. 9.

[2] Pandey, p. 43.

[3] *PS* (Silburn), p. 10.

dealing with the theories of Sentiment (*rasa*) and Suggested Sense (*dhvani*).[1]

(c) *Final or Second Theological Period*

Three principal works are assigned to this period:

(1) *The Compendium on the Gītā* (*Bhagavadgītāsaṃgraha*) is a work which gives a Śaiva interpretation to the most famous of Hindu scriptures.

(2) *The Short Examination* (*Laghuvivṛti*) or *The Examination of the Memorial Verses of the Supreme Lord's Self-Awareness* comments on the *Memorial Verses* of Utpaladeva. This former work is divided into four sections dealing, in successive order, with knowledge (*jñāna*), activity (*kriyā*), the Thirty-six Principles or Categories (*tattvas*) of Triadism, and a final section which deals with the essence of Supreme Śiva and summarizes the three previous sections.

(3) *The Examination of the Gloss of the Memorial Verses on the Supreme Lord's Self-Awareness*, or *The Great Examination* is a commentary on the gloss (*ṭīkā*), no longer in existence, that Utpala wrote on his own *Memorial Verses*.[2] As I have pointed out, these are the last two known works, respectively, of Abhinavagupta for which he is renowned as the principal exponent of Self-Awareness philosophy.

Of his forty-four known works, these are but a few of the most famous. We can only speculate as to the total number of works that came from Abhinava's prolific pen.

Let us now look at the basis of Triadic metaphysics—the categories of primordial unity, separation, and return.

B. Metaphysics

As I remarked, all theology has a tripartite structure: it considers transcendence *in itself*; the emanation of the phenomenal from it; and the *reversion* of the phenomenal to the transcendent. This archetype seems to have been first conceived by the great Upaniṣadic sage Uddālaka (ninth century B.C.).[3] In Triadism, too, there is the Supreme Śiva, undifferentiated Reality or Unity; then differentiation, the Cosmic Manifestations, or the multi-

[1]Ibid., pp. 10-12; see also, Pandey, pp. 55-60.
[2]*PS* (Silburn), p. 18.
[3]*Chāndogya Upaniṣad*, 6:2:1-4.

plicity of beings emanating from the Unity; and finally, a return to Unity (Reabsorption).

Pereira identifies seven Śaiva schools by a clear schema, the "Trident Cluster of Śaiva Theologies."[1] These seven schools are each represented by a black trident arranged in a cluster. Standing erect at the center of the cluster beneath the yoga flame—representative of a school, Śaiva in origin, but Indic in scope and application—is Triadism, greatest of all the schools. The other six tridents are linked in pairs on either side of center (one on the left with its counterpart on the right). The first pair, adjacent to the Triadic trident, in this order, consists of the two rival *śaiva siddhānta* schools—the Southern or Devotional Orthodoxy (*drāviḍa*) and the Northern or Gnostic Orthodoxy (*gauḍa*). The next set consists of the newest of the schools—the Hero-Śaivism (*vīra-śaiva*) of Basava and the Śaiva Nondualism (*śivādvaita*) of Śrī-kaṇṭha. Lastly, there is the Dualist Pastoralism (*pāśupata*) of uncertain foundation and the Monist Pastoralism (*lākulīśapāśupata*) of Lakulīśa. The white tridents at the periphery of the cluster represent the Logicism (*nyāya*) of Gautama and the Atomism (*vaiśeṣika*) of Kaṇāda; they began as Śaiva schools but were demythologized.[2]

Although the black trident schools are more or less distinct, they all have three basic ideas in common—Master, Beast, and Bond; it is on this triad that Śaiva Orthodoxy is built. Later, these contiguous schools tended to become absorbed into Triadism and even began to adopt Triadic language. The Triadic school itself is colored with Yogic mysticism (absorption into an undifferentiated awareness), more so than any other theological tradition; and so, calls itself the Yogic school, as does its predecessor, Buddhist Idealism (*yogācāra*, "The Yogic Way").

Returning to the three categories of Śaiva Orthodoxy, *Master* is Śiva, *Beast* is the individual soul, and *Bond* is the entanglement which leads the soul to be immersed in the transmigratory world—when Bond is unleashed, the soul is liberated. Thus, *Master* is the author of bondage and liberation; *Beast* is the victim of bondage and heir to liberation and the object of both these states; *Bond* is the means by which these two states are achieved—bondage

[1]Pereira, Scheme 8, pp. 434-36.
[2]Ibid.

(by means of Bond) and liberation (by means of dissolution of Bond).

In Triadism, Master, Beast, and Bond are absorbed into *two* universal categories: *Inconceptualized* (Undifferentiated)—Śiva beyond concepts; and *Conceptualized* (Differentiated)—Śiva within concepts, which comprises the Thirty-six Categories of Triadism. In absorbing the triple concept of Master-Beast-Bond into the double concept of Inconceptualizable-Conceptualizable, Triadism is emphasizing the basic problem of theology—the relationship between the transcendent and the phenomenal—basic because it is inclusive of all the themes of theology which are interwoven either in the transcendent or the phenomenal. In attempting to resolve this problem, Triadism poses the question as to why the transcendent or inconceptualizable God, who is plenitude itself, needs to manifest Himself in the phenomenal. ' "But how," ' asks Somānanda, " 'can the Exalted have an impulse to the vile [how can God, quiescent in His connatural joy, have an urge to transform Himself into imperfect things]?' "[1] And, as with most Hindu theologies, Triadism replies that it is due to play or frolic (*līlā*). God has a natural motiveless impulse to indulge in the activities of creation, conservation, dissolution, graciousness, and obscuration, all of which concern the phenomenal. Hence, "Śiva, engaging in them out of delight at His natural impulse, is not deserving of blame."[2]

It follows, then, that the transcendent and the phenomenal are necessarily linked: there can be no phenomenal without the transcendent, and, paradoxically, no transcendent without the phenomenal. Even Catholic theology—because it is concerned not to compromise God's infinity, and hence, affirms the total *difference* between God and creation—maintains that God's infinity is inconceivable without (the possibility of) His creatures.[3]

Here, then, is a theme or "archetype" common to the Difference-in-Identity theology of Triadism and the Difference theology of Catholic Scholasticism—common, but developed by the two traditions with the maximum of individuality and distinctiveness. As I will show in the last chapter, a study of the archetypes, or

[1]Ibid., p. 365, v. 11.
[2]Ibid., v. 12.
[3]Ibid., p. 359.

themes common to various religious traditions, is an indispensable method to determine the distinctiveness of their treatment in each of those traditions.

1. *Cosmic Manifestation: The Thirty-six Categories of Triadism*

First, in order to form a basis for my discussion, I list the categories in sequential order without elaboration.[1] I then present a metaphysical conspectus of their significance, preliminary to examining the categories themselves in greater detail.

[The thirty-six categories of Triadism are indicated by numbers after the categories. The categories are thirty-seven if the Trans-universal, which transcends categories, is included among them. Categories 12-36 are those of Sāṅkhya].

Single (bipolar) ultimate category
CONSCIOUSNESS, INTELLIGENCE OR LIGHT (*cit*, *prakāśa*)
Trans-universal, inconceptualizable (*viśvottīrṇa*, *anuttara*): the Supreme Śiva (*paramaśiva*)
Universal, conceptualizable (*viśvamaya*)
a. Macrocosmic, the "Pure Way" (*śuddhādhva*)
b. Microcosmic, the "Impure Way" (*aśuddhādhva*). The Pure and Impure Ways unfold the elements of the conception innate in the Consciousness, expressible in the sentence 'I am this (unmanifested) universe', and constituted of subject and object.

Subclassifications
a. MACROCOSMIC CONSCIOUSNESS: THE PURE WAY: THE FIVE ENERGIES:
'I AM THIS unmanifested universe'.
Subject
ŚIVA. Energy of Consciousness (*cicchakti*)
'I am this unmanifested universe'. 1.

[1] Ibid., Scheme 34, pp. 496-97.

ENERGY (*śakti*). Energy of Joy (*ānandaśakti*). 'I'. 2.
THE EVER BENEFICENT (*sadāśiva*). Energy of Will (*icchāśakti*). Incipient experience of phenomenal being. 'I am this' ('I' emphasized). 3.

Object

THE SUPREME LORD (*īśvara*). Energy of Knowledge (*jñānaśakti*). Crystallized experience of phenomenal being. 'I am THIS' ('I' not emphasized). 4.

Subject and Object

PURE WISDOM (*śuddhavidyā*). Energy of Action (*kriyāśakti*). 'I am THIS' ('I' re-emphasized). 5.

b. MICROCOSMIC CONSCIOUSNESS: THE IMPURE WAY: 'I am this (un)-MANIFESTED UNIVERSE'.

Subject

SELF-OBSCURATION (*māyā*) 6.
THE FIVE SHEATHS (*kañcuka*)
  Aptitude (*kalā*) 7.
  Knowledge (*vidyā*) 8.
  Desire (*rāga*) 9.
  Time (*kāla*) 10.
  Fate (*niyati*) 11.
SPIRIT (*puruṣa*) 12.

Object

MATTER (*prakṛti*) 13.
INSTINCT (*buddhi*) 14.
EGOISM (*ahaṅkāra*) 15.
  Mind (*manas*) 16.
  The Ten Faculties (*indriya*)
    Five Preceptual (*jñānendriya*) 17-21.
    Five Motor (*karmendriya*) 22-26.
  The Ten Elements (*bhūtādi*)
    Five Subtle (*tanmātra*) 27-31.
    Five Gross (*mahābhūta*) 32-36.

Let us try to re-form these categories into a brief narrative that will help uncover the basic metaphysics behind them and, thereby, make the whole more intelligible.

The Trans-universal Śiva is, as such, incommunicable and supremely perfect, yet there is a dimension of His total being which lies in the multiplicity of creatures. So Śiva, in a manner of speaking, wishes to discover that dimension of His nature which is not evident in the simplicity of His being; He wishes to discover Himself in the multiplicity of the universe. Latent in God's essence is a difference-in-identity—one aspect is His immutable essence (identity), and the other is communicability to the creature (difference). Therefore, there is a dimension of His Essence that can only be realized in multiplicity. God must possess this capacity through His sovereign power and uninhibited freedom (*svātantrya*). However, this can only be accomplished by His unity being, so to speak, annihilated—by His emptying Himself through the Mirific Power of self-obscuration. In an idealist system like the Triadic, the multiplicity or differentiation cannot be *ontological*, in the form of mutable and real modifications supervening God's immutable aspect; it can only be *conceptual*, in the form of ideas projected by an inconceptual substance.

Thus, Śiva is the supreme being beyond concepts (undifferentiated, perfect) and also conceptualized (multiple, complex, seemingly limited). So we have here two contradictory notions coinciding in the same unity; and this division is made possible by the Mirific Power—the wall of self-occlusion that separates the two aspects of the divine being.

Before, we listed the categories of Triadism, and we indicated that the concepts of Master, Beast, and Bond are absorbed into a more universal, dual concept in Triadism—the Inconceptualized and the Conceptualized. Stated another way, we might say that the two reduced concepts are *Master* (Śiva) and *Bond.* Master brings about the Bond or self-obscuration which, in turn, results in Beast; in other words, by means of Bond, He is self-emptied and then becomes Beast.

Initially, then, there is the Supreme, undifferentiated Śiva who wants to realize one dimension of Himself that is only latent in His immutable perfection. But, to realize this He must possess all the powers necessary to attain it. It seems, though, to jump from this plenitude and plunge into the imperfection of this universe is an awesome step to take—too much to realize all at once—so it happens in several stages:

(1) In the first (macrocosmic) stage, there is a movementa way

from unity by which all the "tools" for the comprehension of the universe are forged. In an Idealist system, such as the Triadic, these "tools" can be none but the differentiation of subject and object. In this stage, however, the pure and unsullied essence is still present—although there is a progressive "degradation" of the original undifferentiated entity.

(2) Then, in the second (microcosmic) stage we come to the wall, or curtain, the Mirific Power, and the great plunge into the depth of multiplicity and variety and flux takes place. Again, this blacking-out (masking) or "annihilation" of perfection is necessary to achieve multiplicity.[1] Now the emanations of the first stage (the five Pure Principles) that have been undergoing a progressive devolution (without impurity) come off the wall of the Mirific Power as limited and reveal themselves as five glimmers, and these start to produce the multiplicities of the universe.

Let us look at the thirty-six categories more in detail.[2] The first Five Principles[3] representing the Macrocosmic Consciousness (Pure Way) can be illustrated in the concept, "I am this (unmanifested) universe." The Self-Awareness School holds that in each of the five Pure Manifestations, all the five Energies are present—but, the difference of one Manifestation from another is that a particular power is emphasized more so in it than it is in the others. The first three categories concern the Ultimate Reality.

As *subject*, they are as follows:

(1) Śiva, where the *Energy of Consciousness* has predomination. It is the pure Light of Self-Awareness in which everything is latent. Here, just the "*I*" becomes explicit.

(2) ENERGY, where the *Energy of Joy* predominates. These first two, and most important, manifestations occur almost simul-

[1]It should be remembered that in this theology God is *everything*—Himself, and creatures, and universe—there is nothing outside Himself; thus, there is no question of a creation as in Christian doctrine, where too self-emptying has a salvific purpose. Nor should this self-annihilation be looked at here as selfish. Since nothing exists outside God in Triadic theology (a theology of difference-in-identity), it can only be *for Himself* that He becomes differentiated. To realize His perfection, Śiva must annihilate Himself (supreme undifferentiatedness) in this blackout of illusion which almost occludes perfection.

[2]The thirty-six categories will be indicated in the text by arabic numerals in parenthesis.

[3]*PS* v. 14, trans. Silburn, p. 68. See also her treatment of the five pure manifestations (pp. 27-29).

taneously and enjoy an inseparable union as does the flame and the fire. Here, "I *am*" is emphasized.

(3) THE EVER BENEFICENT, where the *Energy of Will* is predominant. It may be compared to the desire of an artist as the inspiration to paint a canvas arises within him or to the faint outlining sketch on the canvas before the paint is applied.[1] With this principle we are moving away from the subject and about to enter the next realm of objectivity—so the "this," which represents the universe, is still only slightly effective. Consequently, the "I" is predominant in the "*I* am this."

As *object*, there is only one category:

(4) THE SUPREME LORD, where the *Energy of Knowledge* has predominancy. The consciousness of "I" is submerged by the clear consciousness of "this" which now appears as a substratum of "I". Śiva realizes "*This* I am." From here on the rupture of balance between knowledge and activity shows activity the *benefactor*.[2] Using the above analogy of a painting, this category might be seen as a completely finished painting—so much so that the underlying canvas is not seen.[3]

As *subject and object*, there is one final pure category:

(5) PURE WISDOM, where the *Energy of Action* is stressed. Here, subject and object are differentiated. The last two categories concentrated almost exclusively on either subject or object; now, emphasis will be equally divided between the two—"*I* am *This*."

Having arrived at this stage of manifestation, we enter upon the sphere of Illusion[4] which projects the Microcosmic Consciousness (Impure Way) and consists of differentiated subject and object. The *subject* phase is concerned with the following categories:

(6) SELF-OBSCURATION, which I have just explained;

(7-12) THE FIVE SHEATHS or COVERS, which appear as partially limited: *Aptitude*, *Knowledge*, *Desire*, *Time*, and *Fate*; and SPIRIT.[5] The Sheaths are so named because they completely envelop the Self and cause It to lose the intuition of Its true nature

[1]Pandey, p. 365.

[2]*PS* (Silburn), p. 29.

[3]Pandey, p. 366.

[4]Abhinava, in the *PS*, v. 15, when referring to the Goddess, "Māyā śakti," says "She is the mask that covers the Self of Śiva." (trans. Silburn, p. 68).

[5]Pereira, Scheme 34, p. 397.

which is pure selfhood.[1] When they are fully limited, they form Spirit, which is the Individual, and Matter. This is the beginning of the *object* phase-power that forms the multiple evolutes that Spirit enjoys.

Beginning with SPIRIT, we now go into the Sāṅkhya categories: (12-36), which Abhinava adopted as part of his philosophy.[2] Although simple in breakdown, it is the metaphysics basic to all Vedāntic systems:

The Ultimate Categories of Sāṅkhya are: (12) SPIRIT, and (13) MATTER. Spirit is just a witness; in essence, it is liberated. Matter provides Spirit with experience by means of two kinds of factors: (1) the Attribute Triad (*guṇatrayam*)—the three qualities or strands which are the ultimate constituents of experience—consisting of Brightness, Passion, and Darkness. For example, there are some things in us that appear *bright* and make us experience peace or goodness; other things wear and push us down, almost destroy us, and lead to *darkness* and death; still other things in us are in between (not bright or dull and boring) and arouse *passion.* It is a profound description of experience. (2) The evolutes—the factors constituting the multiplicity of experience proceed from these three Attributes; the latter are either in a state of balance or imbalance. When they are in balance (equally represented), there is tranquillity and an absence of Evolutes; this is the "night of creation." Then suddenly, they start to become unbalanced—sometimes one Attribute seems to prevail over others—when this occurs there is one kind of Evolute; when another prevails, there is a different kind of Evolute. Thus, there is an almost infinite variety of admixtures, and from these the multiplicity of the universe proceeds. The Evolutes start with Instinct and move on to Egoism or self-centeredness. Now, both these Sāṅkhya categories have bright forms and dark forms—those of Instinct are not important for Triadism. Those of Egoism, however, are significant and, consequently, only the latter forms will be listed.

(14) INSTINCT, or the Prodigious (*mahat* or *buddhi*, "Mind")

[1] *PS*, vv. 16-18, trans. Silburn, pp. 68-70. See also her treatment of the five sheaths, pp. 31-32. Abhinava considers the sheaths part of the sphere of *māyā*, and, therefore, he calls them the "six sheaths" (v. 17).

[2] Pereira, Scheme 13, pp. 452-53. Abhinavagupta discusses the Sāṅkhya categories in his *PS*, vv. 19-23, trans. Silburn, pp. 70-71; see also her explanation on pp. 32-33.

is the movement toward something impulsive, un-selfconscious. Here, we do things without conscious thought in much the same manner as animals (who have no self-awareness).

(15) EGOISM, the second Evolute, is the Ego Principle or the Individuator and is the fundamental principle of individuality. It collects tendencies and residues from previous experiences and assimilates present experiences, the ensemble of which constitutes the individual ego. This leads to arrogance, a sense of power, and so on.

The first of the sub-classifications of Egoism are the Bright or Modified forms which comprise the following categories:

(16) *Mind*, Inner Faculty, which brings all the others together; it receives, coordinates, and colates information.

(17-21) *Five Perceptual Faculties*, or the Faculties of Knowledge: eye, ear, nose, tongue, and skin.

(22-26) *Five Motor Faculties*, or the Faculties of Action: voice, hands, feet, anus, and genitals.

These bright forms provide different information and have different actions; for example, what information the eye obtains is relayed or coordinated by the mind and activated by the hand; but all have a sense of Egoism.

The second subdivision of Egoism are the Dark or Elemental Forms which are the objects—what is known by the faculties, and consist of the following categories:

(27-31) *Five Subtle Elements*: sound, touch, color, taste, and smell.

(32-36) *Five Gross Elements*: ether, wind, fire, water, and earth.

The Fiery Forms are a combination of the Faculties (Bright Forms) and the object of the Faculties (Dark Forms), with the exception of the Gross Elements. Therefore, they comprise the "Bright Eleven" (Mind and the Ten Faculties, perceptual and motor) and the Subtle Elements.

Thus, all these Sāṅkhya categories are absorbed into the lower categories of Triadism—the Microcosmic Consciousness from Spirit to the earth.

Now that Śiva has attained all the richness of multiplicity and experience, and has become fully differentiated by emptying Himself, the questions must be asked: how does He reclaim His glory; and, how do we return to the indifferentiable Śiva? In other words, how is reabsorption accomplished?

2. *Reabsorption: The Twelve Consuming Energies or kālīs*

Śaivism is a religion in which everything is energy (overwhelming power) and terror; it is not a religion of sweetness and delight. Its favorite images are those of blackness, fire, and death—represented by the figure of the murderous goddess of Consuming Energy. She is not only death personified, she is also the goddess of consuming fire. Śiva, in producing the universe is depicted as surrounded by the Wheel of Energies (we find this in Maheśvarānanda)[1]—the Consuming Energies are imagined as engulfing the universe in their destructive fire, making it more rarified and finally absorbing everything into His substance (fire), leaving nothing of multiplicity but ash, so to speak. Hence, the supreme reality is called *The Tremendous God*; because, in relation to the multiplicity of the universe, the undifferentiated Śiva is like a fearful conflagration absorbing all into Himself. With this devouring of all multiplicity into divine unicity, we have the completion of the triad—The Tremendous God, surrounded by His Consuming Energies reverses the sequence of Cosmic Manifestations (simplicity to multiplicity) by means of His absorptive fire (multiplicity to simplicity).[2]

According to Abhinava, in both the *Light on the Tantras* and the *Gradation Frolic*, as Pandey points out,[3] the number of aspects of the Ineffable Wheel (*anākhyacakra*) or the Consuming Energies are twelve: there are four Consuming Energies of creation, maintenance, destruction, and ineffability, in each of the three groups of Knowable, Norm, and Knower. To put it simply and logically, you must have something to know (knowable), someone to know it (knower), and the means to know it (norm). In these three categories, things must *come* into existence, *continue* to exist, *cease* to exist, and they must be *beyond* all these categories. We see here a progression from the knowable to knower, with the subject always predominant over the object.

[1]Maheśvarānanda in his *MM*, vv. 36-41, speaks of the Wheel of Totality and of the twelve *kālīs* in his discourse on the krama school. We will see more on this in Chapter II when we again discuss the kālīs, a distinctive feature of this school.

[2]Pereira, Scheme 35, pp. 498-99. This reverses the progression depicted in Scheme 34.

[3]Pandey, p. 513.

(1) *The Consuming Energies of the Knowable:* the Consuming Energies of the creation of objects, the experience of objects, the termination of the experience of objects, and doubt about the experience of objects. First, you must create the objects, then you must experience them, and finally, experience must be terminated and subjected to doubt; because ultimately, as far as the Supreme Śiva is concerned, all these finite objects are of no relevance—so they must be doubted.

(2) Similarly, *the Consuming Energies of the Norm* exert a certain destructive or creative action in regard to the several elements which constitute experience—"I am this (manifested) universe." Thus, Śiva reabsorbs the universe through the destructive fire of His energies—the one Energizer and His many Energies.

(3) *The Consuming Energies of the Knower:* this fiery Energizer by means of His fiery Energies absorbs things gradually. After the death rays are turned on the object, then to the means of knowing, they are finally directed to the subject—the knower. The subject (merged object-subject) is reabsorbed into Śiva in the final act which is accomplished by the most awesome of all the Consuming Energies, called the Furious, Violent, and Terrifying Consuming Energy of the Great Tremendous God.

3. *Bondage: The Three Impurities or Ignorances*

In Indic philosophies ignorance is the cause of bondage; knowledge, conversely, is a chief means of liberation. In the Śaiva view, ignorance does not mean a total negation of knowledge, which only occurs in insentient beings, but only imperfect knowledge.[1] In particular, man in his limited conscious state of Beast is bound by three limitations or Impurities, and if it were not for these coverings or ignorances, the individual soul would be uncontaminated and all-knowing.[2]

The three Impurities are as follows:

(1) Innate or Infinitesimal Ignorance (*āṇava*), the primary covering which causes the individual or infinitesimal consciousness

[1]Ibid., pp. 305-6.

[2]L.D. Barnett, "The Paramarthasara of Abhinavagupta," with Yogaraja's commentary (he is referred to here as Yoga Muni), trans. in *The Journal of the Royal Asiatic Society of Great Britain and Ireland* (London, 1910), vv. 24-32, pp. 727-30. See also, *PS* (Silburn), pp. 71-74.

(*aṇu*) to begin experiencing objects as distinct from the Self. This contamination obscures the soul in two ways, either by hiding its original freedom and omnipotence or by obliterating its capacity to know (omniscience). When the plenitude of the Self is obscured, duality and finitude appear in all things. Thus it is the evil of individuation.

(2) Impurity of Illusion (*māyīya*), represents the whole series of categories from the Five Sheaths down to the earth, which were discussed in a previous section. The soul, being thus limited in knowledge and deluded in the perception of external objects, begins to act meritoriously or otherwise, which brings about the third impurity.

(3) Impurity of Action (*kārma*), the body with its organs reaps the results of these acts and as a consequence becomes a transmigrator from one life to the next.[1] Kṣemarāja brings out the soul's entanglement in the continuous cycle of births, deaths, and rebirths in his work, *The Heart of Self-Awareness*, "Through the contraction of Its Energies, the plenary Consciousness becomes a transmigrant soul enveloped in Pollution."[2]

The three Impurities which surround the enslaved man have been compared to the three coverings of a seed of grain without which it cannot grow. When the seed casts off these covers it is "freed" from growth, and the sprouts of existence will be prevented from developing, and, therefore, he cannot be born again. "As a seed, stripped of chaff, husk and awn produces no sprout, so too the Self, stripped of the impurities of Innate Ignorance, Illusion, and Action, does not produce the sprout of transmigration."[3]

At the conclusion of the section on Cosmic Manifestations we posed a two-part question, the first, concerning how Śiva reclaims His glory has been answered. I now turn to the second part, as to how we return to the undifferentiated Śiva. The answer, simply stated, is that Triadism offers four distinct Ways to Liberation through reabsorption in Śiva. Each of the Triadic schools is primarily founded upon one of these Ways—the theme of my next and major chapter.

[1]*PS* (Silburn), pp. 34-35.
[2]*PHṛ*, aphorism 9.
[3]*PS*, v. 57.

CHAPTER II

GNOSTIC TRIADISM: THE WAYS TO LIBERATION

It is, then, the three Impurities or Ignorances which whirl the individual from one existence to another. Liberation comes only through the knowledge ("recognition") of one's true Śiva-nature, a recognition dependent solely on Śiva's grace. Silburn rightly says that Triadism "does not offer us a mystique of *yoga* but a mystique of grace, for everything is grace: Śiva does not appear as the bearer of grace, but as grace itself."[1] Since access to Śiva is entirely a function of grace, she continues, the four distinct Ways correspond to the intensity of divine favor.[2] And grace is communicated by Śiva as a "fall" of His Energy (*śaktipāta*) on the receiver, through its being hurled or fulminated, so to speak. Hence, grace, in Triadism, is an Energic Fulmination.

The theology of the Ways is extremely complex, requiring a detailed exposition of concepts. We can best prepare for this exposition by seven preliminary observations:

(1) *The classification of the Ways.* The Ways may be grouped under two paths—the Inferior Path, and the Superior Path. The Inferior Path consists of the two *lower* Ways, progressive stages in the purification of dualized thought (*vikalpa*), the differentiation between subject and object.[3] They are the Individual Way of the Family School and the Energic Way of the Gradation School. Grace varies from feeble to average in intensity. The Superior Path comprises two *higher* Ways, free of progressive stages. The soul is carried to Śiva spontaneously; duality is overcome and all is one in Śiva. They are the Divine or Śiva Way of the Family School and the Null Way of the Self-Awareness or Vibration School. Grace ranges from intense to most intense.

(2) *Their effectiveness.* Of the four Ways, only the Null directly

[1] *PS* (Silburn), p. 41.
[2] *TA*, VIII, 163.
[3] *PS* (Barnett), vv. 97 and com. p. 746.

realizes ultimate Reality.[1] Each Way is, in a sense, an extension of the one that precedes it. The difference between the Divine and the Null Ways is very slight. Some authors do not even consider the latter as a separate Way but rather as the culmination of the former.[2] Also, the Ways are understood as immersions or absorptions which lead to the final realization or recognition of Śiva.

(3) *Their relationship to the process of the absorption of the phenomenal into the Transcendent.* Now the process of absorption, as we have seen, is the exact reversal of the process of emergence or manifestation of the thirty-six categories.[3] The two lower Ways concern the emergence or manifestation of the Energies of Action, and Knowledge, respectively;[4] the two higher Ways are dominated by the Energies of Will and Joy, respectively. "So in the course of gradual immersion...these very powers similarly merge into one another in reverse order."[5]

(4) *Their correspondence with the five states of human consciousness.* Furthermore, a correspondence can be seen between the five states of consciousness[6] and the Four Ways, resulting in a three-dimensional parallel. The states of wakefulness (*jāgrat*), dreaming (*svapna*), and profound sleep (*suṣupti*) correspond to the Individual, Energic, and Divine Ways, respectively. The fourth state (*turīya*) of ecstasy is not another psychological state differing in degree from the other three; on the contrary, it is the transcendent dimension of consciousness *present in* the three.[7] The state "beyond the fourth" (*turyātīta*) is the uninterrupted fullness of self-realization which corresponds to the Tremendous State of the Null Way.[8]

(5) *Their connection with the intensity of the Energic Fulmination.* The intensity of divine grace increases as the yogī ascends the steps of the mystical ladder, steps which correspond to the Ways of Liberation.[9] Yet, grace does not have to begin as feeble stirrings

[1]*TA*, I, 203.
[2]Ibid., I, 182.
[3]Ibid., I, 205.
[4]Ibid., I, 186-87.
[5]Pandey, p. 313.
[6]*PS* (Silburn), pp. 38-39.
[7]Ibid., vv. 34-35, pp. 75-76.
[8]Ibid., p. 39.
[9]Lilian Silburn, *Le Vijñāna Bhairava*, Texte Traduit et Commente par Lilian

within the heart of the initiated; since it is a gratuitous gift of God, the degree of intensity is dependent solely on His will. Therefore, the Way that best befits the yogī, although of his own choosing, is in reality a question of divine favour.

(6) *The necessary link of certain mystical practices with the Ways.* It must also be realized, as Silburn points out,[1] that certain apparently identical mystical experiences or practices are varied by connection with the different Ways. For example, certain yogic practices peculiar to the Individual Way are often performed from different motives in the other Ways, inspired by a more intense grace, and with widely varying results.[2] Therefore, when a characteristic and dominant trait of a certain Way is discussed, it must not be construed that it is germane to that Way alone.

(7) *The distinctive character of each Way.* This can be expressed in terms of specific categories common to all Hindu theology: the use and non-use of means to achieve the Ways; according to the schools that profess them; the trichotomy—Difference (Individual Way), Difference-in-Identity (Energic Way), and Identity (Divine Way),[3] and then a fourth, the Ineffable (Null Way); the principal triad of divine Energies—Action (Individual Way), Knowledge (Energic Way), and Will (Divine Way), and finally, the supervening Energy of Bliss or Joy (Null Way);[4] the modes of awareness which correspond to the four Energies—differentiated (Individual Way), imaginational (Energic Way), undifferenced (Divine Way), and sudden illuminational (Null Way); and the six states of con-

Silburn, Fasc. 15 (Paris: Institut de Civilisation Indienne, 1961), Postface, pp. 173-94. The overall scheme of this tantra follows along eleven ascending stages of mystical progression.

[1]Ibid., pp. 25-26.

[2]Ibid., pp. 87-88; in Jayaratha's commentary to v. 37 which deals with the yogic practice of meditation on the *bindu*, or luminous point or Nucleus of energy which is a symbol of Śiva, it is clear that this practice can be characteristic of all three Ways (Individual, Energic, and Divine) depending on what location in the yogī's body meditation on the *bindu* is fixed. Similarly, the mystical formula *VB* (Silburn), v. 39 and com., pp. 89-90, successively covers the three Ways: "Cette strophe couvre successivement les trois voies: commençant par la récitation de AUṀ (voie inferieure), elle utilise l'énergie du vide (voie de l'énergie) pour sombrer dans la vacuité totale (voie de Śiva)."

[3]Abhinava only mentions these three (*TA* I. 230).

[4]Pereira, p. 364, from his translation of Somānanda's *Vision of Śiva*, chap. I, v. 2.

sciousness-appeasement of the mind (*cittaviśrānti* state of the Individual Way), awakening of the mind (*cittasambodha* state of the Energic Way), and the absorption of the mind (*cittapralaya* state of the Divine Way).[1]

A. *The Individual Way: Absorption in the Object*

All Indic religions believe man to be enchained to the wheel of transmigration, where he is encumbered by experiences and tendencies encountered in former lives. Besides the physical pain and sorrow of cyclical birth, sickness, old age, and death, he also suffers an endless psychic enslavement due to this "human condition." Unable to satiate his constant worldly desires and "cravings," he undergoes mental as well as physical anguish. New desires create new anguishes, and so on, in an eternal cycle.

To alleviate this condition, the Individual Way strives to liberate thought of its agitation and of its structures by fixing it on an object taken in its concrete individuality, then to absorb it within the Self. It aims to purify thought through the abolition of duality, the distinction between subject and object.

Because it comprises a true and continuous effort of thought and attention, the Individual Way is also called the Way of Activity (*kriyopāya*). Other names include: the Particular Means, Inferior Way, and the Ordinary Way.

Grace is more feeble here than in any other Way because it is addressed to the man attached to his earthly possessions and enjoyment while secretly aspiring for deliverance. Only after numerous rebirths, and when all desire for enjoyment has ceased will this person realize his identity with Śiva. Because of its weakness, grace has a need to be supplemented by a number of yogic practices—postures, mystical attitudes or gestures, control or regulation of the breath, meditation or contemplation, and recitation of mystical formulas or precepts.[2] It is essential that all of these practices be conducted under the direction of a Spiritual Master or *guru*.[3]

Effort, as I have said, must be great and constant. As Abhinava

[1] *VB* (Silburn), pp. 64-65. The author cites (p. 64, n. 3) as her source, Abhinava's *TA* III, vv. 211-14, pp. 202-4; and vv. 216-19 com. pp. 205-6.

[2] Pereira, p. 459, concerning the eightfold yoga.

[3] *PS* (Silburn), p. 43.

warns, the yogī who rests in mid-course or who lapses in his effort—through loss of concentration on the act being performed—will not be sufficiently advanced to reach redemption upon his death; he must pass into a second birth before he can become Śiva.[1]

Since the goal is the purification of dualized thought, the highest stage of the Individual Way is quietude or appeasement of thought.[2]

As I have indicated, yogic practices must be performed under the close direction of a Spiritual Master. I will, therefore, preface my treatment of these practices with a brief comment on the Master's role. It is appropriate to include him in the discussion of the Inferior Path, for, while he may act as an intermediary in the Superior Path, he is indispensable here.

1. The Spiritual Master

Triadism has only one true Master—Śiva, the supreme Guru, the Liberator of the cosmos.[3] When perfect illumination resides undifferentiatedly in both Master and disciple, distinction between them is seen to be imaginary. The disciple identifies with the accomplished Master, and through him, with Śiva.

Now divine grace or the Energic Fulmination may be bestowed on the soul in a threefold manner; spontaneously, without the aid of an intermediary, as in the Superior Path where grace is intense; through the intermediacy of a sacred text or mystical formula; and through the intervention of a Master, where the grace is not very intense.[4] The first two methods are rare.

Not all Masters are equally accomplished, some are yogīs who have experienced ecstasies, while others have a deep knowledge of religious treatises. However, neither ecstasies nor scriptural knowledge can confer liberation. In fact, yogīs such as these, as Abhinava tells us, are inferior to ones who are masters of the range of supernatural states, for even if they have not read the treatises, they will know their contents instinctively.[5]

[1] *PS* (Barnett), vv. 98-102, pp. 746-47.

[2] *VB* (Silburn), p. 27, where she cites the *TA*, III, v. 211 as her authority.

[3] *TA*, XIII. 159.

[4] *PS* (Silburn), pp. 49-50.

[5] TA, XIII. 196, a quote from Abhinava's commentary (*Vārtika*) of the *Tantra on the Triumph of the Engarlanded Goddess* on the four states of consciousness, vv. 327-29.

The true guru is one who is able to confer full consecration on the disciple. Triadism distinguishes Initiation (*dīkṣā*) from Consecration proper (*abhiṣeka*). In *Initiation,* the disciple receives divine power through rites and yogic processes. After a purification ceremony, the guru establishes a series of identifications. First he identifies himself with his disciple, then introduces him to that Way best suited to him and along which he is going to lead him. This interpenetration of disciple, Master, and universe, and of their fusion in the ultimate Reality produces the deliverance (illumination) of the disciple. In *Consecration,* comparable to the coronation of a king, the Master not only confers illumination on his disciple but also divine energy, omniscience, and omnipotence, thus making him a Liberated-in-Life.[1] He confers on him the powers of a Master who is, in turn, able to transfer grace to others.[2]

2. Yogic Practices

The fundamental principle behind all tantric yogic practices is the belief that the "human body...is an epitome of the universe—a microcosm in relation to the macrocosm. There is therefore nothing in the universe which is not there in the body of man."[3] Vasugupta also recognizes this principle in his *Aphorisms on Śiva,* "As in the yogī's body, so also elsewhere."[4] The implication is, therefore, that the cosmic processes parallel the biological processes in man's body; hence, the energy activating the cosmos is latent in the body, and the energy can be located and aroused by yogic practices. Only in this way can a yogī free himself from ignorance and bondage and "recognize" his identity with the Absolute. Yogic practices may be grouped into two categories: *external*—body attitudes, breath control, and recitation of mystical formulas; and *internal*—concentration on objects or concepts leading to medi-

[1]The state of a Liberated-in-Life is the deified Tremendous State and is the goal of one who travels the Null Way, the fourth and highest Way of Liberation. I will treat this topic at the conclusion of this chapter.

[2]*PS* (Silburn), pp. 50-51; see also *VB* (Silburn), p. 8. Here Silburn stresses the necessity of having a master transmit esoteric teaching to his disciples in order to enable the latter to impart this knowledge to others.

[3]Shashi Bhusan Das Gupta, "Some Later Yogic Schools," *CHI*, p. 291.

[4]Vasugupta, *Śiva Sūtra, Part III: Individual Way*, vv. 14, as translated by Pereira, p. 362.

tation and finally culminating in quietude or mystical repose. In the Energic Way, this repose leads to the final stage of yoga, absorption in Śiva.

(a) *Images, Postures, and Gestures*

Mystical attitudes of the body, in particular, postures, and gestures, like movement and positioning of the extremities, developed from the basic and ancient concept of an "image." The worshipper's identification with the god whose image he contemplated was accomplished through a threefold process:

(1) The worshipper first *meditated* on the image of a deity in order to learn its form (attitudes) and understand its symbolism.

(2) Next, he *appropriated* the outward form and inner powers and qualities of the image. This was accomplished by absorbing the external form of the image—the yogī would assume the same body postures and hand positions as that of the image. The external image was thereby transferred to a purely mental plane with the individual.[1]

(3) The final step was *identification* with the god and his powers represented in the image. All the divine powers already latent in him as a microcosm were activated by this internalization, and the god and his powers were one with the yogī and his body.[2]

Yogic posture gives the body a stable rigidity while keeping physical effort and fatigue to a minimum. Only when the posture is effortless and natural can it enhance concentration and cause the yogī to lose awareness of the presence of his own body. The purpose of postures and gestures is always the same—to reach a complete "neutrality" of the senses; consciousness is no longer troubled by the presence of the body. The yogī thereby transcends

[1]Thomas J. Hopkins, *The Hindu Religious Tradition* (Encino: Belmont: Dickenson Publishing Company, Inc., 1971), p. 115. See also *The Yoga Aphorisms*, I.38 with Vācaspati Miśra's comment, trans. by Pereira, *Hindu Theology*, p. 80. In addition, the *VB* (Silburn), vv. 36, pp. 86-87 describes a special gesture which a master teaches his disciple. It consists in placing the ten fingers over the ears, eyes, nose, and mouth thereby blocking the functioning of these sense organs; hence, consciousness is closed to sensory impressions, and vital energy remains stored within. Also, vv. 77-86 describe attributes of the body and eyes (pp. 118-126).

Arthur Avalon, *The Serpent Power*, 7th ed. (Madras: Ganesh, 1964); plates ix-xvii depict this body attitude plus other yogic gestures and postures.

[2]Hopkins, Ibid.

the human condition by a refusal to conform to the most elementary of human inclinations—the desire to move and to be distracted by external stimuli. These are only the first of a long series of refusals of every kind which are to follow.[1]

(b) *Breath Control*

Another means of external yogic discipline, and yet another (perhaps the most important) in a series of "refusals" to conform to the human condition, is breath control (*prāṇāyāma*).[2]

Man measures time by the rhythm in the cosmos and within his own body; he tries to control these rhythms in order to control and eliminate time. The key to this control is regulating the rhythm of breathing,[3] the most basic, life-sustaining function of the human condition. Indeed, the overall goal of all yogic disciplines is to transcend or eliminate time, to bring about a "unification" or "cosmicization" of the most important functions of life—respiration and consciousness. Eliade calls this effort, "the coincidence of opposites." By making opposites, like inhaled-exhaled breaths, to coincide, man hopes to "homologize" his body's rhythms with the cosmic and thereby put time at rest.[4] In this state of equilibrium,[5] time no longer affects him—"he *is*, in the indivisible movement of infinite duration between breathing in and breathing out."[6]

Now there is an interrelationship between the functions of breathing and of the mental states.[7] The rate and intensity of res-

[1]Mircea Eliade, *Yoga: Immortality and Freedom*, 2nd ed. (Princeton: Bollington Foundation, 1969), pp. 53-54.

[2]Patañjali, *Yoga-Sūtras*, II. 49, wherein he defines the term as "the arrest of the movements of inhalation and exhalation, and it is obtained after *āsana* has been realized."

[3]Thomas Matus, "The Christian Use of Yoga: A Theoretical Study Based on a Comparison of the Mystical Experience of Symeon the New Theologian, with Some Tantric Sources," Ph.D. dissertation, Fordham University, 1977, p. 75. Matus claims (p. 38, n. 1) that Abhinavagupta closely links "breath control" with the absorption and destruction of cyclic time, and he cites as his authority, Raniero Gnoli, *Luce delle sacre Scritture* (*Tantrāloka*) *di Abhinavagupta* (Turin: Unione Tipografico-Editrice Torinese, 1972) pp. 208-37 and *Essenza dei Tantra* (*Tantrasāra*) (Turin: Boringhieri, 1960), pp. 136-51.

[4]Eliade, pp. 96-99.

[5]*VB* (Silburn), v. 64 and com., pp. 106-107.

[6]Matus, p. 65.

[7]Eliade, p. 55.

piration is directly affected by external stimuli like physical exertion, and internal ones like emotional stress; it varies considerably from non-stimulated breathing as during sleep or emotionally calm wakefulness. Obvious as this is, it is necessary to underscore the connection between the breath and consciousness if the yogī's goal in breath control is to be understood.

By progressively prolonging and stabilizing the three phases of breathing—inhalation, retention of breath, and exhalation—the yogī hopes to regulate normal arhythmic breathing. Thus he can penetrate the modalities of consciousness in perfect lucidity.[1] This goal is elusive and requires much practice. Initially, concentration on the vital function produces an indescribable sense of cosmic harmony, a rhythmic fullness, and psychophysical serenity. Only later does it bring about an obscure feeling of presence in one's own body, a calm awareness of one's greatness,[2] and a unification of consciousness, breath, and time.[3]

(c) *Mystical Formulas*

In the Vedic sacrificial system, mystical formulas were believed to have creative power; they were sound flows of reality, the proper expression of which would bring forth and establish the realities they represented.[4] These formulas could not only establish identities, but they could bring into reality whatever truth they expressed.[5] However, only qualified Brahmans could transmit them and only to a chosen few. For the Vedic formulas, the *āgamas* substituted *tantric* formulas—which any Master could transmit to any pupil whatsoever.[6] Once "received" from the Master, the mystical formulas bestowed unlimited power.[7]

[1]Ibid., pp. 56-57.

[2]Ibid., p. 58.

[3]Matus, p. 66. For more on breath control, see *VB* (Silburn), vv. 24-29 with com., pp. 76-81; and vv. 35 and 42. See also: *The Offering from Intimate Experience* (Anubhavanivedana) of Abhinavagupta trans. by Silburn in *Hymnes de Abhinavagupta*, Traduits et Commentés par Lilian Silburn, Fasc. 31 (Paris: Institut de Civilisation Indienne, 1970), pp. 37-47. This brief poem of only four verses deals with the exercise of breathing peculiar to the four Ways of Liberation, beginning with the Divine Way (stanza 1) and ending with the Null Way (stanza 4).

[4]Hopkins, p. 127.

[5]Ibid., p. 19.

[6]Ibid., pp. 116-17.

[7]Eliade, p. 214.

These formulas are also tools for altering the state of consciousness through dissolving the conventional link between speech and thought.[1] "Hence *mantra* aids in liberating man's consciousness from time in two ways: by raising his thought beyond the limits of everyday language in which time is noted and observed; and by dissociating his consciousness from the rhythms and vibrations which are the measure of time."[2]

The idea of the creative power of mystical formulas gave rise to the concept of *seed formulas* (*bīja-mantras*)—the minimal sound form of things. *OM* is the primal seed formula; it stands for all the sounds and thus for the entire universe.[3]

> Each God...and each degree of sanctity have a *bīja-mantra*, a 'mystical sound', which is their 'seed', their 'support'—that is, their very *being*. By repeating this *bīja-mantra* in accordance with the rules, the practitioner appropriates its ontological essence, concretely and directly assimilates the God, the state of sanctity, etc. Sometimes an entire metaphysics is concentrated in a *mantra*.[4]

In the last chapter (XIII) of the *Essence of the Tantras*, Abhinava, in discussing the cultic practice of the Family School, says that sacrifice can be offered in a variety of ways, one of which is "exterior reality." But, even in this case it must be performed while *meditating* on the essential unity of "*breath, consciousness,* and *body*"; and while projecting the syllables of the formula "on the head, the mouth, the heart, the genitals, and the whole body."[5]

Reference here is to a system of "placing" or of "ritual projecting" (*nyāsa*), using formulas to establish gods or divine power in various parts of the body. The worshipper *meditates* on the god or power he wishes to appropriate, and, while reciting the appropriate formula, touches areas of the body to establish them at the desired points.[6]

[1]Matus, p. 67.

[2]Ibid., p. 69.

[3]*Chāndogya Upaniṣad*, II. II. 23.3, "As all leaves are held together by a stalk, so is all speech held together by *Aum* [*om*]. Verily, the syllable Aum [*om*] is all this [created universe]." See Radhakrishnan, p. 375.

[4]Eliade, p. 215.

[5]Matus, p. 115.

[6]Hopkins, p. 115. I will again refer to the projection of formulas in this

Mystical formulas are also used by the yogīs as "supports" for concentration and meditation, whether they follow the rhythm of breath control, or whether they are repeated during the phases of respiration. Whatever their historical origin, they had the value of a secret initiatory language. For these sounds revealed their message only during meditation and were not meant for the secular language of everyday experiences.[1]

(d) *Meditation*

The second or internal phase of yogic practices, as I have indicated earlier, begins with concentration (*dhāraṇā*) on any object or concept; successively progresses to meditation (*dhyāna*); and finally to absorption in a state of quietude, appeasement, or mystical repose (*viśrānti*).[2] Now the external disciplines must precede and prepare the yogī for concentration; the body must be in a comfortable, natural posture[3] with the breathing rhythmically retarded[4] for swift and proper concentration to commence. The yogī is then able to pass beyond the "opposites"; sensory activity no longer distracts him; he sinks within himself and becomes invulnerable.[5]

One must take care not to consider, as some do, the terms concentration and meditation as synonymous; although closely related, they are two distinct mental processes both by definition and by yogic practice. Patañjali defines *concentration* as the "fixation of thought on a single point" and *meditation* as "a continuous current of unified thought."[6] It is obvious that one must first fix the entire attention on something before being able to engage in its

---

manner later in this chapter when the subject of the Coiled Potency (*kuṇḍalinī*) is discussed.

[1]Eliade, pp. 212-213. For more on *mantra*, see: *VB*, vv. 42, 81, 90-91, 130, 145, 156-57; *MM*, vv. 46, 49-50; *Stav.*, vv. 20, 84.

[2]Eliade, pp. 69-70. Here the author calls the third component of the internal states "stasis," and later (p. 77, n. 79) "enstasis" and "conjunction." According to Singh (*PHr*, p. 30), *resting* in the condition of ecstasy is *viśrānti*, therefore the former is the "condition," and the latter is the "state."

[3]*VB* (Silburn), vv. 78-79, 82.

[4]Patañjali, *Yogasūtras*, II. 52, 53.

[5]Eliade, p. 66.

[6]*YS*, III. 1, 2.

continuous contemplation. In other words, by prolonging concentration one accomplishes yogic meditation.[1]

Eliade points out that yogic meditation is not the same as secular meditation. The former involves a "mental continuum" which reaches a "density and purity" that only great yogic effort and practice can accomplish; the latter, on the other hand, ends "either with the external form or with the value of the objects meditated upon." In yogic meditation, the meditator can also "penetrate" and "assimilate" objects "magically": in the "fire meditation," for instance, the yogī penetrates the very essence of fire.[2]

It is difficult to remain in any one of these internal yogic states for an extended period of time, for one successively passes automatically and without realizing it from the concentrative to the meditative state and finally reaches the culminating phase of mystical repose[3] which, under the form "appeasement of thought," is the apogee of the Individual Way.[4]

(e) *Appeasement of Thought*

Viśrānti is a word difficult to translate;[5] basically it means appeasement, quietude, or mystical repose. It has various intensities which parallel the extent of the yogī's cognition and meditative absorption. Hence, what begins as discursive, differentiated meditation eventually becomes pure and undifferentiated.

Abhinava tells us that the ultimate goal of all objective consciousness is the Self.[6] Spiritual energy is in effect a dynamism which cannot fix itself in any definite form and can only find its consum-

[1]Eliade, pp. 71-72.

[2]Ibid., pp. 72-73.

[3]Ibid., pp. 76-77. These three internal yogic states are collectively so interrelated that they are called by the same name, which literally means "to go together" (*saṃyama*), the author states that to realize *saṃyama* is to simultaneously realize all three. Silburn notes that "Yogarāja glosses viśrānti by *samādhi*, ecstasy" (*PS*, p. 44).

[4]Yogic meditation is basic to all four Ways of Liberation depending on such variables as intensity of grace, degree and nature of absorption, and object of meditation. Most exercises of yogic meditation, if continuous, will lead from one Way to another as the absorption changes from the self, to energy, to vacuity. Examples of this meditative ascent can be seen in the *VB*, vv. 59, 76, 80, 113 and 115.

[5]*PS* (Silburn), p. 44.

[6]*IPV*, p. 18, v. 9, cited by Silburn, Ibid.

mation in absorption in the undifferentiated Śiva, the Absolute "I"—a place of supreme quietude, the true and unique place of repose.[1]

But this repose is reserved only for those so gifted in the upper Ways of Liberation; in the Individual Way this absorption is in the phenomenal world of objectivity, epitomized in the microcosmic self. The climax of this self-absorption, Abhinava asserts, is the mystical repose of thought,[2] a state of mental serenity in which the intellect is purified of duality and bathes in undifferentiatedness. The mind is immobilized and freed from the perpetual flux of the elements which proceed uninterruptingly in Time. The soul retreats within itself and remains at rest; the personal thirst which motivates transmigration is held in check and fragmented objectivity vanishes.[3]

The *Tantra on the Tremendous Wisdom God* (*Vijñāna Bhairava*), Triadism's classic on the salvific means, has numerous verses on this topic in its various degrees. Verses 27, 52, 79, and 83 in particular underscore the yogī's concentration on his own physical body resulting in the mental quietude of the Individual Way:

Verse 27 concerns the "appeased" energy of retained breath. When the retention of breath is prolonged, a physical and mental quietude gradually takes over the whole person, and the yogī tranquilly resides in a mystical state where abrupt duality, particular to the two inhaled and exhaled breaths, comes to an end.[4]

In verse 52 the yogī meditates on the "fortress of his own body"[5] as if it were consumed by the fire of Time, after which quietude alone remains. This meditation is linked to the exercise of "projecting" (see *mystical formulas* section above) which infuses divine life into the yogī's body as he touches its various parts. Here, only the destructive flames of Time are perceived; dualized concepts no longer exist, and with bodily attachments annihilated, one bathes in an infinite peace.[6]

[1]*PS* (Silburn), pp. 15, and 95, n. 3.
[2]*TA*, III, v. 211.
[3]*PS* (Silburn), p. 44.
[4]*VB*, (Silburn), p. 79; see also v. 24, p. 77, which deals with the repose of breathing (the interval of retention between the inspired and expired breaths).
[5]In her commentary to verse 52 (p. 98, n. 3), Silburn explains that "Indian philosophers since the time of the *Upaniṣads* have enjoyed comparing the body to an eight-sided fortress; here a strong place that can only be defeated by fire."
[6]*VB* (Silburn), p. 98.

Verse 79 speaks of the yogī sitting comfortably on a seat while concentrating on the hollow of his armpits as his arms are pressed forcefully across his chest. This exercise leads to a profound self-absorption; completely enclosed within his repose, his thoughts well appeased, a great silence and immobility is produced within the soul. This physical and mental quietude produces a similar peace of the mystical order.[1]

Finally, verse 83 deals with the continuous and monotonous jolting or rocking of the body in motion (the movement may be either rapid or slow). A sense of disorientation and a somewhat suspended relationship with the visual world results, although the introverted thought remains protected and experiences appeasement. The extreme rapidity or slowness of motion provokes an interior slackening of thought—the first step toward immobility.[2]

But this appeasement of thought is only a prelude to the revelation from movement within the self; the Tremendous State (*bhairava*), under the aspect of a powerful stream, eventually and suddenly, will overflow the heart of the contemplative yogī.[3] First he must relinquish his concentration on objects if he is to move up to the next stage of liberation. It is to this Way that I shall now turn.

B. *The Energic Way: Absorption in Energy*

The Energic Way, characteristic of the Gradation School, is also called the Way of Knowledge (*jñānopāya*). The initiate is to realize the Self through knowledge; correct reasoning (*bhāvanā*[4]) removes the ignorance regarding the true nature of the self.[5] Meditation over the identity of the individual and the universe leads to self-realization.[6]

Accordingly, this Way is primarily concerned with the states of consciousness and the psychological practices that bring about absorption or immersion of the individual's consciousness in the

[1] Ibid., pp. 120-21.

[2] Ibid., p. 123.

[3] Ibid.

[4] The Sanskrit term *bhāvanā* has many meanings such as, correct reasoning, pure energy, and mystical realization; for other definitions see pp. 48-49 below.

[5] L.N. Sharma, *Kashmir Śaivism* (Varanasi: B.V. Prakashan, 1972), pp. 54-55, 353.

[6] *PHr* (Singh), v. 15, pp. 77-79.

divine. Gradually his feeling of duality becomes lessened and his consciousness merges in ultimate Reality.[1]

This subtle Way of Knowledge serves as a transition between the Inferior and Superior Paths and is shorter and more direct than the Way of Activity (Individual Way). It does not respond, as the former does, to a deliberate effort of the will. Rather, it is affected by the intensity of energy aroused spontaneously by the love towards Śiva, or from violent emotions—such as passion, stupefaction, terror, anger—which suddenly unify the entire being.[2]

Sublimation enjoys a predominant role here: the yogī is no longer anchored to the concrete immediate, but works on a concept or an image which he purifies by such intense contemplation until only a single thought exclusively absorbs his attention. Energy in its purest form emerges here, immersed in bliss and in the indivisible consciousness of the unlimited subject.

Silburn identifies five distinct and successive stages in this Way: appeasement, absorption, undifferentiated awareness, reaffirmtion of imagination, and the Tremendous State.

(1) *Appeasement.* In order to reanimate this subtle energy, the disciple must relinquish his concentration on objects and develop a specifically mystical attitude. The impetus of Imagination, accompanied by an intense and total conviction, is thereby led to stabilize the intellect, impelling it to concentrate upon the original energy in its emergent manifestations. These take the forms of bliss; knowledge; desire, in its infant state; introverted breathing arising along the spinal cord, awakening the Coiled Potency; and interior resonance or vibration. In this way, without mental or physical effort, the yogī enters into contact with the undifferentiated energy of his consciousness and attains perfect relaxation, spontaneity, and appeasement of agitation coming from a natural detachment or from adoration.

(2) *Absorption* (*laya*). The yogī then becomes absorbed in this aroused energy at its source. This absorption is the result of the abrupt collapse of the limits and structures of his personality.

(3) Momentary *undifferentiated consciousness* (*nirvikalpa*). The void suddenly becomes deeper, intuition freed from duality flashes

[1]Ibid., p. 18.
[2]*VB* (Silburn), pp. 28-29.

unexpectedly, retaining its awareness of Emptiness for a brief moment.

(4) *Reaffirmation of the Imagination* (*bhāvanā*). The yogī then tries to affirm this instantaneous intuition by again using the universal energy in the form of imagination. Indeed, mystical intuition cannot transform the entire person, nor can it pacify him completely. Only a powerful suggestion (such as—"I am Śiva, omnipresent and omniscient") which gradually penetrates to the source of free energy is apt to put a check on suggestions engendered by subconscious tendencies, to untie complexities, and to recast the personality.

(5) The *Tremendous State*. The entire being then collects and unifies itself in a permanent way in the peace and tranquillity which the yogī has reached. Following repeated contacts with Reality, that which was only a passing stage is gradually revealed as the durable essence of the conscious subject, and the Tremendous State is attained in its immanence. Thus, on this Way, one does not transcend existence—that is, Consciousness in its conceptualizable aspect—as in the Divine Way; but existence spontaneously attracts the yogī in its depths, up to the source of life (the Inconceptualizable Consciousness) where all conflict is absorbed.[1]

I shall first treat jointly the mystical centers (*cakras*), and the Coiled or Serpentine Potency which offers a synthesis of the diverse aspects of the Energic Way. Then, the actualization of the Imagination which constitutes the major trait of this Way will be studied. Finally, Ritual Sex which incorporates these aspects of the Energic Way will be established as an integral part of this Way, and the rite itself will be discussed.

1. The Mystical Centers and the Coiled or Serpentine Potency

Tantric practices can be viewed as comprising two sequential stages. First, the *cosmicization of the human body*, in which all the elements of the universe, its powers and functions are believed to be latent. In the Inferior Way, we have seen, the yogī accomplishes this cosmic-corporeal identification through yogic practices—such as concentration and absorption—using images in mental worship,

[1]Ibid., pp. 29-30.

bodily attitudes and gestures, recitation of formulas, and breath retention. Second, the *yogic experience of a cosmic transcendence through the unification of opposites*. This experience is culminated, in the awakening and ascent of the Coiled Potency, the union of Śiva and Energy in the highest mystical center in the yogī's brain—the abode of Śiva.[1]

To experience this transcendence, he continues to concentrate his attention on the place where the cosmic forces are most accessible to him—his own body; and he continues to utilize the yogic practices developed so well in the previous Way, through which he transcended the cosmos by the immobilization of time. However, in the Energic Way, he employs these practices in their most advanced form, by meditating on the various mystical centers in the body and by using them to awaken the latent forces resting or "coiled" within these centers.[2]

(a) *The Seven Centers*

Hindu Tantrism postulates seven primary mystical centers of consciousness in the body called circles or wheels (*cakras*) situated along the spinal column.[3] While the terms of yogic anatomy refer to a "subtle body" and describe a "mystical physiology,"[4] they seem to correspond to plexuses or nerve centers[5] in the human body as we know it. The names and locations of these centers are as follows:

(1) The Root Support (*mūlādhāra*), situated at the base of the body's vertical axis between the anal orifice and the genital organs.[6] This is where the Coiled Potency, the abode of Energy rests, blocking access to the Central or Gracious channel (*suṣumnānāḍī*).

[1]Eliade, pp. 244-45.

[2]Hopkins, p. 128.

[3]Avalon, Plate I, The Centres or Lotuses (Frontispiece). For a fuller treatment of these centers see his translation of *Ṣaṭ-Cakra-Nirūpaṇa* ("Description of and Investigation into the Six Bodily Centers"), pp. 317-480.

[4]Eliade, p. 239.

[5]Das Gupta, p. 292; see also Lallā, *Lallā-Vākyāni, or The Wise Sayings of Lal Dēd: A Mystic Poetess of Ancient Kashmir*, vol. 17: ed., trans., notes, and vocab., George Grierson and Lionel D. Barnett (London: Royal Asiatic Society, 1920), p. 19.

[6]Avalon, Plate II, facing p. 355.

It symbolizes the earth and has been identified with the sacrococcygeal plexus.[1]

(2) The Own Place (*svādhiṣṭhāna*) sits at the base of the male genital organ; it symbolizes water[2] and has been identified with the sacral plexus.[3]

(3) The Jewel City (*maṇipura*) center is located in the lumbar region at the level of the navel; it symbolizes fire[4] and has been identified with the epigastric plexus.[5]

(4) The Unbeaten (*anāhata*) is situated opposite the heart, the seat of exhaled breath (*prāṇa*); it symbolizes air[6] and has been identified with the cardiac plexus.[7]

(5) The Immaculate (*viśuddha*) center is situated at the base of the throat; it symbolizes ether[8] and has been identified with the laryngeal or pharyngeal plexus.[9]

(6) The Command (*ājñā*) is located between the eyebrows and is the seat of the cognitive faculties and the Supreme Śiva;[10] it has been identified with the cavernous plexus.[11]

(7) The Thousand-Spoked (*sahasrāra*) center is located at the top of the head under the form of a thousand-petaled lotus and has been identified with the medulla oblongata.[12] It is the terminus of the Brahma cavity (*brahmarandhra*), identified with the central canal of the spinal cord (or the anterior fontanelle). Here the Coiled Potency ends her journey, after piercing the six anterior centers, and realizes her final reunion with Śiva. This last center is no longer associated with the plane of the body; it is the plane of transcendence, and, in fact, explains why writers usually speak of the doctrine of "six" centers.[13]

1Eliade, p. 241.
2Avalon, Plate III, facing p. 365.
3Lallā, p. 19.
4Avalon, Plate IV, facing p. 369.
5Lallā, p. 19.
6Avalon, Plate V, facing p. 381.
7Lallā, p. 19.
8Avalon, Plate VI, facing. p 391.
9Lallā, p. 19.
10Avalon, Plate VII, facing p. 413.
11Lallā, p. 19.
12Ibid.
13Eliade, pp. 241-43. Some authors claim that the seventh *cakra* is not merely a site in the cerebrum but the entire brain itself; hence, it is depicted as sur-

These Centers are nourished by innumerable conduits or channels, through which the vital energy (in the form of "breaths") circulates; but for the yogī only three are significant. The right side of the body is the region of Śiva, and here the right or Yellow channel (*piṅgalā*) carries the Descendant or Inhaled breath to activate the centers. The Ascendant or Exhaled breath represents Energy and travels through the region of Energy, the body's left or Vital channel (*iḍā*), and is probably the left sympathetic cord. The goal is to neutralize the two breaths by blocking the left and right channels, forcing the vital air up the central or Gracious channel in the tranquillity of perfect commingling of cosmic energy.[1]

(b) *The "Awakening"*

Since the opening to the central channel is blocked by the Coiled Potency which rests at the base of the body's lowest center, this energy must be first awakened and then sent up the cerebrospinal canal if it is to activate the mystical centers. Although all the yogic disciplines discussed in the previous Way are utilized in the awakening process,[2] the most essential technique employed is arresting respiration.[3]

> The *cakras* are the depository of all the names, forms and gods brought forth in creation. The *Kuṇḍalinī* is Śakti, the creative energy or power of Śiva, resting at the opposite end of creation from Śiva. The Tantric yogin rouses Śakti and brings her back into union with Śiva, bringing back with her all that has been created.[4]

---

rounding the head as a lotus cap in Avalon, Plate I, Frontispiece. Once the Divine Cosmic Energy enters the brain, the whole of the cranium is illumined and a new pattern of consciousness is born.

[1]For a treatment of the three channels see Eliade, pp. 236-41.

[2]Swami Pratyagatmananda, "Tantra as a Way of Realization," *CHI*, pp. 236, 238. Here the author states that "The actual *modus operandi* of the rousing process and of the 'piercing' of the *cakras*...is a very vital mode of Tāntrika and, we may add, of every form of *sādhanā* (p. 236)...It is the basis of every *sādhanā* in every form (p. 238)."

[3]Eliade, p. 247.

[4]Hopkins, p. 128.

The centers are heated by the return passage of Energy[1] and left cold and lifeless as she absorbs the created entities and returns them to their primal place of rest in the summit of the yogī's brain.[2] As she pierces one center after another,[3] the Coiled Potency absorbs, purifies, and otherwise sublimates the elements of the body as though she were a fire that cleansed rather than destroyed. And the yogī, as he meditates on her ascent, experiences that purification on the levels of consciousness represented by those centers—until Śiva and His Energy reunite in the higher center of the brain, and purification of all dualized thought is achieved.[4]

2. Mystical Realization

Mystical Realization is the apogee of the Energic Way; it culminates in absorption (*samāveśa*) in Śiva.[5] Silburn indicates that although *bhāvanā* is a notion rich and complex it remains untranslatable. The term also connotes such abstract concepts as: spiritual efficiency, infused contemplation, intense creative imagination, evocation of the imagination, conviction, and obscure impulse. It indicates, first of all, an imagination conceived as an efficient and creative power which tends to identify itself with an imagined object. However it is actually subjacent to the imagination, as well as to the intellect, dynamic images, and ideas.[6]

[1] *VB* (Silburn), v. 26 and com. pp. 78-79, "flaming intensely, this fire consumes all limitations and permits the yogi to realize his own Self—the supreme conscious Self"; see also v. 35 and com. pp. 85-86, where the ascension of the Goddess up the median canal to unify with Śiva is called "central fire (*udāna*). In v. 52, we see the purifying effect of *Kālāgni*, the Fire of time who burns towards the top in the *kuṇḍalinī* process as the yogī touches, successively, the various mystical centers of his body.

[2] Avalon, pp. 241-42. "*Kuṇḍalinī* when aroused is felt as intense heat. As *Kuṇḍalinī* ascends, the lower limbs become as inert and cold as a corpse; so also does every part of the body when Śakti has passed through and leaves it. This is due to the fact that She as the Power which supports the body as an organic whole is leaving Her centre."

[3] Atal Behari Ghosh, "The Spirit and Culture of the Tantras," *CHI*, p. 249.

[4] *VB* (Silburn), v. 28-29, and com., pp. 80-82; also v. 154-155, and com., pp. 168-170 on the yogī's absorption in energy, elevation toward Śiva, and identification with Śiva-Energy union.

[5] *PS* (Silburn), p. 43.

[6] Ibid., pp. 45-46.

Abhinavagupta uses it, according to Silburn,[1] in the sense of an obscure tendency, both subtle and powerful, towards a goal, without the mode of its attainment being exactly conceptualized. For instance, when a man does something in great haste, he does not have a clear notion of his course of action, and yet, the action is accompanied by a subtle consciousness—a vital energy reaching for the goal. A concrete example would be the breathless haste of a man who runs to save the life of his child, without knowing precisely what means he will employ, without caring for his own welfare, and intent only on the danger to his child. His thought, submerged by the tumult of his emotions, does not burden itself with words.[2]

The same conscious tendency is acknowledged by Somānanda in *The Vision of Śiva*. He gives the example of a man who obstinately searches his consciousness for a forgotten word, and who, after repeated failures still experiences an obscure tendency which moves with precision through a successive process of selection and rejection of terms. Finally, he recognizes the word he was seeking, when it bursts forth in his consciousness "as a direct product of the heart." During the course of this waiting, which in the mystical life is accompanied by fervor, the first vibration of the will is only truly perceptible in the heart at the moment when memory emerges.[3]

Hīnayāna theologians like Vasubandhu also consider Mystical Realization an obscure tendency of vital energy which orients the flow of consciousness in a given direction. It is this energy which forms the key to the association of ideas in different people. This association, for instance, is quite diverse in an ascetic, a son, and a husband with respect to the same woman.[4]

Now on this Way of purification, Imagination seized in the vibrancy of its act as an intuitive and creative power takes on a fuller meaning. This strong and obstinate tendency which turns towards Śiva and Energy links itself to an intimate and sincere conviction

[1]*IPV*, p. 230, 1.2, cited in *PS* (Silburn), p. 46, n. 1.

[2]*VB* (Silburn), p. 31.

[3]*SD*, I, vv. 8-11, cited in *VB* (Silburn), pp. 32, 39-40.

[4]Vasubandhu, *L'Abhidharmakośa de Vasubandhu*, traduction et annotation par Louis de la Vallée-Poussin; nouvelle édition anastatique présentée par Étienne Lamotte (Bruxelles: Institut Belge des Hautes Études Chinoises, 1971), IX, p. 273; cited in *VB* (Silburn), p. 32, n. 1.

and plunges its roots directly into pure energy.[1] For the devotee it is a contemplative act, a psychic force projecting different manifestations of gods and goddesses perpetually evoked in an intense interior vision.[2]

Mystical Realization must not be confused with the concentration and meditation of the Inferior Way that attracts itself to one or several particular objects, implying thereby the bifurcation of the concentrating being and concentrated object. On the contrary, in Mystical Realization the theme and object remain imprecise; the thought, as we have seen, is scarcely outlined, and the verbal expression is faltering.[3] The yogī attains the specifically mystical and obscure zone—silent and calm in emergence, the fringe of intuition which borders on thought where nothing is yet crystallized. Contemplation, rapture, peace, interior word which seeks its own passionate and stammering interest, an irresistible attraction towards the object of one's passion—all these diverse elements are found perfectly blended in the dynamic form of the consciousness; but, at the same time, it is too simple and undetermined to be clearly defined.[4]

Perfectly purified, *bhāvanā* is equivalent to *pure wisdom*—the spiritual realization which depends on an undisguised tension, a powerful evocation constantly directed towards Śiva.[5] The yogī becomes liberated from his individuality and his discursive processes and finally becomes absorbed in Śiva.[6]

(a) *Perfect Compenetration*

Mystical Realization has only one goal for the entire religious experience of the yogī—absorption or compenetration in ultimate Reality.[7] This is characterized by a perfect balance between the

[1] *VB* (Silburn), pp. 30-31.

[2] *PS* (Silburn), p. 46.

[3] *VB* (Silburn), p. 31.

[4] Ibid., p. 33; *bhāvanā* is the theme of various verses of this tantra; see, for instance, vv. 43-46, 59, 61-63, 75, 80, 113, 115, and 145.

[5] "Bhāvanā relates in this sense to the obscure contemplation of Christians. Thus it covers the entire field of mystical life up to illumination and even beyond"—*PS* (Silburn) pp. 46-47, n. 4.

[6] Ibid., p. 47.

[7] Compenetration or *samāveśa* literally means "complete or perfect immersion or absorption." There are four degrees of absorption which correspond to each of the Ways of Liberation—as indicated by the four major subheadings

soul's free activity and enlightenment, on the one hand, and of the universal Consciousness of Śiva, on the other. This compenetration, says Abhinava,[1] is the only thing which is of real importance; it gives sense to cultic acts, to adoration, to practices of concentration and ecstasies, of which it is the true fruit. When the identification of the conscious subject and of the Lord is attained, there is nothing else to accomplish.[2]

> Thus, thanks to mystical realization, he arrives at the state of identity with Śiva in the totality of categories. What grief, what delusion can befall him who perceives all as the Brahman.[3]

And further on he adds:

> Inspired by the stimulant of mystical realization he sacrifices all mental duality in the luminous flames of the Self and becomes one with Light.[4]

The final theme in my treatment of the Energic Way is the mutual participation of the heroic yogī (*vīra*) and his consort (*dūtī*) in the Great Banquet (*mahotsava*), a secret sex ritual whichc ulminates in their act of intercourse under tantric "laboratory" conditions.[5] This rite is the central practice of Hindu (and perhaps Buddhist) Tantrism.[6]

3. Ritual Sex

Although sex ritualism may not enjoy the same distinguished position in the Energic Way as Mystical Realization does, nevertheless, it plays an important role in this Way. Since both Imagi-

in this chapter. Oftentimes the term *samāveśa* is substituted for the term *upāya* (path), Pandey, p. 312.

[1]*IPV* III, II, com. to 11-12, vol II, pp. 231-32, cited in *PS* (Silburn), p. 48, n. 7.

[2]*PS* (Silburn), p. 48.

[3]*PS* (Silburn), v. 52, p. 82; see also v. 59 where the gnostic (*jñānin*) has reached the "state of Maheśvara" in the consciousness.

[4]*PS* (Silburn), v. 68, pp. 85-86.

[5]Sharma, p. 64.

[6]Agehananda Bharati, *The Tantric Tradition* (New York: Anchor Books, 1970), p. 228.

nation and Coiled Potency are integrally related to the sex rite,[1] the latter can be more fully understood here, after having discussed the two former topics.

(a) *Its Rightful Place in the Energic Way*

Now ritual sex is practised by various schools, among which is the Family School;[2] however, it cannot rightly be considered to belong to the Divine Way of that school. Abhinava, admittedly, does describe this ritual as part of the Family School, but it is less in accord with the logic of the Divine Way than it is with that of the Energic—a Way of intense imagination, of pleasure, and of blind impetus.[3]

No spiritual life is possible, writes Silburn, unless the Heart—the mystical Center of the cosmos—has been opened.[4] By the opening of the Center, one attains, according to Kṣemarāja, the compenetration or ecstasy of the supreme yogī.[5] Abhinava enumerates in his *Light on the Tantras* five means in which the votary of the Energic Way must penetrate his own heart: the agitation of Energy; the absorption into pure subjective energy or into the Family (*kula*); the excitation of the nerves, and the relaxation of energy; the contraction of Energy within the Self; and the universal expansion of Energy.[6] And it is through these means that sex ritualism emerges.

(1) In the first means, the agitation of energy (*śaktikṣobha*) is brought about by sexual intercourse—the coagitation of man (sub-

[1] *MM* (Silburn), p. 19: "The Energic Way employs different evocations and practices...[such as]...ritual with a partner..., great reunions of men and women...having for their goal the arousing, in a natural way, of sleeping energies and to consolidate them into a single energy of exceptional intensity (*vīra*)."

[2] Ibid., p. 54. The Family School has a secret ritual, the Familic Sacrifice (*kulayāga*) which corresponds to that of the Gradation Practice (*kramacaryā*), while other schools admit similar rites and observances (n. 3). In her treatment of "the great banquet of *siddha* and *yoginī*" (*mahotsava*), Silburn concentrates on the rite of the Gradation School (pp. 54-59). Abhinava, she says (p. 56, n. 2), describes the Familic ritual in great detail in his *Light on the Tantras*, XXIX, vv. 28-63.

[3] Pereira, pp. 260-61.

[4] *VB* (Silburn), p. 36.

[5] *PHr*, com. to v. 17, cited in *VB* (Silburn), p. 36, n. 3.

[6] *TA*, V, v. 71, p. 317; *VB* (Silburn), vv. 66-70, and pp. 35-47 for her treatment of these five means of entering the heart.

ject) and woman (object)—"The excitement of union with Energy brings about Her possession. The joy of the reality of the Brahman is a reality abiding in ourselves."[1]

(2) In the second means, absorption in pure sexual energy (*kulāveśa*),[2] the object is dropped and only the evoked female image remains to the subject. The absent object which is remembered[3] intensifies the vital energy of the subject—"Goddess, the intense recalling to mind the pleasure a woman has given with her tongue-play and caresses, produces a torrent of joy, even if the energy is absent."[4] Thus, on the one hand, the extraordinary tension and unification of all these psychic tendencies quell ordinary preoccupations and the vibration of thought; on the other hand, the sensual pleasure which pacifies the entire being can bring about the experience of a higher joy.[5]

Somānanda recounts other psychic states which bring about sudden flashes of intense vibrant energy in the region of the heart, such as the sudden reception of joyful news; the spontaneous remembrance of a neglected duty; the soldier's penetrating fear of impending death during battle; or "when...we...are about to discharge semen, or exclaim as we discharge it....In situations like these all our energies commingle [or coalesce]."[6] We have already treated this transitory state of emergent energy and Somānanda's contribution in the section on Mystical Realization.[7]

(3) The third means of entering the heart concerns the excitation of the nerves which leads to the relaxation of energy (*sarvanāḍyagragocara*). Here the object is dropped entirely and only the pure subject remains.[8] All the joys of the senses are relevant to this

[1] *VB*, v. 69, trans. by Pereira, p. 372; also Kṣemarāja's commentary to this verse in *VB* (Silburn), p. 112.

[2] *VB* (Silburn), p. 112, n. 1 and 5.

[3] Abhinavagupta, *Commentary on "The Highest Trigesimal"* (*Parātriṁśikā-vivaraṇa*), v. 1, trans. by Pereira, pp. 369-72; see also p. 370 on "the *agitation* awakened by a memory."

[4] *VB*, v. 70, trans. by Pereira, p. 372; also Kṣemarāja's commentary to this verse in *VB* (Silburn), pp. 112-13.

[5] *VB* (Silburn), p. 38.

[6] Somānanda, *SD*, I, vv. 8-11, trans. by Pereira, p. 365.

[7] See pp. 48-50 above and in particular, p. 49, and n. 3—the same citation from Somānanda's *SD* is applicable here.

[8] *VB* (Silburn), vv. 66-67.

means:[1] their satisfactions refine the sensibilities maintained by them in wakefulness, and also, they give rise to an overflowing joy. Now thought, Silburn says, willingly arrests itself at that point which best pleases it or which provides it with pleasure. A relaxation results from this, and the appeasement of agitation provides a favorable condition for the opening of the heart.[2]

The tantrists and Abhinava, she continues, have always accorded an important place to joy. The Self, foundation of the real, seems to them as dense and indivisible consciousness and joy. The "I", intimate essence of Consciousness, being joy and containing the entire universe as a product of its infinite freedom, will desire nothing but itself in such a way that it cannot experience its own consciousness without its own joy. The slightest pleasure is a reflection of divine joy of the Self, and the enjoyment experienced when one attains the desired goal proceeds from the self-consciousness. The entire being appeased and satisfied is engulfed in its profane joys and experiences plenitude.[3]

Then, if the joy is enriched and invades the entire consciousness, the object—cause of the pleasure—fades away under the rising stream of mystical joy, and, through it, one is lost in the energy of joy itself.[4] Thus, joy, as Abhinava defines it, becomes the best means of access to interiority: "That which is called supreme joy, serenity, wonderment is only a determination of self-consciousness in which the fundamental freedom that cannot be separated from the essence of consciousness is savored in an indivisible manner."[5]

(4-5) The fourth and fifth means, respectively, are the interiorization or contraction of Energy in the Universal Self (*sarvātmasaṃkoca*), and its expansion of Energy or Universal Penetration (*vyāpti*). The *Tantra on the Tremendous Wisdom God* again addresses itself to these last two means: "Let the yogi meditate on the joy experienced at the junction between the fire (*vahni*) and the ever-present poison (*viṣa*). Thought thus detached, or breath thus elevated, he experiences the intimacy and joy of love."[6]

Silburn explains the esoteric language of this verse in her com-

[1]These joys are described in vv. 72-74 of the *VB*.

[2]Ibid., p. 43.

[3]Ibid., p. 44.

[4]Ibid.

[5]*IPVV*, p. 179, 1. 5, tome II, cited in *VB* (Silburn), p. 44, n. 5.

[6]*VB* (Silburn), v. 68.

mentary: the phrase "fire and poison" refers to a practice which works on two different but homologous levels—sexual intercourse, and the ascension of the Coiled Potency by a mystical use of sense joys. The practice involves, she continues, a man engaged in sexual union with a woman; his thought is so profoundly absorbed in the sport of love that he forgets everything else and thus rids himself of all duality. The technical terms "fire" and "poison" (allusive of images typical of Śaivism) have a twofold meaning: first, they signify, respectively, the beginning and the end of sexual intercourse; and, secondly, they refer, respectively, to the contraction (*saṃkoca*) and expansion (*vikāsa*) of Energy during the rise of the Coiled Potency which, as we have seen, have for their goal the opening of the median canal leading to the superior center of the brain.[1]

Similarly, in *The Light on the Tantras,* Abhinava says that this "fire" appears during the entrance of the breath in the median way and also at the commencement of sexual intercourse. It is because Śiva hides His omniscient and all-powerful essence that He is called "poison."[2] But the term also has the sense of all-penetrating reality for those who, endowed with knowledge, repose peacefully in the Energy of Will (*sadāśiva*); hence, this reality is only "poison" for the ordinary man who is ignorant of its true essence.[3]

Therefore, according to the interpretation of Abhinava, the yogī must fix his perfectly appeased and unified concentration on the joy of love, at the intersection of *fire* and poison—namely, the Center which forms their common essence, the point between contraction and expansion, the appeased state at the beginning and end of sexual intercourse. Or, he must meditate on Śiva and His Energy in intimate union, and he will obtain cosmic breath beyond inhalation and exhalation. Here is the true joy of love; for, united to Śiva, he will enjoy the all-penetrating joy of the cosmic order.[4]

And so, the rationale for this logical sequence of means for penetrating the heart is twofold: first, there is the salvific character

[1] Ibid., see Silburn's comments on the above verse, p. 109, also her remarks on pp. 46-47.

[2] *TA,* III, p. 170, l. 9, from the com. to vv. 168-70 as cited in *VB* (Silburn), p. 110.

[3] Ibid., p. 168.

[4] Ibid., com. to v. 170, pp. 168-69 as cited in *VB* (Silburn), p. 111, n. 4, and p. 47.

of limited joy in which any joy however small is a reflection of that plenary joy of the Self and, therefore, is a means of access to it. Second, is the salvific character of instant energy, which flashes at such moments as anger, imagination, and sexual orgasm. Thus, both the elements of joy and vibrant energy give access to the intensity of Selfhood, and are found in sex.

(b) *The Ritual Itself*

Sex ritualism according to Hindu Tantrism is divided into three distinct practices (*ācāras*)— left-handed, right-handed, and the Familic. In the left-handed rite, the consort sits to the left of her male counterpart. During the ritual the participants or votaries (*sādhakas*) actually use five ingredients referred to as the "five Ms" (*pañcamakāras*) because their Sanskrit equivalent terms all begin with the letter "M."[1] The right-handed practice is performed purely on a mental or metaphorical plane (without utilizing these same ingredients). The consort sits on the right of her partner, and the ingredients are used meditatively; or else non-alcoholic, vegetable, and cereal substitutes are used.[2] The conduct of one devoted to pure undifferentiated Energy (*kula*)[3] is called the Familic practice; it is a synthesis of the other two and is considered the highest of the seven rules of conduct.[4]

The purpose of the ritual is two-fold: (1) It is the means to the attainment of spiritual greatness through the identity (union) of Śiva and Energy. The aspirants become identified with the Absolute or the Tremendous God—the highest state realized by a yogī —and remain there even in the most adverse conditions.[5] (2) It is a test to see if the votary can have such control over bodily senses as to remain impassible[6] to emotion and pleasure (especially dur-

[1]Bharati, p. 244, they are—wine or liquor (*madya*), meat (*māṃsa*), fish (*matsya* or *mīna*), parched kidney bean and other so-called aphrodisiacs (*mudrā*), and sexual union (*maithuna*).

[2]Ibid., p. 229.

[3]*VB* (Silburn), pp. 62, 70.

[4]Ghosh, pp. 243-44; see also Sharma, pp. 59-60. Although these two authors disagree as to which of the three classes of votaries (animal, hero, and divine) the seven kinds of conduct usually apply, they both agree that the highest conduct is the Familic.

[5]*TA*, XXIX. 73-74.

[6]*VB*, (Silburn), vv. 68-70, pp. 109-113 deal in general with ritual sex and detached passionlessness.

ing the climax of the sexual union) and to concentrate on the pure Self.[1]

For Triadic theology, supreme joy is simultaneously spiritual and physical. The physical, experienced in sexual union, is not an end in itself, but only a means to the realization of the spiritual.[2] The use of wine and meat invigorates the senses, produces a state of freedom from want, and brings about an increase of bliss in the consciousness.[3] Sexual union is transformed into a ritual through which the human couple becomes the incarnation of the divine couple—this is "the true sexual union...all other unions represent only carnal relations with women."[4]

It should be obvious that the principals in this secret rite—the hero and the consort—must possess certain qualifications in order to properly perform their respective roles. The yogī who personifies the Tremendous State, is the hero or valiant warrior, and "only the valiant warriors (*vīras*) take part in the great Banquet of Life[5] having fully recognized the Self in its cosmicity, since they are the only ones able to enjoy cosmic bliss where the joys of this world and the bliss of the Self are intermingled."[6] In short, only the hero is equipped to pass the test (the second purpose of the ritual), for the *paśu* (beast) is bound by worldly pleasures which seek merely to gratify the senses; but the hero has transcended the sphere of morality. He utilizes these pleasures to attain a high level of spirituality.[7] The votary tries to rest in the divine bliss at the very moment he experiences the height of sensual pleasure. The belief is that he may attain the vision of Energy (*spanda*) if at the rise of an emotion he becomes introvert.[8]

As for the consort, she must personify Energy,[9] and should possess all external excellence. However, since this is practically impossible, it is only essential that she possess a mind capable of

[1]TA, XXIX, 74.

[2]Ibid., 67.

[3]Ibid., 77.

[4]*Kulārṇava Tantra*, V. 111-12.

[5]*MM* (Silburn), p. 167, "The Great Banquet symbolizes the Banquet of Life."

[6]Ibid., pp. 57, 167.

[7]*TA*, III. 296-97.

[8]*Spanda Nirṇaya* (of Kṣemarāja), pp. 39-40.

[9]*TA*, XXXIX. 68-71.

merging in the Tremendous God or State.[1] Also, she should be directly related to the yogī (this too is not an essential requirement), "because...there is greater identity of nature on account of both uterine and spiritual relations."[2] Although the yogī's wife could also participate,[3] Abhinava excludes her because of a strong sexual attraction he would probably feel towards her. The mind, Abhinava says, should be free of all "sex-desire" and other limitations so as to become completely merged in the highest reality.[4]

Now the secret rite itself is divided into two parts, the first being a preparation for the second more important phase (where the five Ms are used). During the initial phase (in which only the male usually takes part) the votary consecrates the site of the sacrifice with incense and mantras.[5] He then purifies his bodily members and identifies with the Tremendous God through the yogic means or formulas, touching areas of his body and concentrating on the deities associated with them, and finally by awakening the Coiled Potency.[6]

The second and secretive part of the sacrifice begins with the introduction of the consort; although she may be a participant from the outset of the sacrifice, most often she sits apart from the ceremonial site and is only brought in at the beginning of the second phase.

The rite begins with the worship of the circle of male and female votaries who sit alternately (female to the left of her male partner); the leader (*guru*) sits in the center with his consort. Formulas are recited to establish her as the Goddess Energy, in a manner similar to the establishment of the yogī as the God Śiva, which occurred in the initial stage. This process of "attributing " is vital to the sacrifice. The votaries must be identified as Śiva and Energy so that their pending sexual union will not be one of carnal gratification but the perfect and intimate union of the Tremendous God and Goddess—the ultimate goal of Familism.[7]

Similarly, the first four ingredients (Ms)—wine, fish, meat and

[1]Ibid., 70-71.
[2]Ibid., 72.
[3]Bharati, p. 230, right-hand practice uses the wife as one's consort
[4]*TA*, XXIX. 72-73.
[5]Ibid., 16, 19-20.
[6]Ibid., 42-44, 56-60.
[7]Eliade, pp. 129.

aphrodisiacs—prohibited by the Scriptures,[1] are first consecrated by various processes of symbolic purification before consumption, in order to establish their Energic natures and to remove therefrom the danger of forbidden elements. Once identity is established, the male worships the female as Goddess. The rite concludes with sexual intercourse, the culminating act of devotion—the union of worshipper with the divine Energy.[2]

Before engaging in intercourse, the yogī, now mystically identified with the Tremendous God, mentally worships the couch upon which he and his "eternal female partner, the Tremendous Goddess" will lie; he then sits on the couch and repeats formulas to his consort. After she is introduced to the circle of worshippers and consecrated, he whispers "seed formulas" to her, bathes her and applies fragrant oil to her hair, combs it, dresses her, and sits her beside him on the couch. He purifies her with formulas while touching her body members (as he previously did to himself). He continues in this manner, "creating the attitude of the oneness of Śiva and Energy," while he simultaneously performs sexual intercourse. In the end "he abandons his sperm."[3]

Although the vast majority of canonical texts (*śruti*) presuppose marriage to consummation, the tantric consecration of a consort is of a higher order than a marriage ceremony in the Vedic tradition; in fact, there is no question of moral right and wrong.[4] Energy is present in all things, in forbidden food and drink, and especially in sexual union—she is the Goddess, the eternal female partner. The problem, the yogī would say, is that men do not recognize their female partner as the Goddess and use her to gratify their senses; instead, they should worship her or the Goddess in her, and redirect their senses from gratification of selfish desires to an expression of devotion.[5]

According to Abhinava, joy, the essential nature of the self be-

[1]Sharma, p. 63.

[2]Hopkins, pp. 129-30.

[3]Bharati, pp. 264-65; the main difference between Hindu and Buddhist tantric practice seems to have been that the Hindu tantric, as described here, ejects his sperm while the Buddhist does not, "although there are some obvious exceptions on both sides." See p. 266 for the author's explanation of wh the semen is ejected or retained.

[4]Ibid., p. 242.

[5]Hopkins, p. 129

comes manifested both in the beginning and at the end of sex-union; and the repose of the self in joy leads to the realization of the true self and identity with the Brahman.[1] The person who has identified himself with the Tremendous God remains unaffected by the use of the five Ms, because he transcends the empirical level at which their use tends adversely to affect ordinary man.[2] Nor does the hero experience any desire, any shame, any doubt; "everything being Śiva, all is pure, all is joy."[3] Abhinava echoes this sentiment when he says: "That alone is pure which is identical to the immaculate Consciousness; everything else is impure."[4] It is for this reason that these ingredients must only be used to bring about the manifestation of the joyful aspect of the self.[5]

Moreover, by transcending the moral distinction between good and evil, the ritualist frees himself from all differentiatedness and dualizing thought, as Gorakṣa clearly points out in his *Bouquet of Great Meaning*:

> Abandoning themselves to the delight of the Great Banquet, where they drink the intoxicating quintessence of nectar from the pots of undifferentiated Energy—the revelers make bold to masticate the sprouts of differentiating concepts.[6]

And, in his own commentary to this verse he adds:

> These supermen whose hearts have been purified by a glance from their spiritual masters and who follow the Way of Śiva demonstrate the power, skill, and unshakable resolve necessary to bite, without hesitation, the sprouts of dualizing thoughts, subject-object, as well as all the doubts which are entrapped there, at the moment of some pleasurable experience, in particular, sexual union.[7]

Similarly, in the *Tantra on the Tremendous Wisdom God,* the author remarks:

[1]*TA*, II. 164-65.
[2]Ibid., XXXVII. 396.
[3]*MM* (Silburn), p. 56; see also Sharma, p. 65, and Pandey, p. 623.
[4]*TA*, III. 266.
[5]Ibid., XXIX. 67.
[6]*MM*, v. 58 as translated by Pereira, p. 387.
[7]*MM* (Silburn), p. 167, her interpretation to Gorakṣa's com. to. v. 58.

This purity which ignorant men espouse is, according to Śaiva doctrine, actually judged to be impurity. In fact, it must be considered pollution. For this reason, (freeing oneself) of dualizing thought means the attainment of real peace.[1]

Thus, the votary believes that sex can be transformed into a means of spiritual attainment, and this is the real contribution of the secret rite. Other philosophies—such as the Vedānta and non-Tantric Buddhism—hold that renunciation of the world as a whole, together with all its enjoyments, is necessary for liberation. They recognize pleasure (*bhoga*) as the major obstacle to this liberation (*mokṣa*). In the secret rite, on the contrary, pleasure is actually a means to liberation, an aid not an obstacle. So, while other systems view the two as antagonistic, the Energic Way, through its ritual sex, synthesizes and harmonizes them.[2]

The Way of Energy in which Imagination reigns as the creative dynamism of the consciousness forms the transition between the conceptualizing duality connoted by the conventional language of the Inferior Path, and the inexpressible intuition of the Superior Path. The Divine Way, first means of the Superior Path, is the next to be discussed.

C. *The Divine Way: Absorption in the Void*

As we have seen in the introductory comments to this chapter, the four Ways were grouped under two Paths, Inferior and Superior: the former motivated by little or moderate grace and composed of sequential stages comprised the Individual and Energic Ways. The latter incorporating the Divine and Null Ways admitted no stages and was motivated by intense grace.

The Divine or Śiva Way is also called the Way of the Will (*icchopāya*) because self-realization is attained in it through the mere exercise of the faculty which predominates over all other aspects of experience, the will—in its initial vibration.[3] It is an ad-

[1] *VB* (Silburn), v. 123 and com., p. 151.

[2] I will return to the interrelationship of pleasure and liberation at the conclusion of the final section of this chapter—the Null Way. Equilibrium between physical and spiritual joy is realized by one who is deified or Liberated-in-Life.

[3] "...his will being moved by the will-*śakti* of Shiva, the Yogic attains the

vanced Way in which observance of external yogic disciplines, such as concentration and meditation, are not regarded as important.[1] All the sensorial and intellectual activities of the soul are naturally introverted—so without concentration and meditation they spontaneously reach their center.[2] Even the evocative and intense power of Imagination, so essential in the previous Way, is left far behind. Now the gnostic is so taken (emotionally) with absolute unity that in his ardent and spontaneous thrust toward Śiva, he roughly brushes aside doubts and alternatives until all apprehension disappears.[3]

Contrary to what happens on the Energic Way intuition which illumines the depths of the Self surges spontaneously from within. The gnostic, having attained the Tremendous God in his transcendence, immediately becomes a Liberated-in-Life.[4]

The perfect compenetration of the Self of the yogī and of the cosmic Self (Śiva) is more profound and total than the absorption in the object or in energy of the two former Ways. In the Superior Path the gnostic's empirical thought is entirely dissolved, and the universe is absorbed in the plenitude of infinite Subjectivity, which no longer differentiates between subject and object.[5]

In the Divine Way, special importance is placed on total and spontaneous Emptiness (*śūnyatā*) and on an intense act of ecstasy (*udyama*) in which the soul is carried to Śiva by an ardent inspiration. These subjects will now be treated.

1. Emptiness

Triadism derives its concept of Emptiness from the Mediatist (*mādhyamika*) or Vacuist (*śūnyavādin*) School of Buddhism,[6] according to which "all our experience is confined essentially to the

---

'divine' means [Way of Śiva] of intuition; in a flash of light, by a simple act of will, he perceives his union with God." Matus, p. 64.

[1]Sharma, p. 353.

[2]*PS* (Silburn), p. 42.

[3]*VB* (Silburn), p. 51.

[4]Ibid., vv. 140-44 and com., pp. 162-63.

[5]Ibid., p. 52.

[6]William Theodore de Bary, *The Buddhist Tradition, in India, China, and Japan* (New York: The Modern Library; 1969), pp. 77-78. The Mādhyamika School of Buddhism was founded by Nāgārjuna, first-second centuries, A.D.

realm of chance or becoming. The transitory and the momentary alone is available to us."[1]

(a) *The Concepts of the Single Moment and the Interstitial Void*

As interpreted by the Triadists, the Buddhist theory of momentariness, or belief only in the existence of the single moment, maintains that everything in the phenomenal world (all objective manifestation), which has its being only within the Self,[2] is continuously undergoing the processes of creation, maintenance, destruction, and ineffability.[3] Moreover, these stages occur with such rapidity that they cannot be observed. An analogy can be seen in the flame of an oil lamp which only appears to be continuous; in reality a new flame is created every instant to replace the one of the previous moment.[4] It is in the flame of the lamp, says Gorakṣa, that being and non-being exist at every moment.[5] A second analogy would be a motion picture. Although composed of single frames juxtaposed in sequential order, when rapidly projected before the camera's eye, these disconnected segments are artificially fused in an apparently continuous animation.

Adhering to the principle of the single moment, the Triadic system rejects the concept of time conceived as a real and homogeneous entity underlying the instants and serving to link them together. In the absence of a real connecting link, the yogī is able to disconnect the "frames" of time and penetrate the interstitial void (*madhya*) which lies between these moments. Thus, he becomes the master of time, which he can create or destroy at will by residing in the instant.[6]

Abhinava calls the breaking of temporal continuity a "rupture of the two modalities of time"—past and future:

It is at this very instant...at the present, actual moment that

[1]Sharma, pp. 162, 164.

[2]*MM* (Silburn), v. 54 states that only the Self is permanent, it only becomes impermanent in relation to the destruction of the *instant*. Abhinava (*TS*, 60) defines the *instant* as the duration of an act of consciousness.

[3]Pereira, Scheme 35, pp. 498-99, re the four *kālīs*. See also Pandey, pp. 530-31.

[4]*VB* (Silburn), pp. 17-18.

[5]*MM* (Silburn), v. 10, p. 92.

[6]*VB* (Silburn), p. 60.

(mystical experience) is realized, while past and future are excluded. Then the present moment is also rejected as dependent upon the other two...

...Having immobilized his own wheel of light and having drunk the incomparable ambrosia, one may be fully appeased in an eternal present, after having put an end to the two times.[1]

In our previous discussion of the Center, we considered it, in one sense, as an interval (distance apart), a point of intersection between two entities. On the Superior Path this separating interval is viewed as a rupture or interstitial void;[2] it is also "the undifferentiated plenitude at the junction of the two poles...the plenary state of Bhairava," wherein the yogī who practices breath retention resides.[3] He directs his undivided attention at the junction of his choice to discover the exact point of balance, the one and only place of repose.[4]

Kṣemarāja remarks: "Since nothing can have an essence without inhering in It as in a wall, the august Consciousness is Itself the Center, subsisting (as it does) as the innermost nature of everything."[5]

Such, then, is the concept of the interstitial void; but how is vacuity itself to be understood? Is it to be understood in the same sense as in the above two references on the Center, namely, the Self?

(b) *The Definition and Implication of the Term "Emptiness"*

Before identifying what this term *is* according to Triadic theology, I shall first stress what it *is not*. Emptiness or Vacuity is not

[1]*PT*, p. 35, as quoted in *VB* (Silburn), pp. 60-61.

[2]*VB* (Silburn), p. 35.

[3]Ibid., v. 24, com. p. 77; see also p. 15, n. 4; and p. 171.

[4]*TA*, I, v. 83-88; see particularly v. 87 where concentration on the Center will lead to identification with the Tremendous God as in v. 24 of the *VB* (in the previous note).

[5]*PHr*, aphorism 17. See also *VB* (Silburn), v. 89, com. p. 128; here she remarks: if one is totally absorbed in the interstitial void, which ruptures subject-object duality, one retreats (within himself) into the secret recesses hidden from the world, and there "the Self or the ultimate Consciousness will be manifested." For more on the interstitial void, see *VB* (Silburn), vv. 25-26 and com. (pp. 77-79); 155-56 and com. (pp. 170-71); and *MM* (Silburn), v. 56 and com. (pp. 163-65).

to be interpreted as "nothingness" or "non-being." As Sharma argues, denial or rejection of something as unreal is possible only if there is some positive reality. If everything is denied, so is the denial itself; or otherwise, denial itself becomes a reality[1]. Thus, Emptiness is conceived not as nothingness, but as the ineffable absolute, which is in reality fullness itself.[2] The void, when considered in itself, as the interstitial void, and as the great or absolute void (*śūnyātiśūnya*) is Consciousness as Pure Act (*spanda*), generic energy taken in its undifferentiated and fundamentally free source (*svātantrya-śakti*).[3]

In the *Quintessence of the Ultimate Truth* (*Paramārthasāra*), Abhinava identifies the Self with the void—the absence of body, breath, and finite intelligence, or that which remains after the world has been annihilated—and calls it "the expanse of ether."[4] In his *Light on the Tantras*, he further remarks that the Emptiness experienced by Consciousness is this ether and nothing else. Characterized by the thought, "It is not, no, it is not (*neti*, *neti*)," it is for the yogī the supreme state.[5]

In her introduction to the *Aphorisms on the Mad Lord* (*Vātūlanātha Sūtra*), Silburn says that the author, in the manner of the Buddhist Idealists or *Yogācārins* and the *Tantra on the Tremendous Wisdom God*, conceives Emptiness as being, void of all determination: "If one plunges into the non-dual void, in that place is the Self illuminated."[6] Therefore, the Absolute Itself is a void in that It is free of duality and discursive thought. Emptiness constitutes the method par excellence which frees Reality of its limitations.[7]

In his commentary to the verse referred to above from the *Light on the Tantras*, Jayaratha calls this condition the Absolute Void (*śūnyātiśūnya*).[8]

[1]Sharma, pp. 165-66.

[2]Lilian Silburn (*Vātūlanātha Sūtra, avec le Commentaire D'Anantaśaktipāda*, Traduction par Lilian Silburn, Fasc. 8 (Paris: Institut de Civilisation Indienne, 1959), p. 41.

[3]*VB* (Silburn), p. 54.

[4]*PS* (Barnett), v. 32, pp. 729-30.

[5]*TA*, VI, v. 10.

[6]*VS* (Silburn), pp. 40-41; quote from the *VB*, v. 89.

[7]*VB* (Silburn), p. 54.

[8]*TA*, com. to VI, v. 10, pp. 8-10.

(c) *The Absolute Void*

The authors of the *Tantra on the Tremendous Wisdom God* uphold the primary relativity of the absolute Consciousness which they call "the receptacle of the great void."[1] In order to manifest a separate and varied universe latent within Himself, the Supreme Śiva initially flashes forth as Light (of Consciousness) in the Absolute Void.[2] This void is presented as a necessary phase of manifestation, for, if the Absolute "I" does not obscure His plenitude (through the Mirific Power), He can neither reveal categories and worlds nor enter bodies by taking on the appearance of limited subjects. This divine energy[3] thus seems to fragment the indivisible totality of absolute Consciousness by making it mirror (with varied reflections) the intellect, breath, and body; then, it engenders the notions of the self and the non-self. This is the process of emanation, which we examined in detail in chapter I.

The unique Center is bifurcated, and the resultant duality causes a disturbance and incessant agitation; but the undifferentiated plenitude (the Consciousness or Center), latent in the heart of things, replenishes the interstices of duality. It is sufficient, then, that the Center be freed from its dualizing processes and recover its native purity so as to reflect the universe in its integrity and no longer in its fragmentation. Nothing must be denied in the true self-consciousness, for nothing opposes it. All is Consciousness.[4]

We have described how the yogī penetrates within himself by residing in the Center or the void of the heart. At this point, it is necessary to discuss the pure act which functions as a catalyst, "shaking" the depths of the heart. In turn, it is this stimulus that sends the yogī racing to Śiva.

2. Mystical Fervor

Udyama or *udyoga* are the Sanskrit terms denoting this pure act in its initial vibration. Freely understood, they can include the

[1] *VB* (Silburn), v. 149. This verse alludes to the Vedic fire (*agni*) sacrifice into which offerings are thrown. The true oblation is seen here as the yogī casting, as his own body, the entire universe into the sacrificial fire of ultimate Consciousness—the "Great or Absolute Void."

[2] *PHr* (Singh), aphorism 4, p. 43.

[3] *VB* (Silburn), v. 2, 95.

[4] Ibid., pp. 14-15.

following meanings: flame of desire, thrust, and innate impetus;[1] ardor;[2] mystical fervor;[3] act of intense ecstasy;[4] act of illumination;[5] and ardent inspiration.[6]

The pure act,[7] so understood, blocks the present moment, and time suddenly stops; it alone constitutes the brief path to Śiva—that of mystical fervor. For the master yogī (hero among the yogīs) who resides solely in his act (of ecstasy), there is no other experience possible except this act itself.[8] However, before this impulse becomes a consuming ardor, it begins as a secret and subtle movement of the heart, an innate impetus without measure, an unforeseeable and powerful "gushing out" towards Śiva. The *True Import of the Tantras* (*Tantrasadbhāva*) compares the mystic rushing towards Śiva, whom he clutches with all his might, to the predator who descends upon its prey "seizing it immediately with its inborn impulsiveness."[9]

This initial vibration is also found at the level of our ordinary knowledge and is always carried out in three stages: from the *will* to the level of *activity* having passed through the level of *knowledge*. At the *first* stage, the consciousness one has of a sensation, intuition, or desire is live, intense, and undifferentiated. Instantaneous vibration penetrates with an extraordinary impression the person who experiences it; illumination flashes forth in an instant. The *second* moment belongs to the mental constructions of the conceptual and logical domain, and the *third* to objectification in the realm of activity. Now the Divine Way accords great importance to the first instance in which the yogī feels a sudden pulsation of his will towards Śiva which takes place in the intimacy of his

[1]Lilian Silburn (*La Bhakti: Le Stavacintāmaṇi de Bhaṭṭanārāyaṇa*, Texte Traduit et Commenté par Lilian Silburn, Fasc. 19 (Paris: Institut de Civilisation Indienne, 1964), pp. 39-40.

[2]Ibid., v. 77, p. 129.

[3]Ibid., p. 151.

[4]*VB* (Silburn), p. 52.

[5]Ibid., p. 210.

[6]*PS* (Silburn), p. 42.

[7]*MM* (Silburn), p. 47. It is the pulsation of the will that takes place at the stage of Energy of Will, and, at the beginning of emanation, manifests the universe as flashing energy.

[8]*VB* (Silburn), pp. 59-60.

[9]A lost tantra cited by Kṣemarāja in his *Śivasūtravimarśinī*, II, 2, p. 49.

heart.[1] Always undifferentiated, this impulse is situated on the universal plane where the cosmic Heart beats, and the conscious awareness of this pulsation corresponds to cosmic awakening and to the highest illumination (*unmeṣa*).[2]

This spontaneous thrust beyond all differentiation no longer belongs to the individual, but to the Tremendous God Himself: "The concentration of the myriads of energies everywhere perceived is Śiva the supremely independent, His essence the impulse of the Heart."[3] This energy of pure desire is so intense that the yogī grasps Śiva and possesses Him instantly and eternally.

D. *The Null Way: Absorption in Bliss*

The fourth and highest of all the Ways is called the Null Way or No-Means because it neither prescribes nor proscribes performances or rituals.[4] Pandey says it receives this name, "not because there is no use of any means whatsoever,[5] but because the elaborate means are of little importance."[6] The use of means is indeed minimal, and not arduous or disciplined as in the three lesser Ways. Specifically, the spiritual master utters some "identity" formula as, "You are It," and sudden illumination flashes in the pupil's mind. Many years may be spent in numerous practices, and suddenly, through his master's recalling to mind the disciple's identity with Śiva, illumination is realized.

The Null Way is also called: Blissful Means (*ānandopāya*), since the experience of joy is predominant in it; and the Way of Recognition (*pratyabhijñopāya*),[7] since it constitutes the recognition of the true nature of the self,[8] enabling the individual to attain self-realization without the need of Initiation.[9] Gorakṣa devotes the last section of the *Bouquet of Great Meaning* to the Null Way;[10] he

[1] *Stav* (Silburn), p. 37.
[2] *MM* (Silburn) p. 47.
[3] Pereira (translation of MM v. 13) p. 382; see also commentary to this verse in *MM* (Silburn), p. 98.
[4] Sharma, pp. 53-54.
[5] *TA*, II. 3.
[6] Pandey, p. 315.
[7] Sharma, p. vii.
[8] *TA*, II. 39-40.
[9] Ibid., VIII. 107.
[10] *MM* (Silburn), vv. 64-72, pp. 175-85.

calls it the Way of Self-Awareness (*vimarśopāya*), which leads to Self-Recognition.[1]

Recognition in the case of the Self consists in realizing the perfect free-will power of the Self—in the self. The veil of ignorance clouds the individual's real nature causing an imaginary distinction between it and the Supreme Self. Perfect Self-recognition consists in removing this veil, resulting in the identification of the individual as the universal Self.[2]

Now the concept of freedom is the chief doctrine of the Self-Awareness School—it is the doctrine of self-discipline or sovereignty of the Lord's will which is responsible for all manifestation.[3] "Freedom," Abhinava says, "represents the Supreme Energy of the highest Lord and includes all the powers that can be attributed to Him."[4] Kṣemarāja also brings this out in the following verse which depicts the first of the Supreme Śiva's fivefold powers —the creative power: "By His will, on Himself as the wall, He unfolds the universe."[5]

Abhinava tells us that the Null Way is the highest stage of the Divine Way; in its fullness the latter is identical to the former.[6] In this sense, the fourth Way is a synthesis of all the Ways of Liberation.[7] The differences between the two higher Ways are mostly confined to attitudes and practices; for instance, while the Family School has certain prohibitions, the Self-Awareness School gives perfect freedom to the gnostic.[8] This freedom is attained only through divine grace (*anugraha*)—Energic Fulmination, the fifth and last activity of God which leads to final release.[9]

[1]Ibid., p. 44.

[2]Pandey, p. 303.

[3]J. Rudrappa, *Kashmir Śaivism* (Mysore: Prasaranga, University of Mysore, 1969), p. 42.

[4]*TA*, I. 107-8.

[5]*PHṛ*, aphorism 2.

[6]*TA*, I. 182.

[7]Some authors, for whatever reasons, do not mention the Null Way in their treatments of the Ways of Liberation. Perhaps they do not recognize it at all as a Way, or they do not deem it worthy of separate distinction since it is said to be identical with the highest stage of the Divine Way and therefore should be included in that Way.

[8]*TA*, III. 286 and 288-89.

[9]*PHṛ*, aphorism, 2; the first four acts of Śiva are cosmological, but the fifth, grace, is soteriological; also Rudrappa, p. 102.

1. Energic Fulmination

In the Null Way, man, without personal effort, receives the grace (of the highest intensity) of the Supreme Śiva and spontaneously realizes Him.[1] In fact, Abhinava says, not only is it independent of human action,[2] but it is the only cause of Self-recognition.[3] Modern authors commenting on original Triadic sources also assert the Null Way's relationship between grace and human effort. Rudrappa remarks that redemptive grace of the first degree will immediately release the soul from bondage. This is called Intense Energic Fulmination (*tīvra śaktipāta*)—"such sexalted selves who are fit to receive this divine grace do not require any psychological practices, rituals, or initiations. They get light from within and not from external sources."[4]

Divine grace is operative everywhere and at every time. The very desire for God arising in the heart of the individual presupposes the operation of grace.[5] Abhinava concludes that it is undetermined and unconditioned. If it were dependent upon some condition, it would not be absolute and independent grace. It is the uncaused cause of the release of the soul. What appears at first as the condition of grace is in reality the consequence of it. The postulation of conditions or qualifications would be contrary to the doctrine of free will of the Absolute which carries on the sport of self-bondage and release.[6]

Now the one upon whom such intense grace descends is delivered at that very moment and becomes identified with Śiva, although he is still united to the body. He thereby enters the Tremendous State and is filled with the highest form of joy—cosmic joy (*jagadānanda*)—the ultimate goal to be realized by the gnostic of the Null Way.[7]

[1] *IPV*, I, 7, 14, cited in *MM* (Silburn), p. 15; see also *PS*, v. 96.

[2] *TA*, VIII. 173.

[3] Ibid., 163.

[4] Rudrappa, p. 132; see also Pandey, p. 305; *MM* (Silburn), p. 15; *PS* (Silburn), p. 42; Sharma, p. 341.

[5] When grace is spoken of in the context of "the descent of grace" it is referred to as *śaktipāta*; when it is simply referred to as "grace" it is sometimes called, *anugraha*, *VB* (Silburn), com. to v. 110, p. 143.

[6] *MVV*, vv. 611-90.

[7] Pandey, p. 80.

2. The Tremendous State

Final release can be either gradual or immediate, as we indicated above. When grace descends, illumination becomes equally manifest in all the realizing souls. However, these souls differ in regard to the degree to which freedom is achieved. The degree varies according to the extent to which objects are assimilated in the Self. Final liberation consists in the attainment of perfect Freedom, wherein the entire objectivity is assimilated in the subject. Abhinava brings out the urgency of this quest for true freedom in the following verse:

> Even though the Master of the universe always shines in us as our Self, nevertheless His true nature is not recognized in its transcendence and its sovereignty; the heart is not full of the plenitude of His Light. But when the soul becomes aware of the true freedom of the Self and of its liberation from this life, perfection will be attained.[1]

But the goal to which the gnostics of the Self-Awareness School aspire is not so much to liberate themselves as to realize the Self in all its manifestations and to attain the Tremendous State—Tremendous because it is dreadful to all differentiation in the manifested cosmos. Hence, as Abhinava tells us, this State is nothing more than Śiva in His relations with the cosmos. When a man is conscious of this relationship in all his ordinary actions, this consciousness causes him to abide in the Tremendous State.[2] The gnostic who reaches this highest spiritual goal becomes a Liberated-in-Life.[3]

However, not all those who follow the four Ways of Liberation attain to Liberation-in-Life (*jīvanmukti*). We have seen that those on the Inferior Path who, because they retain some desire for sensual enjoyment, stop midway do not attain liberation while "yet in the flesh." Others who have adopted the Individual Way are freed from nature and its bonds because they are no longer tied to the individual and illusory universe; although they will not be born again, they have not reached identity with Śiva. They have

[1] *IPV*, IV, II, 2.
[2] *TA*, IV. 206, com. p. 236; see also, I, vv. 96-100, and XIV, vv. 24-26.
[3] *VB*, v. 142.

stopped on the threshold of the pure categories where their own efforts have led them. Only the merciful grace of Śiva will allow them to proceed further on the mystical path to supreme Consciousness (*vijñāna*).

Those followers of the Energic Way are absorbed in divine Energy without being capable of union with Śiva unless a still more intense grace allows them mystical favor higher than Energy.[1]

The votaries of the Divine Way, privileged to become immersed in Śiva alone, without the accompanying revelation of divine Energy, only experience luminosity or Light, while Self-Awareness remains encapsulated in that Light—which means that their self-consciousness remains imperfect; they have gnosis but not freedom, and their bliss is only conscious bliss (*cidānanda*).[2]

Finally, truly perfect beings are those who are elevated on the Way of Bliss or the Null Way up to the Supreme Śiva. They both enjoy Śiva-union, and are endowed with his Energy; they are at once replete with full self-consciousness and the power of divine liberty. Having become the Supreme Śiva, they possess cosmic plenitude; hence their joy is the highest (cosmic joy), the experience of perfect unity of Śiva and Energy.[3] This is the Tremendous State.

Now the propagators of the Self-Awareness School give evidence of a constant concern not to separate mystical life from ordinary life, contrary to the general tendency in Indian religion.[4] Like the followers of Zen,[5] they are at pains not to disregard or deempha-

[1]*PS* (Silburn), p. 52.

[2]Using the *Tantra on the Tremendous Wisdom God* as my source, earlier in this chapter (p. 62) I mentioned the gnostic who was Liberated-in-Life while a devotee of the Divine Way. Although this seems to be a contradiction to what I have just said above, actually it is not. The tantra referred to only treats the first three Ways to Liberation; hence the author does not specifically mention the Null Way. But Abhinava, we have seen, held that the Null Way was the highest stage of the Divine Way. Thus, what is treated here as the highest goal of the Divine Way is in essence the same for the Null Way.

[3]*TA*, V. 356. On the subject of cosmic bliss, see also: *VB*, vv. 15, 65-66, 72, 74, 150, 152, and 155.

[4]*IPV*, I, VI, 7.

[5]Hakuin, *The Zen Master Hakuin: Selected Writings*, trans. by Philip B. Yampolsky (New York and London: Columbia University Press, 1971), passim, especially p. 58.

size everyday experience. They only reject as erroneous, the truncated and illusory conceptions that we tend to superimpose arbitrarily on the practical life.[1]

Consequently, Somānanda[2] and Abhinava hold practical daily experience in very high esteem; in fact, Abhinava gives personal experience the first place of importance in supersensuous matters, the second place to reason, and only the third place to ritual practices.[3] It is through daily experience, they say, that the yogī strives to elevate himself to the ultimate experience.[4] By contrast, these philosophers show a great disdain for pious and devotional practices,[5] claiming that practical life cannot be considered as an obstacle in the path of union with the Lord, because it has the supreme Self as a substratum. Not only does Abhinava connect the absolute Brahman to bliss, but goes much further by saying that bliss is the effect of the sensual enjoyment of daily life:

> the hero (*vīrasādhaka*), in availing himself of the three prohibited means: meat, wine, and sexual enjoyment becomes a *brahmacārin*[6] 'and the *brahman* is bliss (*ānanda*) and the bliss resides in the body thanks to these three.'[7]

Whether he walks, eats or attends to his ordinary occupations, the Liberated-in-Life enjoys a nectar of immortality made of bliss and wonder.[8] "As soon as a man has tasted this nectar," Abhinava says, "he is liberated and acts according to his good pleasure. Yoga, fasting, formulas, and ecstasies now seem to be only a poison to him."[9]

3. Liberation-in-Life and Impassibility

When through reflection, contemplation, and other methods

[1] *PS* (Silburn), p. 53.
[2] *SD*, I, the theme of which is on this topic.
[3] *TA*, I. 149.
[4] *IPV*, I, VIII, Intro.
[5] *PS*, vv. 74-80 expose ritualistic practices since the Liberated-in-Life has no further duty to accomplish.
[6] One who leads a chaste life, or a young, celibate brahman—Silburn, *Hymnes*, pp. 87, 93.
[7] *TA*, XXIX, vv. 97-98, quoted in *VB* (Silburn), p. 195.
[8] *PS* (Silburn), p. 54.
[9] *TA*, III. 264-270.

ignorance is destroyed, the individual becomes the Liberated-in-Life. "He that has burst the bond of ignorance, whose doubts have passed away, who has overcome delusion, from whom merit and guilt alike have vanished, is redeemed, though he be still united to the body."[1]

At the conclusion of discussion on the Energic Way, I pointed out how pleasure was used as a means in the attainment of liberation, rather than being in its path. I also stated that this relationship would again be stressed in connection with the Liberated-in-Life, "one who enjoys the complete liberty of the Spirit while yet in the flesh."[2]

As we have often seen, Triadic liberation is chiefly the manifestation of absolute freedom, the attainment of fullness (*pūrṇatva*)—consisting precisely in the realization of non-difference between pleasure (*bhoga*) and liberation or release (*mokṣa*).[3] "Release in life is nothing but equanimity between *bhoga* and *mokṣa*. When the experiencer and the experienced become one, their unity might be referred to as *bhoga* and *mokṣa*. Indeed, the equanimity in the experience of *bhoga* and *mokṣa* alone constitutes *Jīvanmukti*."[4]

He who has obtained deliverance in this life sees the world of the senses in a liberated way, and no longer views things as desirable or hateful.[5] Thus divinized, the liberated soul persists irreversibly in a state of impassibility, impervious to merit and demerit, pleasure and pain, and the entire range of emotions common to the human condition. "Removing from himself conceit, joy or gain, wrath, lust, misery of loss, dread, avarice, and delusion, ...he will walk like a senseless creature, without speech or perception."[6]

[1]*PS* (Barnett), v. 61 and com. p. 736; also *PHṛ*, aphorism 16.

[2]Matus, p. 20.

[3]Defining the term *mokṣa* as "freedom" rather than "liberation" seems to accent the positive and not the negative aspect of the term's meaning. This, says Silburn (*MM*, v. 65 and note 3, p. 177), also conforms to Abhinava's interpretation of the word: "*Mokṣa* does not mean to be liberated from something,—to free oneself from sorrow and *saṃsāra* is a totally negative goal; true *mokṣa* consists in the revelation of one's proper essence—self-awareness." (*TA*, I. 156). It is only a question of rediscovering one's innate freedom.

[4]Sharma, p. 359.

[5]*PS* (Silburn), v. 72 and com., pp. 86-87.

[6]*PS* (Barnett), v. 71.

Abhinava speaks of this in his commentary on the *Memorial Verses on the Supreme Lord's Self-Awareness:*

> The man who has continuously practised burying himself (*samāveśa*) in Śiva and has fully recognized his energies of knowledge and activity as being the pure freedom of the Lord can then know and do all he desires even though he is still associated with the body. He is not only deified (*jīvanmukta*), in the ordinary sense of the word, but he is fundamentally free because he uses at will the divine powers belonging to Parameśvara and lives in eternal freedom.[1]

If he is omniscient and all-powerful, it is not because he knows perfectly or acts upon beings or objects which exist independently of himself, but it is because he exteriorly projects and absorbs into himself the phenomenon of knowledge as a dreamer does dreams. For these phenomena, like dreams, do not exist but in the consciousness; and it is thus that he creates and destroys the universe. "All the realities of the universe which he previously mistook for bonds henceforth appear as a 'sport' overflowing with innate joy,"[2] as the free blooming of his conscious and divinized energies.[3]

Abhinava devotes almost all the concluding part of his *Quintessence of the Ultimate Truth* to both the Tremendous and the Liberation-in-Life States. He clearly describes this characteristic trait of the theopathic state, consisting in the "sport " of bondage and release.[4] He first treats the manner in which one absorbs the universe in Śiva[5] and how one acquires the revelation of the self as well as the divinization of his being; Abhinava then describes the activity belonging to the Tremendous God—the perfectly pure "I" which turns anew towards the universe and displays His divine Energies there.[6] This Tremendous God is Śiva, the sovereign

[1] *IPV*, IV, I, 15, p. 269, 1. 13.

[2] *PT*, p. 18, 1. 1. the goal of this literary work, the acquisition of the Liberation-in-Life State is developed here.

[3] *PS* (Silburn), p. 55.

[4] *PS* (Barnett), v. 33, com., p. 730.

[5] Ibid., vv. 43-45.

[6] Ibid., v. 46.

of the wheel of Energies which He controls at will—by the force of His "sport."[1]

In the course of the next three verses,[2] Abhinava exalts the almighty Energy of this Tremendous God. Perceiving only the undifferentiated Consciousness, always and everywhere, the yogī attains the divine state—the All. His impassibility is unshakable; whatever the circumstances, he remains inaccessible to grief, fear, worry and delusion.[3] No longer enslaved to actions nor by them, he will not be born again: "When knowledge is once gained, works performed thereafter can bear no fruit; how then, can he be reborn? The union with the bond of birth has left him, and he is revealed in the lustre of the Self, a sun consisting of Śiva."[4]

The glorified soul of the Liberated-in-Life is fully restored to its natural splendor.[5] Abhinava compares his divine actions to those of a madman because they have lost all significance, and his exalted feeling of plenitude inebriates the gnostic with divine folly.[6] Henceforth, he perceives in all things nothing but the undifferentiated fullness; consequently, he no longer cares about anything—neither clothing, nor nourishment, nor the place where he lives.[7] Indeed, he who views his own body as a temple in which to worship the Self could feel no other way:

> His own body...is a temple, i.e. the seat of Consciousness (*saṃvid*), the home of the divine Self. As a temple has windows, so the body has its organs of sense....the whole phenomenal world is to the thinker a temple of His own indwelling Consciousness.[8]

Now Triadic mysticism attempts to synthesize knowledge and action. The path which the mystic propounds is neither the strict path of knowledge nor the path of blind devotion (*bhakti*) totally lacking in knowledge. He strives to harmonize knowledge and

[1]Ibid., v. 47
[2]Ibid., vv. 48-50.
[3]Ibid., vv. 51, 52, 55, 58-59.
[4]Ibid., v. 56; see also vv. 57, 62, 70, 83-95.
[5]Ibid., vv. 64-66.
[6]Ibid., vv. 71-73.
[7]Ibid., v. 69.
[8]Ibid., com. to v. 74, p. 739.

devotion. Liberation is the state of attainment of consciousness-bliss, or the rapture of supreme egoity. The element of consciousness in this state represents knowledge, and that of bliss, devotion. Accordingly, liberation is the state of perfect identity of consciousness and freedom—it is the supreme Self-consciousness which is the basis of all devotion.[1]

I turn my attention in Chapter III to the theme of devotion as exemplified in the works of the devotional poets of Kashmir.

[1]Sharma, pp. 350-51.

CHAPTER III

DEVOTIONAL TRIADISM

Triadic thought combines the rigor of theological analysis with the depth of emotional experience; it demonstrates, to a high degree, the harmony between mysticism and theology so characteristic of the Indic faiths—as contrasted with the Semitic religions, so preoccupied with God's *otherness*, and so dubious about the possibility of a union between a finite creature and a transcendent God. However, Semitic though it is, "Christianity is the exception because it introduces into a monotheistic system an idea that is wholly foreign to it, namely, the Incarnation of God in the Person of Jesus Christ. Such an idea is as repulsive to the strict monotheism of Islam as it is to that of the Jews."[1]

Thus, from its very inception, Christianity reneged upon much of its Semitic character, and appropriated insights specific to the Indic religions—as the belief of a plurality in the divine consonant with divine unity (interpreted by Christians as the Trinity); the humanization of God (the Incarnation); supreme bliss as union with the divine (for Christianity, the Beatific Vision); the realization of this bliss through gratuitous divine election (grace); and the accessibility of the divine through numinous visible symbols (image cults—devotion to persons through their images). These insights, most favorable to mystical experience, were also the basis of Christian orthodox theology. Hence, among the faiths of Semitic origin, it is in Christianity that the concord between theology and mysticism is most complete—though by no means free of dissonance—giving rise to a mystical tradition of profundity and brilliance.

Of comparable splendor was the mysticism of Christianity's successor religion, Islam; although in the latter, orthodox theology and mysticism were in perennial conflict—Muhammad having reaffirmed the unmystical Semitic values that Christianity had radi-

[1]R.C. Zaehner, *Hindu and Muslim Mysticism* (New York: Schocken Books, 1969), p. 2.

cally modified. Orthodox Islamic theologians "maintained that there could be no love between God and man because there can only be love between like and like, and God is totally unlike any created thing: when the Qur'an speaks of love, then it means no more than obedience."[1] For mysticism to flourish, the "Indic" values had to be reintroduced. This was accomplished by the esoteric Shia and Ṣūfī traditions which were initially inspired by Neo-Platonism; later, perhaps, they were influenced by Indic religion itself. Islam, having become a combination of Semitic dogma and Indic mysticism, was subsequently to confront Hinduism on the latter's own soil. But their encounter on the plane of mystical theology was never deep, and the two faiths were not (until modern times) to realize their profound mystical affinities.

A. *Conflict between Knowledge and Love*

Whether or not tension exists between Christianity and mysticism, there is an undoubted tension innate to mysticism itself—between its aspects of knowledge and love, or its gnostic and devotional elements. Christianity affirms the preeminence of love; yet Catholic theologians debate on what constitutes the Beatific Vision—whether it is beatific knowledge (Aquinas) or love (Scotus) or both (Suárez). In Hinduism this tension is seen in the controversy as to which is the superior way to liberation—gnosis or devotion. The ultimacy of devotion, hinted at in the predominantly gnostic Upaniṣads, is part of the central message of the *Gītā.* But in the systematization of Hindu theology, the Era of Knowledge preceded the Era of Devotion, the latter subsequent to the tenth century. Abhinava can therefore be considered the last great theologian of the gnostic schools, and Rāmānuja (1056-1137), the first systematic thinker of the devotional.

Love thus came to triumph over knowledge, but the triumph caused no great upheaval in Hindu theology. Indeed, Triadism itself came to acquire a devotional speculation of its own, as seen in the writings of Bhaṭṭa Nārāyaṇa in the ninth, Utpaladeva in the tenth, and Lallā in the fourteenth centuries. At the same time, a conflict between knowledge and love was occurring in a neighboring theology, Islam, which was soon to engulf the home of Tri-

[1]Ibid., p. 91.

adism, Kashmir. Unlike Hindu mystical theology, Islamic mysticism had been mainly ascetic and devotional at its inception in the eighth century; but from the ninth century onward, it began developing monist and gnostic orientations. At the time of Islam's confrontation with Triadism in the thirteenth century, Muslim mysticism (Ṣūfism) exhibited a tension between love and knowledge, with knowledge dominant in speculative mysticism, and love in the poetic.

The confrontation between Semitic and Indic religions was, respectively, between an intolerant and proselytizing faith and a philosophy of tolerance—between a legalistic orthodoxy and ritualistic gnosis. However, as I have suggested, the opposition between the two faiths on the level of mystical theology was minimal. In Islamic mysticism, Plotinus had triumphed over Muhammad, and the creationist God of Qur'ānic and Asharite dogma had been supplanted in mystical speculation by the One manifested in emanations, and encompassing the world of created spirits as well. Many Indic traditions identify all phenomenal reality, spiritual and material, with the divinity; but Islam went only so far as to identify the spiritually phenomenal, or created spirits, with God—spirits which emanated from the divine substance and were later to be reabsorbed into It.

This absorption, the realization of the state of "Identity" was described, not long after Abhinava's time, by Abū Ḥāmid Al-Ghazzālī (1058-1111) as follows:

> And they [the ordinary mystics] are passed by others, among whom are the Few of the Few; whom 'the splendours of the Countenance sublime consume', and the majesty of the Divine Glory obliterate; so that they are themselves blotted out, annihilated. For self-contemplation there is no more found a place, because with the self they have no longer anything to do. Nothing remaineth any more save the One, the Real; and the import of His words, '*All perisheth save His Countenance*', becomes the experience of the soul.[1]

And further, as though describing the Null Way, he remarks:

[1]Abū Ḥāmid Al-Ghazzālī, *Al-Ghazzālī's Mishkāt al-Anwār* (*The Niche for Lights*), trans. by W.H.T. Gairdner (London: The Royal Asiatic Society, 1924), p. 97.

> Some of these souls had not, in their upward Progress and Ascent, to climb step by step the stages we have described; neither did their ascension cost them any length of time; but with their first flight they attained to the Knowledge of the Holiness and the confession that His sovereignty transcends everything that it must be confessed to transcend. They were overcome at the very first by the knowledge which overcame the rest at the very last. The onset of God's epiphany came upon them with one rush, so that all that is apprehensible by the sight of Sense or by the insight of Intelligence was by 'the splendours of His Countenance utterly consumed.'[1]

Al-Ghazzālī affirmed the superiority of gnosis, but his younger brother, Ahmed (died 1123) composed one of the classics of Islamic love mysticism. The superiority of love was ardently proclaimed in the poetry of the greatest of Islamic mystics, Jalāl al-Dīn Rūmī (1207-73), as the following four examples clearly indicate:

> Be drunk in love, for love is all that exists; without the commerce of love there is no admittance to the Beloved.[2]

> Is it not the case with everything in the world, that love is its vital soul? Apart from love, everything you see remains not eternally.[3]

> I am that lover of your love who have no occupation but this, for I have nothing but disapproval for him who is not a lover.[4]

> The girdle and cap of his love are enough for me in both worlds; what matter if my cap falls? What care if I have no girdle?[5]

Rūmī, however, endeavored to combine his mysticism of love with the monist gnostic theology; the latter continued to produce mystics of genius, like Shihab al-dīn Suhrawardy (1153/55-91),[6] and one whose thought was to have such great impact on Indian Islam—Ibn al-'Arabī (1165-1240).

[1]Ibid.

[2]Jalāl al-Dīn Rūmī, *Mystical Poems of Rūmī*, trans. from the Persian by A.J. Arberry (Chicago: The University of Chicago Press, 1968), no. 54, v. 2, p. 48.

[3]Ibid., no. 96, v. 3, p. 82.

[4]Ibid., no. 198, v. 1, p. 162.

[5]Ibid., no. 200, v. 3, p. 164.

[6]Pereira, p. 358.

However, despite their geographic proximity, the Triadic and Islamic traditions, for all their mystical fermentation, remained isolated. It must be remembered that Srinagar, capital of Kashmir, is but five hundred kilometers from Kabul, one of the centers of Islamic culture, while it is about eight hundred kilometers from Banaras, Hinduism's sacred city. Nevertheless, it was in Abhinava's own lifetime that Islam's major confrontation with Hinduism began, with the raids of Maḥmūd of Ghazni in 1001. But Kashmir, under the reign of its King Sangrāmarāja (1004-29) was strong enough to repel his two attacks.[1] It might have ever remained untouched by Muslim ferocity had it not been for the thirteenth century Mongol assault on the Muslim world, which almost annihilated Islam. The onrush of Chingiz Khan's armies (and later those of Tīmūr) sent great multitudes of Muslim Central Asians fleeing into India—whose outermost province is, of course, Kashmir.[2]

Suhadeva (1310-20), the last Hindu king of Kashmir, was overthrown by Zuljū, a descendant of Chingiz Khan, in a raid on the province in 1320. The king's throne was then usurped by the Tibetan Rinchana, or Rinchin (died 1323). Born a Buddhist, he desired to convert to Śaivism, but was rejected, only to be received with open arms into Islam by the Central Asian Ṣūfī Sharaf ud-Dīn Bulbul Shāh (died 1327). It was the latter who started the conversion of Kashmir to Muhammadanism.[3] Rinchana was ousted by Suhadeva's brother, Udhaṇḍadeva, who, in turn, was deposed by his Muslim minister, Shah Mīrzā, in 1349. The latter, under the name of Shams ud-Dīn, became the first Muslim Sultan of Kashmir, and established the Shahmiri dynasty which was to last till 1561.[4]

Most important among the immigrants from Central Asia, fleeing the advance of Tīmūr's armies, was Mīr Sayyid 'Alī Hamadānī (1314-85). He was a member of a Ṣūfī order founded by an opponent of Ibn al-'Arabi named 'Ala 'u'd-Daula Simnānī (1261-

[1]Girdhari L. Tikku, *Persian Poetry in Kashmir*, 1339-1846: *An Introduction.* (Berkeley, Los Angeles, and London: University of California Press, 1971), p. 10. See also P.N.K. Bamzai, *A History of Kashmir: Political, Social, Cultural.* New Delhi, Metropolitan Book Co. 1973, ch. 9, passim.

[2]Tikku, p. 9.

[3]Ibid., p. 11.

[4]Ibid., p. 12.

1336). Mīr Sayyid's dialogue with Kashmir's Buddhists and Hindus is reported to have resulted in the conversion of many to Islam. However, although one of the Hindus he discoursed with was the devotional poetess Lallā, he was not successful in converting her. Nevertheless, he must have communicated to her the Ṣūfī ideas which her poems exude. Combined with the sublime concepts of Triadism, they occasioned the mysticism of love that is comparable in ardor to that of Islam's greatest woman mystic, Rabi'a (died 801).

B. *Devotion and the Devotional Poets of Kashmir*

The term devotion (*bhakti*) means an intense or supreme love, respect, and adoration for God. "Supreme" devotion has a threefold meaning: 1) an undivided devotion for God, free of all worldly attachments; (2) it is not overshadowed by knowledge and action, and it is the highest end and not a means to any other higher end; and (3) it is manifested in both word and deed.[1] Hence, it might be looked upon as the total annihilation of desire for worldly pleasures and the over-abundance of desire for divine love.

We do not find the term *bhakti* used by Vasugupta, founder of the Self-Awareness School, in his *Aphorisms*. However, his *Aphorisms on Vibration* does speak of a continuous veneration toward Śiva (v. 34).

Since devotionalism was not systematized in Kashmir during Vasugupta's scholastic period (ca. 825-50), it is difficult to say with certainty who were the advocates or propagators of this trend within the Triadic schools at that time. However, three significant representatives of devotionalism emerged in Kashmir in the five hundred years between the last half of the ninth and the end of the fourteenth centuries, they were: Bhaṭṭa Nārāyaṇa, Utpaladeva, and Lallā; the major literary work of each one will be the subject matter of this chapter.[2] Predominant in all three is the advocation of a path of love unencumbered by techniques and means. Mystical fervor or "the flame of desire" and spontaneity alone are re-

[1]Jadunath Sinha, "Bhāgavata Religion: The Cult of Bhakti," *CHI*, p. 148.

[2]I follow here the format and subject matter of Silburn in her fascicle on *Bhakti*, previously cited. This work is primarily a translation of the *Wishing Jewel of Praise* (*Stavacintāmaṇi*) of Bhaṭṭa Nārāyaṇa.

quired of the mystic. For them, this path is the highest, indeed the only, path, for it is its own reward.

Bhaṭṭa Nārāyaṇa (855-83) was the direct disciple and successor of Vasugupta and lived in Kashmir. We know little about him or his family other than the names of several descendants. He wrote the *Wishing Jewel of Praise*; Kṣemarāja, Abhinava's disciple, wrote the commentary. The major theme of this love poem of 120 verses is the union of Śiva and Energy under the form of Light and Self-Awareness.[1]

The second poet whose work will be discussed is Utpaladeva (end of ninth and first half of tenth centuries). I have already mentioned him in the historical section of Chapter I as being the son and pupil of Somānanda, the teacher of Abhinava. Silburn says of him, "Both mystic and genius, powerful metaphysician, astute psychologist and above all, great poet, Utpala was next to Abhinava the most notable and audacious figure of the Self-Awareness School."[2] His love poem, the *Series of Hymns to Śiva*, is perhaps the most beautiful of the Śaiva love songs. Written in a simple although personal and touching style, its emphases are profound and true. However, since it contains allusions to spiritual truths rather than images and concepts, Silburn notes that the translation is particularly difficult.[3]

Lallā, a mystic poetess who lived in Kashmir in the fourteenth century was, as we have seen, a contemporary of the great Ṣūfī, Mir Sayyid, who was instrumental in converting Kashmir to Islam (1380-86). Although she belonged to the Śaiva religion, she was strongly influenced by Ṣūfism. She is also called Lalleśvarī by the Śaivas and Lal Dīdī or Dēd ("Granny Lallā") by the Muslims. After an unsuccessful marriage within a noble family in Kashmir, she became a wandering ascetic.[4] Lallā is to this day revered by Muslims and Hindus alike for her many four-line verses filled with a strange musical charm. Her style is simple and direct; her images (in the manner of Ṣūfī writers and unlike that of Sanskrit poets) are drawn from the everyday life of her time. Some of her images are seldom if ever employed by the Sanskrit writers, but

[1]Silburn, *La Bhakti*, pp. 8-9.
[2]Ibid., p. 9.
[3]Ibid., p. 10.
[4]Lallā, pp. 1-3.

are popular among Persian poets, such as: "jasmine," "garden," "wine," and "sugar candy." However, she utilizes Persian words only sparingly, substituting the Kashmiri equivalents even for Ṣūfī words such as "the Beloved." But the literary form of her poems is the Arabic or Persian quatrain, or *rubā'ī*.[1]

Her quatrains depict her own mystical life and thus serve as an autobiography. Unfortunately, not a single authentic manuscript of her works has come down to us, but there are several incomplete collections of her verses in existence; however, they are often in disagreement.

All three authors share "the sharp feeling of the divine presence." Their poetry stems from an intense resignation to the divine will, and it appears that much of it was written after emerging from states of ecstasy. The verses, reflecting the vivacity of the authors, are alive with such originality and devout sincerity, that we tend "to share their emotions, struggles, sufferings, intoxications, madnesses, and a little of their wonder." They ridicule the ascetic practices of yogīs as well as "outward signs of ostentation" and scorn the respect of others—their only goal is divine servitude.[2]

C. *The "Personal" God of Devotionalism*

Triadic philosophy, it is true, does not adhere to a personal God, that is, to a God whose subsistent individuality is emphasized over and above His conscious or intelligential nature.[3] The Tremendous God, and the Supreme Śiva are names it gives to the ultimate Reality, the Absolute and indivisible All, the Supreme Consciousness—names that connote non-personal entity. Nevertheless, ultimate Reality, as I have noted before, is the Self or Consciousness, and Its manifestations are separated from the Self as reflected external objects are from a mirror.[4]

[1]Antonino Pagliaro and Alessandro Bausani, *Storia della Letteratura Persiana.* Milan: Nuova Accademia Editrice 1960, "La Quartina", pp. 527-78.

[2]Silburn, *La Bhakti*, pp. 10-12.

[3]"Est autem advertendum, in divina natura dari substantiam completam et singularem, quae secundum praecisum conceptum persona non est, scilicet haec Deitas, vel hic Deus...Divinitas singularis est et individua, non tamen persona, quia communicabilis est." Francisco Suárez, *Opera Omnia* (Paris: Vives Edition, 1856), *De Trinitate*, lib. 1, cap. 1, num. 6.

[4]*TA*, II, 3-4.

But even though the votary realizes that he and the entire manifested universe is Śiva—all in All; it is still difficult for him to pay homage to an impersonal or non-personal God. The concepts of impersonality and compassionateness seem to be contradictory, and yet the devotee worships Śiva, the "compassionate" God,[1] the dispenser of "universal grace" and his "only refuge"[2] whom he clenches and "holds in his fist":

> 'Here You are, I *hold* You in my fist! Here You are, I've *seen* You—where are You fleeing?' With words like these the lucky ones, dilated with the Sentiment of Devotion, rush to Śiva, the Lord Weighted with Matted Locks.[3] (Italics mine.)

It is for this reason (in addition to that suggested in the previous chapter, in the section on *Images*) that images and idols were created, namely, to depict God in human form so that man could establish a personal relationship with his Creator. Hence, the votary, in addition to recognizing the inexpressible Consciousness also envisaged a personal aspect of God, linked to His manifestations and identified by such names as: *Śiva*-the-Beneficent; The Great Lord (*maheśvara*); The Tranquilizer (*śaṅkara*);[4] The Lord (*īśa*); The Supreme Lord (*Īśvara*); The Benevolent One (*śambhu*);[5] The All-Powerful One (*prabhu*);[6] and The Lord, "Weighted with Matted Locks" (*dhūrjaṭi*),[7] toward whom the votary's veneration was directed.

In a comparable way, as the Eucharistic Prayer from the Catholic liturgy at the Midnight mass of Christmas clearly indicates, devotion to the personal God, Jesus Christ, encourages greater love for God the Father, and the Holy Spirit:

> In the wonder of the incarnation your eternal Word has brought

[1] *Stav*, v. 35.

[2] Ibid., v. 52.

[3] Ibid., v. 68. See also v. 36 in which reference is made to "contact" as a mystical stage in the devotee's ascension toward Śiva; "he *touches* Him," says Kṣemarāja in his commentary to this verse, "he *embraces* Him with all his being."

[4] Ibid., v. 3.

[5] Ibid., v. 57.

[6] *SA*, XIX, 17.

[7] This is Śiva, the divine ascetic.

to the eyes of faith a new and radiant vision of your glory. In him we see our God made visible and so are caught up in love of the God we cannot see.[1]

Utpaladeva also experiences the worship of Śiva as a real and personal encounter, as these words suggest: "You are the Great Person (*mahāpuruṣa*), the unique one, the refuge of all persons."[2] And in another passage he says, "You are the Supreme Person (*adhipuruṣa*) always vigilant in a profoundly dreary world."[3]

We see, in the verse quoted above, from *The Wishing Jewel of Praise*, that the lucky ones enflamed with an intense desire of love rush toward their personal God, Śiva, in His form of the divine Ascetic. But why toward Śiva-the-Ascetic, asks Silburn? Because, she replies, like Him, they have renounced everything. Thus, this total renunciation or self-emptying of all worldly cares, desires, and attachments coexisting with an ardent and disinterested love—a passionless devotion for God alone, forsaking all else, are the marks of the ascetic. Where could you find these two traits more in evidence than in Śiva—who, for the votary, is the very personification of passionless detachment?

D. *Śiva, the Archetypal Ascetic*

Śaiva mythology envisages the Supreme Ascetic, Śiva with His hair rolled up in a "bun," with a serpent as a sacred cordon and holding fire in His hand. In His cosmic dance, the garland of skulls about His neck leaps up and down in a weird animation.[4] Under this form He symbolizes the universal Consciousness, The Tremendous State, which gives movement and animation to individuals who are deprived of life and consciousness of their own. It is this Tremendous God who haunts the huge cemetery of the universe, drinking from a skull the intoxicating nectar which has the savor of the cosmos.[5] It is also the sacrificial fire into which one commits

[1] *The Roman Missal: The Sacramentary* (New York: The Catholic Book Publishing Co., 1974), p. 379.
[2] *SA*, III, 14.
[3] Ibid., XIV, 18.
[4] Ibid., XX, 2.
[5] *PS* (Barnett), vv. 79-80.

the differentiated universe in sacred oblation[1]—the fire of spiritual asceticism, "whose purifying splendor," Utpala says, "is covered by the great ashes of (the universe) which it consumes."[2]

Śiva, the primordial ascetic, smeared with ashes, and wandering alone in the arid places of cremation and in desert solitudes, is the typical image of the yogī. In the course of His wild dance, He tramples on the bonds and the impurities of the mystic; as carrier of the destructive fire, His purgative flames burn their way into the votary's heart, changing it into an arid, passionless desert without feelings, pleasures, or a will of its own.

Although Triadic ascetics are vehement renouncers, they are opposed to ascetics who seek to imitate Śiva but fail to find Him despite their self-torments and bodily abuses.[3] True renunciation, the former ascetics insist, must be purely interior—the total death to oneself, total detachment from pleasure, pain, knowledge, and personal effort. Such detachment can only be acquired by perfect and uninterrupted contemplation of Śiva. For it is by this complete detachment from the world and heroic attachment to Śiva that results in the utter forgetfulness of self—even as "the All-Creator, who Himself became lost in forgetfulness."[4] The ascetic renounces everything and everybody and thirsts for the nectar of undifferentiation alone, generously offering the gift of self in mystical immolation.[5]

Bhaṭṭa represents the true ascetic as "he offers himself as victim to Śiva by thrusting himself into the ardent fire of the Tremendous Consciousness which consumes corporeal and subtle differentiations."[6] Its purifying flames cause him to act like an automation which responds only to the divine will.[7] From this point on, Śiva

[1]*VB* (Silburn), v. 149. *PS* (Silburn), vv. 68, 75, on the Consciousness identified with the Fire and sacrificial oblation.

[2]*SA*, II, 2.

[3]Ibid., II, 24. Silburn, *La Bhakti*, p. 54, n. 1. The reason for this failure to find Śiva is that the mortification of these ascetics lacks love and is, therefore, in vain. Full of selfish, mundane pride, they rely on their personal effort instead of acquiring the selfless, cosmic pride of "depending on Śiva" (v. 103) by putting themselves under the power of divine grace. This asceticism results in a mystical destitution which blocks the thrust of the heart toward Śiva.

[4]Lallā, q. 59.

[5]Silburn, *La Bhakti*, p. 54.

[6]*Stav*, v. 11, and com., pp. 105-06.

[7]*MM* (Silburn), v. 66.

reigns supreme, the divine will replacing the human.[1] Having thus become Śiva's slave, the saint realizes his utter "nothingness" before the Lord. In Lallā's words:

> When I beheld Him, that He was near me
> I saw that all was He, and that I am nothing.[2]

Similarly, Al-Ghazzālī says, "the meaning of dominion is that all is He and nothing else whatever exists beside him."[3]

The concept of servitude is rich with imagery and is popular among the devotional poets. Utpala often expresses the wish of becoming Śiva's slave to constantly seek ways to serve him.[4] "If" he says, "I had not savored with a profound respect and without interruption the nectar whose savor is the undifferentiated union with You, I would not be worthy of undergoing Your slavery here on earth even for an instant."[5] Utpala seems to suggest that in order to become a slave one can no longer belong to oneself, and it is in this servitude that he places his honor and glory. Lallā takes this one step further by saying that the loss of self-possession means universal servitude,

> He who hath slain the thieves—desire, lust, and pride—
> When he hath slain these highway robbers, he hath thereby made himself the servant (of all).[6]

Only those, Utpala claims, are truly free who are the slaves of Śiva and depend on Him in order to subsist.[7] He further comments, "Of what importance are others to me: parents, friends, and masters as well. For me You replace all."[8] Now the slave of an earthly master is a "conquered" soul who is looked upon by

[1]Silburn, *La Bhakti*, p. 55, n. 2. "The saint, in ignorance but through love conforms first of all to the will of Śiva; then he accepts it with clarity of spirit and heart; and finally he becomes identified with it."

[2]Lallā, q. 31.

[3]This is quoted in Zaehner, p. 169.

[4]*SA*, IV, 3.

[5]Ibid., IV, 18.

[6]Lallā, q. 43.

[7]*SA*, III, 2, quoted in Kṣemarāja's Commentary to *Stav*, v. 103, p. 137.

[8]Ibid., XI, 1; *Stav*, v. 75 has the identical quote.

all with scorn, but the slave of the heavenly Master is a "conqueror" who should be highly revered by all; for, exclaims Utpala, "those who have conquered the world and are Your slaves, O Omnipresent One, must be venerated by the universe. The turbulent sea of transmigration itself is for them but a vast lake where they play."[1]

As the divine model of renunciation, Śiva, according to Bhaṭṭa Nārāyaṇa, is the example par excellence of the ascetic with total absence of desire: "Among those who (follow) the difficult path of renouncement, who possess the supreme splendor of wisdom and carry to the highest degree the absence of desire, You, O All-Powerful One, You are the (most) powerful!"[2] Commenting on this verse, Kṣemarāja identifies renunciation, wisdom, and passionlessness as the three qualities possessed by the servants of Śiva: (1) *Renunciation*, which leads to the final goal—perfect comprehension of Reality. (2) The glory of *wisdom*, which surpasses the limited knowledge of the followers of Viṣṇu, Lakula, and Paśupati,[3] by revealing the Self-without-second, freedom, full of bliss, and of knowledge, immanent in the universe and equally transcendent to the universe. (3) *Passionlessness*, which consists in rejecting such yogic practices as mystical formulas, gestures, and meditation: "Your Reality is present everywhere, evident and well established. Those who pretend to manifest (You) with the aid of means, certainly do not know You."[4]

Śiva performs the perfect act of love and self-sacrifice when He willingly subjects Himself to us as a divine oblation. The ascetic follows His example, for the only one who can become supreme, Utpala assures us, is the one who in Śiva's image makes a gift of himself:[5] "Glory to You, Lord, Master of the Universe, who goes so far as to give Your own Self!"[6] This gift is understood on the *macrocosmic* level, when Śiva forms the Universe from Himself;

[1]*SA*, III, 15.

[2]*Stav*, v. 73; re Śiva, the Ascetic without desire who fulfills all desires, see also: vv. 19, 42, 51, and 63.

[3]Reference is made here to monist Pastoralism, "the dionysiac religion of joy." For a description of this see Pereira, ch. XXII, pp. 346-56, and schema, 33.

[4]*Stav*, com. to v. 73, pp. 127-28.

[5]Bhaṭṭa has already given us an example (above) of his own self-offering as an example of the "true ascetic."

[6]*SA*, XIV, 12.

but there is also the gift of grace on the *microcosmic* level, when the Lord penetrates the heart of the devotee and unites Himself to it by a bond of love.[1]

The following examples from the sayings of Lallā give further testimony[2] to the great importance she placed on renunciation and the resultant indifference to life and death, honor and dishonor; it is, in fact, a theme that recurs repeatedly throughout her verses.

On total indifference to either abuse or exaltation, she says:

> Let him utter a thousand abuses at me.
> But, if I be innately devoted to Śiva...disquiet will find no abode within my heart.[3]

> Let him bind abuse upon me, let him orate blame against me,
> Let each one say to me what pleaseth each.
> Yea, let him worship me with the offering of his own soul for the flowers.
> Still keep I myself untouched and undefiled by all these;...[4]

Disinterest in bodily welfare prompts the following remark:

> Don but such apparel as will cause the cold to flee.
> Eat but so much food as will cause hunger to cease.
> O Mind! devote thyself to discernment of the Self and of the Supreme,
> And recognize thy body as but food for forest crows.[5]

Her ardent desire to realize the passionless state is evidenced in an expressed suggestion to deliberately inhibit the proper functioning of one's own faculties:

> Though thou hast knowledge, be thou as a fool; though thou canst see, be thou as he that is one-eyed;
> Though thou canst hear, be thou as one dumb; in all things be thou as a non-sentient block.[6]

[1]Silburn, *La Bhakti*, p. 55.
[2]See Lallā, q. 43 quoted above.
[3]Lallā, q. 18.
[4]Ibid., q. 21; see also, *SA*, XII, 3.
[5]Lallā, q. 28; cf. *SA*, XVIII, 4.
[6]Lallā, q. 20.

Lallā renounces all but Śiva-union:

...the material world dried up within me.
With the fire of love I parched my heart as a man parcheth grain,
And at that moment did I obtain Śiva.[1]

Once wast thou a swan [flamingo], and now thou hast become mute.
Some one, I know not who, hath run off with something of thine.
As soon as the mill became stopped, the grain channel became choked,
And away ran the miller with the grain.[2]

In the first part of the last quatrain, it seems Lallā is saying that her voice, once melodious, has now fallen silent, and she has thereby attained mystical wisdom.

The last part continues this theme of silence and wisdom through the metaphor of ground grain. When the grinding operation of a millstone stops, the orifice in the upper stone becomes blocked by the grain hidden beneath the surface. Here, again, Lallā seems to be alluding to her newly found salvation and state of silent rapture. Now that she has experienced God, her preaching has ended and her voice is silent. God is represented here as the miller[3] "who turns the mill of worldly experience in order to grind out the grain of the chastened soul." His work completed, the mill at rest, the channel blocked, "the miller has taken to Himself the grain."[4]

Now, as I indicated at the beginning of this chapter, Lallā was greatly influenced by Ṣūfī mysticism, an influence which is clearly evidenced here in the concept of "silence." It is so pervasive a theme in the mystical poetry of Rūmī, that his exhortation to "be silent!" is present in many of his poems: speech, he says, is a wind that distracts the heart;[5] and "when the lip is silent, the heart has

[1]Ibid., q. 25.
[2]Ibid., q. 86.
[3]Rūmī uses the similar imagery of a mill operation in which the *miller* is God, the *mill* is man, and the *grain* is the human heart—see no. 21, vv. 1-5, p. 22.
[4]Lallā, com. to q. 86, p. 100.
[5]Rūmī, no. 7, v. 8, p. 13.

a hundred tongues."[1] Therefore, he repeatedly insists, we must be silent and listen to the heart:

> Close your lips and open the window of the heart; by that way be conversant with the spirits.[2]

And again he says:

> Wash your hands and your mouth, neither eat nor speak; seek that speech and that morsel which has come to the silent ones.[3]

And so, by falling silent and listening to the heart ("soul"), God will come and dwell therein, and His promptings will impart divine wisdom:

> Rational soul, be silent and depart into hiding like the thought, so that he who thinks of causes only may not find my track.[4]

> Like a mirror my soul displays secrets; I am not able to speak, but I am unable not to know.[5]

> Speak no more the grief of your heart, for I have carried your heart to the presence of Him who knows all secrets.[6]

> Reason says to me 'Be silent! Enough; for God who knows the Unseen has come'.[7]

> I have fallen silent, do you speak the rest, for I am shunning henceforth my own speaking and listening.[8]

And finally, returning to Lallā, we see from the following excerpts that although she is alive, her wish is to be as one dead:

[1]Ibid., no. 111, v. 7, p. 96.
[2]Ibid., no. 13, v. 9, p. 17.
[3]Ibid., no. 115, v. 11, p. 100.
[4]Ibid., no. 182, v. 12, p. 152.
[5]Ibid., no. 181, v. 1, p. 151.
[6]Ibid., no. 189, v. 16, p. 157.
[7]Ibid., no. 126, v. 14, p. 108.
[8]Ibid., no. 193, v. 10, p. 159.

...the soul that is free from desire will never die.
If, while it is yet alive, it die, then that alone is the true knowledge.[1]

I, Lallā, passed in through the door of the jasmine-garden[2] of my soul.
And there, O Joy! I saw Śiva seated united with His Śakti.
There became I absorbed in the lake of nectar.
Now, what can (existence) do unto me? For, even though alive, I shall in it be dead.[3]

Die, Sir, even before thy death,
Then, when thy death cometh, great honour will increase for thee.[4]

In quatrain 68, the union of Śiva and Śakti is the highest form of the Supreme Self, and Lallā discovers them in the tranquil repose of loving union within her own self—the "Joy" of her soul. The "lake of nectar" is a metaphor for the bliss of this tripartite union. "Drowned in this lake, though alive," the ascetic poetess is as if dead.[5]

This then is Śiva, the archetype, master of yoga and the supernatural powers, who reduced to ashes the god of carnal love. But beyond Him is the ineffable Tremendous God. Yielding to this Absolute, the relinquisher heroically follows the path of emptiness and undifferentiation—the dark and painful Night of Śiva opening upon the Night of inexpressible joy and silent bewilderment.[6] The ascetic is not unprepared for this journey, for the true renouncement that the mystical night requires must be purely interior—total death to oneself, and we have seen that self-annihilation is the seal of the ascetic. As Rūmī says:

[1]Lallā, q. 12.

[2]Here, we have an example of the Ṣūfī language influence mentioned above on pp. 85-86; with regard to the term "jasmine", see Rūmī, no. 25, vv. 4 and 8, p. 25; no. 72, v. 3, p. 64; and no. 141, v. 11, p. 118.

[3]Lallā, q. 68.

[4]Ibid., q. 87.

[5]Ibid., com. to q. 68, p. 85.

[6]Silburn, *La Bhakti*, p. 15.

The mystic's soul circles about annihilation, even as iron about
a magnet,
Because annihilation is true existence in his sight,...[1]

E. *The Dark Night of Śiva*

Abhinava pays homage to the undifferentiated and ineffable Śiva, the Mystical Night (*Śivarātri*): "Light of all Lights, darkness of all darknesses! To these lights and to these darknesses, Brightness without equal, homage!"[2] And Utpaladeva exclaims: "Let this inexpressible Night of Śiva reign supreme, Śiva whose radiant essence spreads its own brightness. It is in it that the moon and the sun as well as all the other (dualities) penetrate when they set."[3]

The Mystical Night is characterized under various titles, each representing an aspect which leads the soul to final undifferentiatedness. One such title is the Night of Undifferentiation; another is the Dark Night of Annihilation, where the soul plunges into the secret life of the Self, and the Night progresses in silence and emptiness to the mysterious brightness of the light of love, without a clear understanding, even though it is fortified by a subtle and hidden nourishment. Something the soul does not know makes it desire it knows not what, without its knowing how: "In a way that I did not know," says Utpala, I acquired the nectar of Your love, that I had not known previously. May it now, in the same manner nourish me, O Sovereign One!"[4]

This Night spreads to the various faculties which lose their dualistic functioning: *Night of the Will*, when the mystic burns with the fire of love before enjoying illumination; *Painful Night*, because Śiva, Who reveals Himself from time to time also hides Himself for extended periods; *Night of Thought*, for love pours out a completely "new knowledge," full of savor and delicacy which replaces, little by little, the differentiated and false knowledge of the senses and of understanding. The faculties are suspended and exterior occupations are interrupted while the prestige of the Mirific Power is erased.

[1]Rūmī, no. 32, vv. 10-11, p. 31.

[2]*IPV*, I, I, Introduction; see also Abhinava's *Fifteen Verses on Consciousness* (*Bodhapañcadaśikā*), v. 1, trans. in Silburn (*Hymnes*), p. 25.

[3]*SA*, IV, 22.

[4]Ibid., XVI, 5.

Then, in this profound and pacified night the agitation of the spirit having calmed, the saint plunges into Śiva. Utpala describes in a few words this *Night of the Heart* that Kṣemarāja identifies with an interfusion of Śiva and the Soul:[1] "The lover adores you perpetually, Lord, in the state of the *Night of Śiva* when there is not the slightest sign of a light, and when the entire universe is very drowsy."[2] Whether he sleeps or is awake, the lover knows the yogic or "vigilant sleep" (*yoganidrā*)[3] of love which will awaken him to non-duality. By the ardor of the will, the thought is as if asleep to the world, the entire being resting within the quietude of love. This sleep not only concerns the understanding, it also involves the heart. For the spirit must be stripped of its concepts and images by absorbing itself in the undifferentiated in order to allow only the pure consciousness to subsist without states. The heart, in like fashion, must empty itself of all that is not Śiva: memory, feeling of devotion, and spiritual delights, in order that the naked feeling of Śiva alone remain. Such is for the loving heart true mystical asceticism.[4]

Whereas Utpala has recourse to the symbolism of "night," Nārāyaṇa, like John of the Cross after him, uses the image of the "cavern":

> O that we may see Your interior cavern, enchanting and profound, in darkness dissipated on all sides by the Brightness Supreme![5]

According to Kṣemarāja's commentary to this verse, the poet desires to sink deeply into the bottomless cavern of Śiva—His Energy of Illusion, the Mirific Power—perceived in the brightness of the Supreme Light which dissipates the darkness of ignorance without and within. This strophe also insists on the ambivalent

[1]Ibid., com. to IV, 22.

[2]Ibid., XV, 18, and com.

[3]Kṣemarāja, *The Ascertainment of Vibrancy*, III, 1-2, in which he defines sleep as the "vigilant sleep" of the yogī who ardently desires Śiva and remains continuously in a contemplative attitude. In order to illustrate this mystical sleep he cites: *VB*, vv. 79 and 99.

[4]Silburn, *La Bhakti*, pp. 57-58.

[5]*Stav*, v. 12; note the similarity in the words and meaning from stanza 3 of St. John of the Cross' *Living Flame of Love* quoted below, p. 144.

nature of this Energy, which is at once the sterile and servile darkness of Illusion for the ignorant, and freedom and Independence for the liberated being.

Rūmī employs a similar metaphor in the divine "lamp of light", which he prays will dispel the darkness of "confusion":

> On the day when you pass over my grave, bring to mind this terror and confusion of mine;
> Fill full of light that bottom of the tomb, O eye and lamp of my light,...[1]

From the point of view of mystical experience, Bhaṭṭa searches the fertile darkness of the unexplored depths of the heart; for it is there that the Absolute Subject secretly reposes—invisible to the man blinded by duality. Yet, Śiva is visible to the mystic in the abysmal light of the "torch of unity," which, illuminated by the sacrificial flame, consumes the ego offered in "oblation."

Man, Kṣemarāja continues, needs "boldness" and courage to venture into the cavern of the heart in order to "purify it" from its unconscious residues or conceptual latencies (*vāsanās*), and to attain the naked will of the undifferentiated Consciousness which is the profound unity underlying memory, intelligence, and sensibility.

The cavern, "emptied" of all its distinctions, appears in its infinite capacity and under the form of a free energy,[2] as soon as it is found to be illuminated in the interior by divine splendors. In other words, man's entire being, including his "faculties," flourishes fully; and it is in these depths, those of the Self, at the moment of "cosmic illumination," that he can discover the universe, the cavern manifesting itself to him as the very "heart of the cosmos."[3]

This cavern is not only the birth of the universe, according to Abhinava, but also of the wonder-struck self-awareness.[4] From this, obscure nature emerges, for it is at the same time a cavern of illusion and a cavern of absolute Consciousness. Will, under-

[1] Rūmī, no. 193, vv. 1-2, p. 159.
[2] *Stav*, v. 29.
[3] Ibid., com. to v. 12, p. 106.
[4] *PT*, p. 55, 1. 22.

standing, and sense are darkened illusions which must be purified from their unconscious tendencies.

Now Lallā sometimes uses the symbolism of night to express her demand of self-annihilation:

The day will be extinguished, and night will come;
The surface of the earth will become extended to the sky;
On the day of the new moon, the moon swallowed up the demon of eclipse.
The illumination of the Self in the organ of thought is the true worship of Śiva.[1]

Here, "night" is the undoing (paling) of the multiple and varied world, and the sky and earth will mix in the *Night of Undifferentiation*. Then, at the new moon the moon (symbolic of the Conscious Subject) will swallow the demon of eclipse (dark demon of ignorance). The illumination of the Self in thought is the true worship of Śiva. The full moon is the illuminated world transfigured after emerging from the total night. The full moon is weak, if we compare it to the illusory day of differentiation. In the "silent" night all is appeased and undifferentiated.[2]

Lallā, however, prefers the symbol of emptiness to express the *Night of Śiva*. She accedes to the ineffable Supreme Śiva by progressing from one emptiness to another—always more perfect until she attains total undifferentiatedness.

There is there no word or (thought of) mind. There is there no non-transcendent or transcendent.
Not by vow of silence,[3] not by mystic attitudes, is there entry there.
Not there dwell Śiva and his Śakti.
If there remaineth somewhat, that is what the doctrine teacheth[4].

According to the author's commentary, the "there" in the above

[1]Lallā, q. 22.

[2]Ibid., com. to q. 22, p. 44. See also Silburn, *La Bhakti*, p. 60, no. 1.

[3]This interior "silence" is empty insofar as it is perfect forgetfulness of the self and the external world. Silburn, *La Bhakti*, p. 59, n. 3.

[4]Lallā, q. 2.

quatrain is the Supreme; a "vow of silence" cannot lead us to Him directly, "it can only lead the mind to that knowledge of the Supreme which brings it into union with Him." The "somewhat" stands for the ineffable Supreme—it does not mean Śiva, or His energic power, "for these have form and name, while the Supreme has neither."[1]

Darkness accompanies this secret and inviolable silence until all is absorbed in the Void:

When the sun disappeared, then came the moonlight;
When the moon disappeared then only mind remained;
When (absorbed in the Infinite) mind disappeared, then naught
  anywhere was left;
Then whither did earth, ether, and sky go off (absorbed) together
  (in vacuity)?[2]

Proceeding from absorption to an always simpler absorption until only the mind remains; finally this too disappears and nothing subsists—emptiness loses itself in Emptiness.[3]

1. The Painful Night

The dark night which accompanies the progression of the mystic toward illumination differs according to the stage and the degree of the lover. Although it ends as a night of gaiety for one who has realized union with Śiva, it has moments when it is "sweet" and moments when it is "bitter." The devotee advances slowly, gropingly, disoriented, often oppressed with the feeling that he is deprived of the divine presence after having enjoyed it for some time: "Even though Your essence of great Light is permanent and evident everywhere, Lord," exclaims Utpala, "why then did I venture into darkness?"[4]

That which is darkness for the understanding becomes "bitterness" and "aridity" for the heart. Cries Utpala: "For those of us who take delight in You, there is no pain, neither in the beginning,

[1]Ibid., com. to q. 2, pp. 24-25.

[2]Ibid., q. 9.

[3]For this same refrain—"void merges in the Void," see qs. 11, 30, and 69; see also Silburn, *La Bhakti*, p. 60.

[4]*SA*, X, 21.

nor in the middle, nor in the end. Nevertheless, Lord, it is pain which causes us to weaken! Explain to us, how can this be!"[1]

Mystics of every age and faith seem to be united in their assertion that there is no greater suffering than the separation experienced in mystical love; next to this, all other pain is insignificant: "Pain is separation from You, and joy is union with You."[2] Utpala briefly describes this feeling: "Even if I am separated from you for only a moment, O Lord, soon, I consume myself with torments. Remain, therefore, always visible."[3]

This separation has produced unbearable "wounds of the heart"[4] for those who have lost their direction on the path to divine oneness: "When will your essence, Lord, which reveals itself at the precise instant when one contemplates upon it, fill forever with the wave of its supreme ambrosia, the gaping wounds made by (my) ignorance of the true liberation?"[5] Only the mystics who are used to ecstasy and those whose hearts overflow with love know this suffering; nevertheless, this inexpressible torment is dear to the heart of the lover, to whom night and pain are fertile with meaning: "They alone enjoy, they alone suffer, they alone see the beauty of the universe!"[6]

2. The Painful and Purifying Phases of Progression

The suffering deepens as the mystic advances. In the beginning, he is afflicted by his own "imperfections." Lallā describes the pain and difficulties of her progress toward true knowledge by means of the metaphor of a cotton-pod:

> I, Lallā, went forth in the hope of (blooming like) a cotton-flower.
> Many a kick did the cleaner and the carder give me.
> Gossamer made from me did the spinning woman lift from the wheel,
> And a hanging kick did I receive in the weaver's work-room.

[1]Ibid., XX, 13.
[2]Ibid., XIII, 1.
[3]Ibid., VI, 1.
[4]Ibid., VIII, 8.
[5]Ibid., XIX, 7. The true liberation is the "non-separation from Śiva." See also Silburn, *La Bhakti*, p. 61, n. 5.
[6]Silburn, quoting an unknown mystic in *La Bhakti*, p. 61.

When the washerman dashed me (or turned me over) on the
washing-stone,
He rubbed me much with fuller's earth and soap.
When the tailor worked his scissors on me, piece by piece,
Then did I, Lallā, obtain the way of the Supreme.[1]

This metaphor is one of the esoteric sayings of Lallā which is difficult to understand specifically, although its general meaning is clear enough. The various stages in the manufacture of a finished cotton garment (from pod to tailor) are delineated and metaphorically compared to the stages of Lallā's painful progress; the suffering she endured at each phase of her spiritual growth is compared to the harsh treatment of cotton during its purification, refinement, and final production.

In another saying, Lallā affirms, also metaphorically, her own misery—alone, she does and can do nothing; or, if she does act, her efforts prove as useless as one towing a ship across the sea with weak (defective) rope:

With a rope of untwisted thread am I towing a boat upon the
ocean.
Where will my God hear? Will He carry even me over?
Like water in goblets of unbaked clay, do I slowly waste away.
My soul is in a dizzy whirl. Fain would I reach my home.[2]

The fervent cry of helplessness and frustration to God is clearly evident here. Lallā sees all her spiritual efforts as utterly fruitless as if she had tried to tow the ship of her soul across the sea of existence with a rope of untwisted thread—both tower and tow line are too weak for the task.

Utpala expresses the same sense of frustration with his personal weakness. Śiva has revealed Himself to him, and yet, the chain which continuously links the Self to the physical body will not slacken for a moment.[3] He deplores his inner and subtle impurity, owing to the "non-revelation" of God who does not allow the

[1]Lallā, qs. 102-103, and com., pp. 114-15.
[2]Ibid., q. 106.
[3]*SA*, IV, 24.

pure luminous Essence to manifest itself.[1] He prays, still burdened by his frailty: "Make me penetrate forcefully, Lord, into my own home."[2]

Thus, Utpala feels his heart painfully divided between two incompatible attitudes—one tending toward the joys of the senses, and the other toward fervent absorption in Śiva.[3] Although he has denied his faculties their natural satisfactions, he is, nevertheless, incapable of remaining steadfast in annihilating himself in God.[4] New fears torment him: "I turn away from the pleasures of the world as I am sprinkled with a drop of ambrosia from Your union with me, but this is so rare and the drop so little! Will I not be (from now on) deprived of both at the same time?"[5]

Lallā knows a similar anguish and discouragement when, deprived of the sweetness of ecstasy, she lived neither in her self nor in Śiva:

> The sling of the load of candy hath become loose upon my (shoulder).
> Crooked for me hath become my day's work. How can I succeed?
> The words of my teacher have fallen upon me like a blister of loss.
> My flock hath lost its shepherd. How can I succeed?[6]

Lallā finds herself in the same painful situation as Utpala, as we have just seen—a soul suspended in the emptiness between two worlds, one which she has just left and one whose threshold she has not yet crossed, but whose door, soon to close again, had opened slightly. She carries the weight of worldly illusion and pleasures on her back, sweet and enticing as candy[7] in taste and appearance. However, her entry into the mystical life has loosened the knot in the rope that holds this load on her back. The burden now seems much heavier, and the support rope "wounds" her;

[1]Ibid., XIII, 2.
[2]Ibid., V, 1.
[3]Ibid., V, 20.
[4]Silburn, *La Bhakti*, pp. 61-62.
[5]*SA*, VIII, 9.
[6]Lallā, q. 108.
[7]Ṣūfī influence, see Rūmī, no. 76, v. 2, p. 68; and no. 81, v. 15, p. 71.

the sweet things in life are now but an unbearable burden which weigh her down. Lallā, still with divided loyalties, has recourse to her *guru.* His words—far from consoling—cause her intolerable pain, for she is told to spurn the external world and to restrict her thoughts to meditation on her inner self; but her inability to do so, due to human frailty, causes her mental anguish.[1] Finally, she learns that the "whole flock" of factors that make up her sentient existence have lost their "shepherd," the mind, for it is steeped in ignorance of the Self.[2]

Utpala voices a similar complaint: "Why does the thought of Your slave wander off on the wrong road, avoiding its intuitive sense of direction toward identity with You, (knowing all the time) that there exists no other glory here on earth, no other joy?"[3]

And so, the devotee at the entrance portico to mystical life begins by penetrating his own heart in search of Śiva; if unable to do this, he can never succeed in keeping a permanent memory of Śiva in his mind and can never advance in the spiritual life. What is a love that cannot fix itself upon the beloved even for a brief moment and which wanders carelessly in diverse paths ever more distant from the seat of all love?

3. The Anguish of Possession and the Pangs of Desire

This inability to fix attention (concentration) on Śiva because of innate ignorance and illusion is an agonizing pain which must be endured by the devotee who is determined to persevere. Moreover, in the advanced stages of mystical life this anguish does not abate but becomes more acute. In the earlier phases there were the desire to possess Śiva and the yearning for this possession to become permanent:

> O Happy Existence! who does not desire to realize Your Reality, so adroit in dispelling the fear of repeated existences? O Master of the universe, all throughout our lives we must obtain through Your grace the permanence of Your presence by forever concentrating our minds on You.[4]

[1]Lallā, q. 94.
[2]Ibid., com., p. 119.
[3]*SA*, IV, 7.
[4]*Stav*, vv. 14-15.

But in the later stages, after possession has been realized, the votary suffers even more severely. He fears he will lose Śiva, whom he now possesses; and, once lost, even momentarily, he is consumed by the fear he will never be able to repossess Reality.

This intensification of suffering caused by separation from Śiva creates the feelings of helplessness and abandonment: "What shall I do, impotent that I am? Thus, as I am lacking confidence in all things, the all-gracious Energy of Śiva is my help!"[1]

The feeling of anguish reaches the point where the mystic senses a spiritual death: "And if now my spirit, although lifted by ardor, does not even approach the Essence of the Self, then, alas, I die!"[2] It would seem from his writings, therefore, that Utpala knew an abandonment that was as bitter and prolonged as union was sweet and enduring: "Since you approached the field of my vision, Lord, why do you move farther from me, Your slave? Do You not make Yourself seen within the fraction of an instant to all living beings on earth?"[3]

If, in the higher mystical realm, the lover experiences his greatest pain, his closeness to God permits him a certain familiarity—a "boldness" not experienced earlier. Utpala demonstrates this when he reproaches Śiva for the feeling of abandonment which plagues his own soul; Śiva, Utpala asserts, is acting most illogically: "There cannot be one thing in Your heart, another in Your word, and still another in Your actions, O Śambhu! If You are Truth itself, adopt only one way of acting: grace or disgrace."[4]

Even though the mystic has realized the Self and attaches himself to Śiva in a union of incomparable sweetness which has filled the frightening "abyss of separation,"[5] the lover is still saddened at not being able to contemplate God without interruption; for divine splendor shines only occasionally, during ecstasy, as a "flash of lightning,"[6] but it is fugitive at other times. And so he suffers deeply from his yearning to regain Śiva and to remain permanently in the quietude of His sweet embrace: "Alas, how unimaginable are the loving games of the Lord! He offered me the cup of His

[1]Ibid., v. 52.
[2]*SA*, v. XVIII, 3; see also, v. IV, 16.
[3]Ibid., v. XII, 16.
[4]Ibid., v. XI, 7.
[5]Ibid., v. XVIII, 19; also, VIII, 8.
[6]Ibid., v. IV, 8.

essence full of ambrosia but without permitting me to drink from it."[1] This causes Utpala to cry out in frustration: "I cry bitterly before You, Omnipresent One! for the sole reason that, even while knowing everything, I remain in error!"[2] Kṣemarāja explains that the poet, after having come out of ecstasy and active in worldly affairs continues to desire ecstasy; therein lies his error, he says, for Śiva finds Himself as much in one state as in another.[3]

Only love can appease the anguish, the frustration, and the pain which seize the votary and which at times seems too much to bear. He will only find peace and tranquillity if he cries out to Śiva and awakens Him from within the secret and silent cavern of his own heart. Lallā expresses this beautifully in her following sayings:

At the end of moonlight to the mad one did I call,
And soothe his pain with the Love of God.
Crying 'It is I, Lallā—it is I, Lallā', the Beloved I awakened.
I became one with Him, and my mind lost the defilement of the ten.[4]

The "end of moonlight" is the early dawn after the night of ignorance, and the "mad one" refers to the mind intoxicated and maddened by worldly illusion. The "Beloved" whom Lallā "awakened"[5] was the Self, alone and silently at rest within the secret cavern of her heart. The "ten" refers to the organs (impediments) of sense and action.[6]

Lallā's tearful cry is eventually heard, and she finally attains illumination:

Absorbed within Thyself, Thou remainedst hidden from me.
The livelong day I passed seeking for 'me' and 'Thee'.
When I beheld Thee in my Self,

[1]Ibid., v. XIII, 19.
[2]Ibid., III, 21.
[3]Silburn, *La Bhakti*, p. 64.
[4]Lallā, q. 105.
[5]Here, the soul awakens Śiva, at other times, however, Śiva awakens Himself within the soul, as in *Stav*, v. 117, where the divine presence reveals its "hidden" essence by "purifying " the heart and thought of the devotee.
[6]Lallā, com. to q. 105, p. 116; alluded to here are the Five Perceptual and Five Motor Faculties (of the Sāṅkhyas).

I have to Thee and to my Self the unrestrained rapture of (our union).[1]

F. *Illumination and the Path of Love*

Now, although illumination was the *sine qua non* of the two Paths of Liberation studied in the previous chapter, it is of secondary importance with the respect to love, a path complete in itself. It is infinitely more important than Yoga or knowledge, whose "supreme stage"[2] it represents. Bhaṭṭa, therefore, implores Śiva:

> Lord, may Your Torch of Illumination (Awakening)— tearing the web of hostile darkness and burning the fuel of transmigratory lives—be for me Your Torch of Devotion![3]

Silburn translates "burning the fuel of transmigratory lives" as "consuming the wood of all existences."[4] According to Kṣemarāja's commentary, the poet wishes to see the Torch of Illumination—which, as such, is unable to penetrate the deep cavern of darkness and ignorance—transform itself into a "lamp flame (*dīpaśikhā*) of love." This alone is capable of purifying the heart by consuming "phenomenal becoming" (transmigration), as wood is purified by consumption in fire.[5]

Utpaladeva goes even a step further: "Because I have tasted the ambrosia of Your love, O Master, illumination, even at its summit, seems to me only a sour liquid."[6]

Love plays an essential role in preparing the way to illumination and in stabilizing it once it has been attained. It is from love that the two conditions favorable to illumination flow: quietude and exceptional intensity which activate the movement toward illumination in the votary.[7] "Even though Your essence is inconceivable

[1]Ibid., q. 44.
[2]*SA*, IV, 9.
[3]*Stav*, v. 58.
[4]Silburn, *La Bhakti*, p. 122. I will refer to her rendering of these words when discussing parallels in St. John's Dark Night in Chapter IV in order to make the comparison more explicit (see p. 155).
[5]Ibid., com. to v. 58, p. 123.
[6]*SA*, I, 11.
[7]Silburn, *La Bhakti*, p. 87.

—therefore, beyond contemplation—it shows itself to those who love You as soon as they begin to contemplate."[1]

When the mystic turns toward Śiva in contemplation, he is thrown into an abyss of love; possessing simultaneously the mysterious light, peace, and joy, he passes through alternating phases of mystical intoxication, ecstasy and madness, mystical sleep, drowsiness, and quietude in which he forgets all that is external. Having reached this stage, he is completely immersed in God and living with His life: "He who knows how to taste the nectar of love and how to bathe within it enjoys the greatest of all bliss."[2]

The gradual conquest of love, as we have seen, follows alternations of abundance and deprivation, with respect to the free gifts of divine grace and divine love. Deprivation is no less essential than abundance, for both lead to self-annihilation on all levels of mystical progression. Dying in his various psychic states the devotee, plunged in darkness without his knowledge, directs himself toward a new and undifferentiated knowledge while the "flame of love" is nourished within the secret cavern of his heart.

Love becomes progressively simpler, unadorned, and delicate as his intelligence and sensitivity are refined. In the course of this profound and obscure immersion from one emptiness into another more perfect one, his very will is transformed: true slave of Śiva, the devotee renounces his own desires; he does not know, does not feel, loves nothing, wants nothing. Progressing in this passionless state, he reaches the ardent Center where blaze the consuming flames of love, immolating to the Tremendous Consciousness all the dualities of sense and thought.

Regardless of whether the progression was slow or rapid, the saint must finally leap into the infinite and release his hold on the relative if he wants to obtain the Absolute. By means of this brief journey to Śiva, the fearless being attains illumination.

Now totally absorbed in Śiva, his faculties fulfilled, his heart surfeited, his will divinized, he achieves harmony between the self and the universe.[3] Having been stripped of all modalities, having become limitless and immense, he identifies with the undifferentiated God. He has now achieved the triumphant love of Divine Majesty; he spreads this love freely to all, for he resides in the efficacious Center, within Śiva's will, in the plenitude of grace.

[1] *SA*, XX, 19.
[2] Ibid., XVI, 17.
[3] *VB* (Silburn), v. 64.

CHAPTER IV

TRIADIC AND CATHOLIC PARALLELS

Before discussing the various archetypes chosen for comparison in this chapter, certain preliminary comments are in order as to the meaning applied here of the term "archetype" and the importance of the comparative method in the study of religion; also, why the Catholic variants of the archetypes are selected and not those of other religions; and finally, how Catholic theology treats the same archetypes differently from the Triadist.

Basically, the term "archetype" means a prototype or primary model. Therefore, I consider two aspects in my use of this concept—that of a fundamental principle, which also serves as a subject for comparison. At first, one experiences an intuitive sense of similarity existing between two or more concepts; next, one systematically attempts to reduce these principles to maximal conceptual unity. The fact that the concepts one seeks to relate can be widely diverse, either in their language or interpretative meaning, is understandable, especially when one is dealing with vastly divergent theological traditions.

It might be wondered, in general, why the comparative method is important and, more specifically, why there is need to compare varying treatments of theological archetypes. Comparison is well recognized as a basis of scientific study. Our knowledge would be otherwise unrelated. Comparison, moreover, increases our knowledge of the common category, as well as of the specific one. This principle can also be applied to philosophical or theological investigation. When the explicit treatment of one theological interpretation is contrasted with that of another, not only is one's knowledge of the broad area in question increased, but the specificness of each interpretation is underscored. Thus, when we compare the Triadic and the Catholic versions of a common archetype, besides increasing our general knowledge of the archetype itself, we also deepen our understanding of its distinctively Triadic (and Catholic) interpretations.

Admittedly, there are religions other than Catholicism that could furnish the material for comparative study with Triadism; and in our last chapter we selected Islam for comparison; but if only one religion were to be chosen, the best choice, it appears to me, would be Catholicism, for it seems to have the maximum number of archetypes in common with other faiths. At the beginning of Chapter III, we saw that although Christianity belongs to the Semitic group of religions, many of its tenets run counter to the Semitic traditions, while concording with the Indic; and I listed several examples to elaborate this point. Furthermore, among the Semitic faiths, it is in Christianity that theology and mysticism are most in accord. In addition, many of the insights basic to Catholicism are also basic to Hindu religious traditions. So, in effect, Catholicism serves as a bridge between the *prophetic*, or Semitic, religions and the *mystical*, or Indic, religions of which Hinduism is a prime example. Catholicism, to my knowledge, contains more of these "ecumenical" or "inter-faith" archetypes than any other doctrine; hence, it is, I believe, the best of the major theological traditions with which to compare Triadism.

Finally, Catholicism handles the same archetypes differently from Triadism. The former describes the relationship between the phenomenal and the transcendental (or between creation and the Creator) in the language of Difference; the latter, in that of Difference-in-Identity. A doctrine postulating the identity of God and the world as reality's true condition seems eminently suited to describe the experience of the divine, the most transcendent available to any awareness—its intense and overwhelming intimacy with the Godhead, making it seem indifferentiable from the Godhead's entity itself. But Catholicism is emphatic about the transcendence of God, asseverating that "one cannot discover so much similarity between the Creator and the creature, without being able to discover an even greater dissimilarity among them."[1] But while Difference—or the otherness of the creature from God—is the proper language for expressing the transcendence of God, it seems singularly inadequate to describe the intimacy of the mystical and beatific experience of the divine. To do so it reverts to the language of Identity—not indeed an *entitative* (or real) identity, but a *representative* or *figurative* (or symbolic) one. The concept of a representative

[1]The Fourth Lateran General Council, quoted by Pereira, p. 38.

identity will be further elaborated in our scrutiny of the four archetypes that form the theme of this chapter.[1]

These archetypes describe the relationship between the phenomenal and the transcendental. The first three focus on this relationship as experienced intellectually, from the viewpoint of gnosis or wisdom, expressed through the metaphors of light and darkness or of fire and combustible matter. The last focuses on the relationship as an emotional state of tranquility deriving from the acquisition of gnosis.

For both the Triadic and Catholic theologies, light generally connotes the transcendental, obscured from our sight by a veil that needs to be pierced for the transcendental to be experienced. In Triadism, the undifferentiated Consciousness is obscured by Illusion or the Mirific Power, but it is intuited when the latter is pierced by the Energic Fulmination. In Catholicism, the Godhead is obscured by faith whose veil is pierced by the gifts of the Holy Spirit, leading the soul, elevated by the Light of Glory, to intuit the Godhead in the Beatific Vision.

For both theologies, light or fire symbolizes the glory and infinity of God, in comparison with Whom the phenomenal is darkness or combustible matter destroyed by divine radiance or inflammation. This destruction can be conceived as a cosmic ritual or sacrifice. In Triadism, the phenomenal is sacrificially "annihilated" in the fire of the Tremendous God, Whose sole subsistence supervenes the conflagration. For Catholicism, adoration is ideally the annihilation of the creature—never to be realized in fact, but only symbolically in sacrifice—by reason of which God's infinity and sole right to subsistence is affirmed.

Both systems, however, also symbolize the transcendental as darkness, conceived as a splendor of mystery exceeding the comprehension of phenomenal intelligence, obliterating the dim lights illuminating it, and replacing the latter with its own overwhelming glory. In Triadism, the faint glimmers of Consciousness flickering through the veil of Illusion constitute the differentiated and conceptualized universe, which are obliterated by the dark blaze of the undifferentiated and inconceptualizable Consciousness. In Catholicism, Divine Wisdom is a blackness which blots

[1]Allusions made without specific reference to these terms, pp. 114-18; terms mentioned, pp. 112, 129, 131-42, and 146.

out the glimmers of creaturely imperfection, and transforms the creature (representatively) into the flames of the Holy Spirit.

As the creature is being so transformed, or as differentiation is being dissipated, the phenomenal world and its turmoil loses its capacity to pain, to bewilder, or to obfuscate. Liberation, or the Beatific Vision, is realized only after death, but the soul is already Liberated-in-Life, and hence impassible.

A. *Archetype I: Breaking through the Energy of Śiva and the Return to Light*

The first archetype comprehends the role of the Mirific Power in the Triadic metaphysics of cosmic manifestation and the return absorption in the luminosity of the supreme Śiva through this concealing veil of Illusion—and also the idea of the Gifts of the Holy Spirit, breaking through the obscurity of faith into the light of divine contemplation, as presented in the writings of John of St. Thomas (1589-1644).

A few words about this Dominican theologian will place him in historical perspective.[1] Born of an Austrian father and a Portuguese mother, he was a staunch devotee of the Angelic Doctor as his chosen religious name indicates. In fact, he is one of the greatest Thomistic thinkers of Baroque Scholasticism and of the modern era. His ministry was spent in the service (as companion, advisor, and confessor) of King Philip IV of Spain (1621-65). The literary work from which I shall draw parallels to Triadism is a treatise on the gifts of the Holy Spirit that forms the fifth and final part of his second[2] major work, the *Cursus Theologicus*. The material for this treatise, one of the masterpieces of systematic theology, was collected during his twenty or more years of teaching, and its composition dominated the last years of his life.

And now, I will compare the two systems. As we have seen in Chapter I, the Trans-Universal Śiva, pure self-luminosity, wills to discover another dimension of His essence in the multiplicity of creation. In order to accomplish this, however, He has to obfus-

[1]John of St. Thomas, *The Gifts of the Holy Ghost*, trans. from the Latin by Dominic Hughes (New York: Sheed and Ward, 1951), pp. 3-13.

[2]His first major work was the *Cursus Philosophicus*, "an exposition of the philosophical disciplines according to the doctrine and the order of St. Thomas." Ibid., p. 11.

cate His perfection—to annihilate, so to speak, His unicity. This self-emptying is brought about by the omnipotent Mirific Power's obscuration of the undifferentiated Reality with the black veil of illusion, thus concealing the divine essence in the darkness that enwombs the emergent multiplicity. Then partial glimmers begin to appear and to bounce off the curtain of the Mirific Power; finally they solidify into Matter and Spirit from which evolves the differentiated universe. Abhinava clearly stresses this process of Light, obscurement, disclosure, and plenitude:

> The Self is embodied Light and is Śiva, the sovereignly free. Impelled by the exhilaration of His Freedom, He obscures His essence, and then discloses It in plenitude—with or without sequence, or in triple phasis...[1]

The liberation process, we will also recall, is the exact reverse of the manifestation process; there is a piercing of the concealing veil, and the universe is reabsorbed into the plenitude of Light. This reversal is brought about by the Goddesses of Consuming Fire (the *kālīs*), whose destructive holocaust engulfs the cosmos in its purifying flames, absorbing Matter and Spirit into the absolute Reality. Hence, as the Ṣūfīs also expressed it, "annihilation" brings forth the created universe (simplicity to multiplicity) and "annihilation" returns it (multiplicity to simplicity) to its original uncreated condition.

We can find striking parallels to this aspect of Triadic metaphysics in the treatise on Faith by John of St. Thomas. The author quotes St. Thomas, who says in his *Summa*, "We love and know God imperfectly."[2] The reason, as John of St. Thomas points out, is because we are separated from God by the veil of faith; our love is imperfect due to the imperfection of faith.[3] He elaborates further on this point:

> Faith, ...is of its very nature *imperfect, inscrutable, and obscure*. The eyes remain *enshrouded in darkness*; ...This defect is

[1] *TS*, ch. 1; trans. by Pereira, p. 375.

[2] St. Thomas Aquinas, *Summa Theologica*, in *Basic Writings of St. Thomas Aquinas*, gen., ed., Anton C. Pegis, 2 vols. (New York: Random House, 1945) I-II, Q. 68, A.2, p. 531.

[3] John of St. Thomas, p. 17.

> removed by a further perfection, which is called a gift,[1] because it exceeds the ordinary manner of human operation. In this case it is the gift of *understanding*. This gift enables the intellect to *penetrate* more clearly the suitability and credibility of the things of faith.[2] (Italics mine.)

The contemplative life is also adversely affected because this "solitary and naked faith...leaves the *soul in obscurity*." Men weary and lose interest when they meditate by faith alone. "Those contemplatives," John of St. Thomas continues, "who desire to *penetrate* the mysteries of faith need to use the gift of *understanding*." For the souls who rely on "solitary and naked faith" alone, seem to have "the things of heaven" closed rather than opened to them. The heavens "are hidden by the *shroud of faith*."[3] (Italics mine.)

> The heavens must at times be opened, therefore, so that the soul will not fail in its contemplation. The Holy Ghost accomplishes this through the gifts of *understanding*, of *wisdom*, and of *knowledge*....The more the soul increases in understanding, the wider is the aperture...[until]...the heavens are torn asunder and the soul sees the glory of God. It no longer dwells in the *obscurity of faith* but it now explores and contemplates the magnitude of God.[4] (Italics mine.)

So our obscure faith enshrouds our love for God, our vision (understanding), and our very soul in "ignorance" of God's glory. Whereas, the gifts of "understanding," of "wisdom," and of "knowledge" remove this veil of "ignorant faith" and open the heavens and the eyes of the soul to a partial "recognition" of the majesty of God. Now in Triadism, the veil of Illusion also causes ignorance—of God's glory, our true Śiva-nature. So too, this veil is removed by "understanding," "wisdom," and "knowledge"—a "recognition" that we ourselves are identical with Śiva. Thus, the Catholic concepts and their Triadic counterparts touch each

[1]The author also says: "They are called gifts, because through them He gives Himself to men and dwells in them." p. 31, sec. 10.

[2]Ibid., p. 32, sec. 11.

[3]Ibid., sec. 12.

[4]Ibid., p. 33, sec. 13.

other here as to terminology and, for the most part, the denotation of these terms. However, as we will soon see, they tend to separate and have wide variance in regard to connotation or practical application.

Then, in the next section, John of St. Thomas, continuing this theme, presents what can be interpreted as an excellent parallel to the Triadic metaphysics of manifestation and absorption. Concepts such as: concealment, illumination, darkness, breakthrough, fire, annihilation, and absorption—are all present and linked here as they are in Triadism; the same *caveat*, of course, is to be observed concerning specific terms and their application as was just mentioned above. Our theologian begins by stressing the need to remove the concealing shroud of faith:

> It is necessary, therefore, for the soul to cast off the shroud of unadorned faith and to leap up to run with God. Through the illumination of the Gifts of the Holy Ghost, the soul enjoys... a variegated understanding of divine things.... Faith, however, cannot, in this life, be illuminated or attain to the vision of its object. It is founded upon the testimony of authority, and it cannot extend beyond that testimony, the specific object of faith, to vision.[1]

The "gifts of the Holy Ghost" are equivalent in Triadism to the Energic Fulmination—the flashing light of the divine Essence. So the analogy is that there is a concealing Energy which obscures the plenitude; in this case it is faith that is obscuring and vision (understanding) that is illuminating or revealing. In an earlier section, the author says, "An analogy exists between the clear eye that has perfect vision and the clear mind that alone is capable of seeing God, whether with the darkened sight of faith or the bright vision of heaven."[2]

Only by an inflamed love which gives way to a clear understanding can the veil be lifted:

> Held captive by the bonds of faith, the soul remains in darkness. The flame of love, however, can benefit the soul in this regard,

[1]Ibid., pp. 33-34, sec. 14.
[2]Ibid., pp. 22-23.

> for love makes things clear. From love proceed the gifts of understanding, of wisdom, and of knowledge. They break through the mist of faith, thereby opening the heavens.[1]

This "breaking through the mist of faith" has its Triadic counterpart in the penetration of the veil of Illusion. But here is where Catholic and Triadic concepts separate as to connotation, for the obscurity of faith is not the same kind of obscurity as the Mirific Power, as I have already indicated.

The author continues on the theme of burning love:

> These gifts, therefore, are attributed, in a special way to love or to the Spirit (Who is Love).... Inflamed by love, the intellect rises from the obscure knowledge of faith to the luminous and clear contemplation of the magnitude and certitude of the mysteries, and the *brightness of a flaming fire in the night.*[2] This night is the veil of creatures enshrouding and hiding the majesty of His eternity, for *over all the glory shall be a protection.*[3] Among the nocturnal shadows of this life the mind becomes aware of that lamp burning in the darkness.[4]

We here encounter the theme of love, central to Christianity and to Devotional Triadism. The author elaborates on the idea of an "inflamed love" briefly mentioned at the beginning of the paragraph. He also introduces the idea of the "dark night" which "conceals the majesty of God"; both themes were extensively developed in the previous chapter. The "Night of Śiva," we recall, conceals the Undifferentiatedness (Majesty here) of the Absolute. The "flame of love" and "that lamp burning in the darkness" have a perfect parallel in Bhaṭṭa's expression, "Your Torch of Devotion" which, commented Kṣemarāja, "penetrates the darkness of ignorance" and is transformed into a "lamp flame of love."[5]

From the theme of the fire of love which consumes the soul,

1Ibid., p. 34, sec. 14.

2The author quotes from Isaiah, 4:5.

3Ibid.

4John of St. Thomas, p. 34, sec. 14.

5*Stav*, v. 58; also, in the com. to v. 68 Kṣemarāja speaks of Śiva as the "brilliant light of consciousness" and of the ascetic "inflamed by the desires of Love." See p. 107 above for a translation of v. 58.

John of St. Thomas moves logically to the Fire of God which both consumes and transforms the soul:

> 'Fire', he says [quoting St. Bernard], 'goes forth from Him, and yet He Himself is the fire'. With this difference, however, the fire which precedes Him brings pain but does not torment, nor does it vex. It moves, but it does not accomplish the work. It is sent in advance only to arouse, to prepare and to recall to mind what the soul is by itself so that it may appreciate what it will be by the grace of God. The fire which is God Himself consumes, but does not cause suffering. It burns pleasantly and cauterizes with joy, for it is a very devastating ember which attacks vices, ...Hence, souls understand that the Lord is present in the power by which they are transformed, and in the love by which they are inflamed.[1]

These words might well have been those of any of the devotional poets of Triadism. But, again, though the words are Triadic, the application and at times the meaning are quite different. John of St. Thomas' message is clear. The consuming "Fire of God," which causes spiritual pain is sent "to arouse" man so that he will recall "what the soul is by itself"—an immortal creation made by God in His own image and destined for reunion *with* Him in eternity. Although His fire is "devastating," it attacks and destroys man's "vices"; he is thereby "transformed" *by* the "flame of love," so that his destiny can be realized. Thus the consuming fire performs only *one* function which influences the soul in *one* continuous action—it "moves," it "arouses," it "enlightens," and it "transforms "

To the theologian of Triadism, the above passage could say the same thing—and indeed much more. For him, the Fire of God serves a double function: as an arousing flame of devotion and a holocaustic flame of total destruction. The first corresponds in general, if we stretch the point a bit, to the function delineated by John of St. Thomas. Namely, in the form of a flame of ardent desire it too causes mystical pain, as we have seen, and it "arouses" in man a recollection of "what the soul is by itself"—but, for the Triadic mystic this is a self-awareness of its Śiva-nature. Also, in

[1]John of St. Thomas, pp. 34-35, sec. 14.

a sense, it attacks "vices," for it annihilates the desire for worldly attachments. However, there is another meaning to the Flame of God. Its second function is to be the "destroyer"—not only of vices, but of man himself, and of the entire universe. The Supreme Śiva is One, before Whose oneness multiplicity trembles, so to speak, in fear of its destruction; which is why He is the Tremendous God. Man's destiny is, therefore, reunion *in* Him; he is "transformed" *in* the "devastating ember"—all is "transformed" in the absorptive Fire of Śiva; even the "embers" are incinerated. Only ash remains.

In the second archetype I will concentrate on the French School of Bérulle, Condren, and Olier. However, I have found an excerpt in one of Olier's letters that echoes the words of John of St. Thomas, his contemporary in Spain. It is for this reason that I briefly introduce him here, before I formally treat him in connection with the French School in the next section of this chapter.

In a letter to an intimate friend, written in 1641, he has this to say about the gift of faith:

> Your soul is denuded and stripped of all, even of God in His gifts, *except those of faith,...*
> *I see it* (*the soul*) *like a dark night, obscure*, vile, detached, separated from all, even from God, Who wills not that any should be known in His gifts, nor should lean upon aught else save Himself in His Own Substance. It is in Him that we must live, move, and have our being. *It is this Essence*, vivifying sustaining, *illumining a dark and shadowy faith* (*when it illuminates purely and without the grosser mists of a dull light*) *which alone is resplendent and makes Itself visible through the latter's very impurity. A lively faith though dimmed*, still nourished in purity, sustained in simplicity, that is all, is it not?[1] (Italics mine.)

[1]Henri Bremond, gen. ed. *A Literary History of Religious Thought in France*, vols. 1-3 (New York: Macmillan Co., 1936), vol. 3: *The Triumph of Mysticism: The French School*, trans. K.L. Montgomery, p. 389.

As I have been unable to consult the original works of the French School (with the exception of one work of Condren's cited below), I have found it necessary to rely heavily on Bremond. Therefore, in order not to clutter the text with references to this work, I will, with rare exception, only cite Bremond in direct quotes; all other factual information in this section, not otherwise cited, is to be understood as having Bremond as their source.

Here the Light of God's "Essence" penetrates a "shadowy," and "dimmed" faith thereby "illumining" it. The soul, also "dark," and "obscure" is penetrated by the Light which "makes Itself visible" to it through the soul's "very impurity."

Although the cause and effect relationship between obscure faith and obscure soul is not as clear here as it is in John of St. Thomas, Olier is clearly saying substantially the same thing—that the shroud or mist of faith keeps the soul in obscurity. Divine Light, by penetrating the mist, illumines both the faith and the soul it was concealing.

B. *Archetype II: Sacrificial Self-Annihilation*

The subject matter for this section will be those aspects in the mystical theology of the French School (Oratorians) described by its major representatives, Bérulle, Condren, and Olier, that lend themselves, I believe, to comparison with Triadic theology.

The founder and first Superior-General of the French Oratorians[1] was Cardinal Pierre de Bérulle (1575-1629). His doctrine formed the basis of the school's mystical theology, and although Condren and Olier adhered strictly to its basic tenets, they each in turn added their own unique contributions to its overall development. I will start with the founding principles of Bérulle, to which shall be added the innovations of Condren and Olier; major emphasis shall be given to Condren, who outshone all the school's proponents—even his master, Bérulle. My purpose, again, is not to write on the teachings of French School, per se, but to stress only their "Triadic peculiarities".

1. Theocentrism: Foundation of the French School

Bérulle's rather innovative contribution to the spirituality of his day was to reemphasize what formerly had been taught; namely, the theocentrism of Christian thought, rather than the anthropocentrism that traditionally held sway in the Church for some time

[1]The French Oratory is not to be confused with the Italian Oratory founded by St. Philip Neri (1515-95) around 1564. Although the two orders were founded for the same general purpose, "the restoration of the ideal and of the virtues of sacerdotalism" in their respective countries, they follow the spiritual doctrines of their individual founders and are, therefore, quite dissimilar. See Bremond, pp. 140-41 for more by way of comparison.

prior to Bérulle and which was so cogently espoused soon after Bérulle by Pascal (1623-62). Père François Bourgoing,[1] a disciple of Condren, clearly distinguishes between these two "conflicting" approaches when he writes:

> Our devotions...must be inspired and consecrated not to our own spiritual profit and advantage, but to the sole glory of God, with no consideration of our private interest or satisfaction; so that we must...*recognize and adore the sovereign majesty of God, as He is in Himself* [theocentric], *rather than as He is towards us* [anthropocentric], and to love His Goodness for Itself rather than what it may accomplish for us.[2] (Italics mine.)

Now the anthropocentric point of view: "God is for *us*," was the traditional approach some twenty years before Bérulle, when souls observed more of a familiarity than reverence for God, and, as Père Denis Amelote, another disciple of Condren, remarks: "though many Christians love God, there are few who respect Him." But, however, thanks largely to the efforts of Bérulle, emphasis on "the necessity of adoring the Perfections of God, His Designs, His Judgments, and the Mysteries of His Son,—is now the first precept in every book of devotion."[3]

So it was theocentrism—the idea of the grandeur of God as affirmed through adoration rather than through familiarity—that was now "revitalized" by Bérulle. Of all the divine attributes, it was greatness that impressed Bérulle most deeply. Not only Bérulle, but all Oratorian mystics—as Condren, Olier, and Eudes—were profoundly, as if by nature, theocentric.

Now theocentrism is also thoroughly Hindu: as Madhva, the great Hindu theologian of Difference, declares, the one great import of Revelation is the majesty of God.[4] The following quote is also rich in Hindu metaphysics concerning the "Attributes" of God:

[1]He succeeded Condren as the third Superior-General of the Oratory after the latter's death in 1641.

[2]Bremond, pp. 23-25; see also, p. 99, n. 1.

[3]Ibid., pp. 28-29.

[4]See Jayatīrtha, *Nyāyasudhā*, quoted by B.N.K. Sharma, *Śrī Madhva's Teaching in His Own Words* (Bombay: Bharatiya Vidya Bhavan 1961), p. 35.

> This Divine Being, adorable in all His Attributes, possesses qualities apparently contradictory. He is infinitely present, yet infinitely distant; infinitely exalted, yet stoops to all His creation; infinitely to be delighted in, yet infinitely stern; infinitely to be desired, yet infinitely unendurable. And when it pleases Him to have to do with His creature without proportioning Himself to the creaturely capabilities, it feels itself crushed, engulfed, destroyed by this Infinite Power dominating a creature so small and so subordinate, but this overwhelming shall one day be converted into consolation and this destruction into the recreation of the soul.[1]

Speaking of God, the Hindu theologian Vallabha (1481-1533), says: "In whatever thing opposing attributes inhere, that thing is indeed great. And those opposing attributes are *both* real, else greatness would not be proved, as in the case of an actor [who is two persons, himself, and his role; but only *one* of these is real]."[2]

In the last two chapters, we have seen examples of the Majesty of God and the nothingness of the creature—the pervasive theme of Triadism and of much of Hindu theology. This dual doctrine is clearly evident in the following variant reading from the opening verse of *The Tantra on the Tremendous Wisdom God*:

> We bow to that par-excellent Supreme Spirit (Lord Bhairava) the Creator, Protector and Destroyer of this whole universe, who relieves from the miseries of existence the hearts of those, who, horrified by the fury shown by Him in the shape of fires, earthquakes, etc. throw themselves at His mercy. He is the fulfiller of their desires, the conqueror of death, the propeller of the sun, the moon and other planets and in the form of superknowledge, remover of all kinds of fears from the hearts of Yogis.[3]

Lallā's sayings, we recall, indicated her estimate of the utter wretchedness of the creature: "recognize thy body as but food for

[1]Ibid., p. 31.

[2]Vallabha, *The Lamp of the Meaning of Truth* (*Tattvārthadīpanibandha*), com. on v. 88; the latter is trans. by Pereira, p. 326.

[3]From an unpublished translation of the *Tantra on the Tremendous Wisdom God* (New York: TheKuṇ ḍalinī Research Foundation), no date.

forest crows";[1] "I saw that all was He, and that I am nothing";[2] and, "all that is, is ashes."[3] Finally one reads in the *Tantra on the Tremendous Wisdom God*: "One must recognize the epidermic portion of the body as a wall. Meditating that there is nothing within it, he will participate in what is beyond meditation."[4]

(a) *Christological Approach: Self-Renouncement and Adherence to God*

Bérulle, in keeping with his theocentrism, considered the Incarnation the greatest Christian mystery. Although, in truth, the Trinity is the principal mystery, the greatest devotion in the Christian religion is directed rather to the Incarnation. For, as an early biographer of Bérulle states "God does not reveal to us the Trinity, except through the Incarnation." The Trinity is hidden in obscurity and sublimity. As the oratorian Jean Eudes expressed it, "the Infinity of His Perfections baffles our intelligence...that which most strikes us is His dazzling Majesty, His overwhelming Almightiness, His dreadful Justice...The God of the Crib, the Calvary, and the Altar, is more within our reach."[5] It is through the Son that we gain easiest access to the Father.[6] Thus, Bérulle worshipped the "whole" Christ, inseparable in His two natures, "the Life Divinely human and humanly Divine of the God-Man."

For Bérulle, the idea of self-annihilation and total adherence to God, so much a part of his spirituality, is founded on the dogma of the Incarnation. A year after his ordination in 1599, he writes of his contemplations while on a Jesuit retreat:

> Meditating on the Incarnation of Jesus Christ, I have long and profoundly dwelled, in the depths of my soul, on the sovereign goodness of the Word Eternal...dwelled deeply also upon how great should be the annihilation of self....I was instructed and

[1]Lallā, q. 28.
[2]Ibid., q. 31.
[3]Ibid., q. 43.
[4]*VB*, v. 48.
[5]Bremond, pp. 35-36.
[6]Matthew 11:27 and parallel, Luke 10:22, "No one knows the Son except the Father and no one knows the Father except the Son—and anyone to whom the Son wishes to reveal him." All biblical references in this work are from the *New American Bible*.

drawn to adhere entirely to God, to depend wholly on Him in perfect forgetfulness of self and of all conditions.[1]

Now Christ—brought to nothingness in our nature—is our divine model in the practice of self-annihilation. He is, as it were, deprived of His own subsistence, emptied,[2] and wholly given over to God.[3] This self-emptying, again, is the metaphysical foundation of Triadic theology, without which the divine manifestations would not be possible.

It is quite understandable, according to the early (1599) contemplative quotation from Bérulle just cited, that the French School considered "adoration" under its twofold aspect: renouncement of self and adherence to God. Self-renouncement means basically a self-offering and is also called self-annihilation, self-abnegation, and the like. It does not, however, represent the entire religious thrust of the French School; a colateral and simultaneous impetus is toward adherence to God. The humanity of Christ is "emptied" so that it may be filled with God. "It is so much one single thing," says Walsh, "that the adhering to God *is* the renouncement of self; the filling with God *is* the emptying of the self." Thus, in the Bérullian conception, "to adore is to be in a 'state' of utter self-annihilation and of such complete adherence to God as to be utterly possessed by Him and filled with Him." The only aim of the French School, he continues, is to have its disciples "worshippers" of God, always in an "attitude of adoration" according to the example of Christ, "the perfect 'worshipper' of God, not only in Himself and for Himself, but principally for all men."[4]

[1]Bremond, p. 12.

[2]Cf. the Christological Hymn of Philippians 2:5-11.

[3]"The vigorous expression 'dispossession' or *kenosis* emphasizes the extent of the renunciation that Christ accepted. Instead of assuming in his human nature a rank consonant with his divinity, he took the status of a slave or servant, that is to say a human nature like our own and subject to all its limitations, including suffering and death." François Amiot, *The Key Concepts of St. Paul* (New York: Herder and Herder, 1962), p. 112.

It should be understood, of course, that only Christ as the preexistent *Logos* could make this choice; the historical Jesus did not have this option, since He was already "in the flesh." Thus, at the moment of Incarnation, this renunciation was a *fait accompli*.

[4]Eugene Aloysius Walsh, *The Priesthood in the Writings of the French School: Bérulle, De Condren, Olier* (Washington, D.C.: The Catholic University of America Press, 1949), p. 10.

Bourgoing sums up Bérullian thought well when he says that the Christian life should be one of "elevation" and "adherence." By elevation, the French School understood a "kind of prayer" tending wholly and simply to honor and glorify God in His infinite greatness, which they held was the first end of piety, and the most essential act and exercise of religion.[1]

2. Sacrificial Adoration

Now Condren, being totally Bérullian, could not have agreed more; however, his concept of adoration took the form of "sacrifice." This was his unique contribution to the French School. While Bérulle, as we have just seen, teaches self-renouncement and a more general adherence to the Person of the Word Incarnate, allowing the God-Man "to appropriate to Himself our states," Condren advocates "an adherence to the annihilation and the 'consummation' of the God-Man, who 'absorbs' and 'consummates' us in the very sacrifice of the Incarnation and of Calvary." In this sense, therefore, Condren emphasizes *sacrificial adoration*—a more special adherence to the dead and risen Christ. Olier, as I will briefly show at the end of the discussion on this archetype, adheres to the most profound *self-annihilation.*[2]

Before I review Condren's doctrine of adoration by sacrifice, it would be helpful first to give some indication of his Bérullian character. As Bremond tells us, Charles de Condren (1588-1641)—almost the exact contemporary of John of St. Thomas—"was as Bérullian as Bérulle himself, and had been so, long before meeting Bérulle." One day while at study, the twelve year old Condren had what might be termed a "visionary dream" that remained vivid all his life. The seeds of theocentrism and sacrificial annihilation were implanted at this time. Amelote, his disciple and biographer, tells us of this vision:

> He was suddenly aware of his mind being encompassed with a wonderful light, in the radiance of which *the Divine Majesty appeared to him so immense and so infinite that it seemed to him that this One Pure Being alone should subsist, and that all the universe should be destroyed for His Glory.* He saw that God

[1]Bremond, pp. 98-101.
[2]Ibid., pp. 298, 316-17, 418.

> had no need of any creature; that His own Son, ...had of necessity offered up His Life to Him; that only the disposition of offering up himself and all things in Jesus the Victim was worthy of His Greatness, and that it was not enough to love Him, if one were not ready, with His Son, to lose oneself for love of Him.
> This light was so pure and mighty that *his soul was as if struck with death*, an impression never effaced from it. He gave himself with all his heart to God, to be reduced to nothingness for His Honour and to live henceforth in that mind only.[1]

Thus his devotion to the divine Majesty and his desire for self-annihilation were firmly established before he was yet a teenager. But this was only the first phase; as Amelote continues, we see that Condren's penchant for sacrificial adoration, which was to be his hallmark, also shone forth at this time.

> For being in the abyss of his nothingness before the Divine Holiness and desiring ardently to be sacrificed for His Glory, he was suddenly filled with a particular joy in seeing that the Son of God was ever the Victim of the Father...He recognized that the Sacrifice of Jesus Christ was the fulfilling of the zeal of all who themselves desired their immolation, but who were incapable worthily of honouring God by their sacrifice. That to present to the Father the Son who died was to praise in infinity the Divine Holiness,...acknowledging before the Father Eternal that not only the universe, but He Himself, merited destruction before Him; and he saw that only the Unique Sacrifice of Jesus Christ was worthy of God.[2] (Last three capitalized pronouns were not capitalized in the English translation.)

Condren held, therefore, that sacrifice demanded the consumption and entire destruction of the victim; he also felt that naught should live save God, Himself—"all must be cast into the fire of sacrifice, taken away from its place to be consumed and vanish utterly."[3] This is in accord with Abhinava's affirmation of the supremacy of God through the destruction of the creature.

[1]Ibid., p. 294.
[2]Ibid., p. 295.
[3]Ibid., pp. 318-19.

The mystical experience at the age of twelve is worked out by Condren in his treatise on Sacrifice and the Priesthood of Jesus Christ. His theology of sacrifice is intricately structured, and even a brief treatment of it (like the present one) requires considerable space. However, a careful analysis of this treatise, so rich in parallels to Triadism, is rewarding. Its systematic structure brings out the multiple nuances of the distinctive Catholic combination of the archetypes it shares with Triadism; it also demonstrates both the compatibility and incompatibility of some of these nuances with respect to the two traditions. Condren's doctrine may be summarized under the following six headings:

(1) *Preeminence of sacrifice* over love as an act of adoration.

(2) Its *nature* as symbolic self-annihilation.

(3) The *reasons* for its celebration: honor, thanksgiving, and expiation.

(4) Its *five essential constituents*: sanctification, oblation, immolation, consummation, and communion.

(5) Its central act, the *inflammation* of the victim, and the seven reasons for it—the purification, glorification, and perfuming of the victim, its communication with God, and the affirmation of His sovereignty, holiness, and plenitude.

(6) Its *fulfilment* in Christ's life, passion and death.

The first and second points constitute the preamble to the others; the third, fourth, and fifth points constitute sacrifice in the Old Law; and the sixth point is sacrifice in the New Law.

Walsh tells us that "the very creatural relationship that a man bears to God by the fact that he is a created being is the 'state' of adoration."[1] For the French School, he continues, "It is adoration with love. To adore for them is to express more than creatural dependence; it is to express all the love and joy consequent upon creatural awareness."[2]

Although Condren adheres to this basic teaching of Bérullian spirituality, love for him is not the first duty that the creature is obliged to render to God. He insists that adoration by means of "sacrifice" is man's first obligation and one that is more ancient than love; it is man's way of expressing the gratitude he owes to God for the very gift of existence. Love on the other hand, is owed

[1]Walsh, p. 10.
[2]Ibid., p. 11.

God only in consequence to the kind of social relationship He has created between Himself and the creature, and to which the condition of created being gives him no right whatsoever. Sacrifice is therefore the first act of religion, without which the latter could not subsist.[1] The perfect sacrifice would be to annihilate the creature entirely—this, Condren says, is the intent of sacrifice because it affirms the supremacy of God. But it is "as impossible for us to annihilate as to create;"[2] we can only *transform* the victim. However, even if human agency could do this, it would, nevertheless, have no effect, positive or negative, on the almightiness and glory of God. Human sacrifice, therefore, is of no value to the transcendent God.

Consequently, man is faced with a dilemma—on the one hand, his duty to sacrifice to the sovereignty of his Creator through some kind of symbolic self-annihilation; on the other, the inconsequentiality of all his efforts, however well-intentioned, human sacrifice being imperfect at best. The only solution is to find a third element capable of bringing these two seemingly exclusive concepts together, namely, the Incarnation. Through the sacrifice of the divine Redeemer the act of self-annihilation becomes infinitely meaningful.

(a) *Sacrifice in the Old Law*

Now Condren, as I have indicated, suggests three reasons for sacrifice: honor, thanksgiving, and expiation. I will only develop the first, homage to the majesty of God, since it is the most important and the only one of true significance for Triadism. Thus, the primary reason for sacrifice is to adore God and to *honor* His infinite perfections, in particular: His *holiness*—so great, and so distant from the creature;[3] His *sovereign domain*—not only over life and death, but over being itself—thereby God is recognized as the Author of all being;[4] and His *plenitude*—self-sufficiency and independence from any other creature.[5] We briefly encountered

[1]Le R.P. de Condren, *L'Idée du Sacerdoce et du Sacrifice de Jèsus Christ* (Vitry-Le-François: E. Hurault, 1849), p. 45.

[2]Bremond, p. 311.

[3]Condren, p. 46.

[4]Ibid., p. 47.

[5]Ibid., p. 49.

the same concept at the beginning of discussion on the Null Way.[1] The ultimate Reality in Triadism is plenitude and infinite freedom. These terms are considered synonymous, and, as applied to the Supreme Śiva, absolute freedom has the exact meaning of self-sufficiency.

The holocausts of the Old Testament were offered for this primary purpose of homage.[2] However, the sacrifice of Our Lord, Condren says, is self-sufficient and answers perfectly all three types of sacrifices. "He is the total holocaust, totally given and totally offered to God, for whom He is totally immolated. He represents all mankind."[3]

In Śaivism, we will recall, the All-Powerful Tremendous God is the all-devouring fire which annihilates the multiplicities of the creature and so demonstrates His transcendence. Abhinava's idea of sacrifice brings out this idea of destruction:

> Sacrifice—the dissolution of all beings in the ardor of the fire of the Supreme Lord's Consciousness, a fire possessed of a yearning to devour all beings in itself, and uniquely subsistent on their dissolution—is [performed] to realize in its intensity the idea that all beings are in essence the ardor of the Supreme Lord Himself.[4]

Śaivism and the Vedānta began to merge in the thirteenth century in the theology of Śrīkaṇṭha. Especially significant in this contact between the two systems was the concept of the destructive nature of the divine. The following excerpt[5] from Śrīkaṇṭha in which he cites the *Upaniṣads* and the *Ṛgveda* attest to this common theme:

In the words of the *Atharvaśiras*—

> To the Destroyer, the Great Devourer, adoration![6]

Revelation proclaims the Supreme Lord, and not any mere soul, to be the All-Destroyer. And from its words:

1See p. 69 above.
2Condren, p. 50.
3Ibid., pp. 53 and 59.
4*T.S.*, ch. 4.
5Śrīkaṇṭha, "The Compassion and Pitilessness of Divine Terror," translated by José Pereira, pp. 389-91.
6Ibid., p. 390; from the *Atharvaśiras Upaniṣad*, no. 3.

He who offers all these worlds in sacrifice,[1]

we understand the Brahman's nature as sacrificer of the holocaust of the universe in the fire of His own radiance. This cannot be true of the soul, who is only one among the myriads of the holocaust offerings. When the Supreme Lord has absorbed into His being everything other than Himself, movable and unmoving, conscious and unconscious: then—...all this survives only as Darkness. Nothing then remains besides that one Supreme Lord, unconstrained in His splendor, the Witness of all. Hence Revelation declares:

> When there is darkness, there is no day or night, no being or non-being. Only Śiva.[2]

Other references to fire oblations are contained in Triadic literature. In the *Tantra on the Tremendous Wisdom God* one reads:

> The mind swiftly offers the oblation—such as the elements, the faculties, and the objects of knowledge—in the fire, the receptacle of the great Void. Such is the offering: the illumined Consciousness is the sacrificial ladle.[3]

This verse alludes to the Vedic fire sacrifice into which one throws offerings. Accordingly the true oblation is the sacrifice of the entire universe seen figuratively as the yogī's own body that he throws into the fire of the ultimate Consciousness, which consumes all aspects of phenomenal reality.

Bhaṭṭa touches upon the same subject in the following verse:

> Even while united with the differentiated,....You remain undifferentiated; we bring the offering to Your Reality, the only realization of the ultimate Truth.

In his commentary, Kṣemarāja notes that Bhaṭṭa offers himself as victim to Śiva by throwing himself into the ardor of the Tre-

[1]Ibid., from the *Ṛgveda*, 8:3:16.

[2]Ibid., p. 391; from the *Śvetāśvatara Upaniṣad*, 4:18.

[3]*VB*, v. 149 and com. pp. 166-67; see also p. 66, n. 1 above, where reference is made to this verse.

mendous Consciousness which consumes all, until the Essence alone remains.[1]

Abhinava also speaks of the "fire-oblation" in his *Quintessence of Ultimate Truth:*

> When in the blazing flame of Consciousness he offers the pile of the great seed which consists in the manifoldness of outward and inward figments of thought, this is his fire-oblation, done with labour.[2]

Here, the yogī's oblation consists in effacing from his mind all mental duality. In another verse of this work, Abhinava repeats this theme of the purification of thought through sacrificial oblation; the yogī "sacrifices all mental duality in the luminous flames of the Self and becomes one with Light."[3]

Having indicated briefly how pervasive is the subject of self-sacrifice in Śaiva literature, I will now continue with Condren's treatise.

Perfect sacrifice, Condren declares, has five essential parts:

(1) *Sanctification or Consecration of the victim*, which demands four things: first, the natural perfection of the victim.[4] In the Old Testament, deformed, sick or otherwise imperfect animals were attributed to man's sin; also, the natural perfection of the victim represented its spiritual perfection as well, and only such perfection was a suitable offering to the majesty and infinite grandeur of God.[5] Second, supernatural elevation of the offering. Only God has the authority to elevate the victim above the order of nature and cause it to be a proper offering by drawing it away from the domain of man. Third, separation of the victim from all profane use, and its setting apart for God alone. And fourth, the commitment to immolation—the victim is "owed to God" by virtue of its consecration.[6]

(2) *Oblation.* The victim is offered to God by means of certain prescribed words in much the same way that the yogī would employ certain formulas in ritual sacrifice.

[1] *Stav*, v. 11 and com. pp. 105-106; reference is made here to *VB*, v. 149.
[2] *PS*, v. 76.
[3] *PS* (Silburn) v. 68, quoted above on p. 51.
[4] Condren, p. 53.
[5] Ibid., p. 54.
[6] Ibid., p. 55.

(3) *Immolation or destruction of the offering* (*victim*) by death or other means.

(4) *Consumption of the victim,* ordinarily by inflammation; however, other means were employed—for instance, eating, in the case of bread offerings. Here Condren makes reference to the "bread of the presence," which, in the Old Testament, was placed in the sanctuary for the priests of the temple and originally, probably symbolized a food offering to the deity.[1]

(5) *Communion or participation in the victim,* which can be divided into three parts: The first is for the fire—the communion of God; in "holocaustic sacrifices," however, the entire victim is destroyed by fire, and only God (as the fire) "eats" the victim. The second part is for the priest—in the "propitiatory sacrifices," only God and the priest partake in the Communion. The third part is for the people—in the "peaçeful sacrifices" of thanksgiving, all (God, the priest, and the people) eat of the victim.[2]

Condren enumerates seven reasons for the inflammation of the victims. One can see many parallels here to Triadism. His reasons are as follows:

(1) The fire consumes all the victim's superfluities and imperfections.[3] This is also what happens in the Tremendous State—all the imperfections of the universe are consumed and only pure luminance, Śiva, remains.

(2) The victim is inflamed, and so glorified as a symbol of the risen Christ, the true victim, who was glorified after His crucifixion (immolation on the cross).[4] This glorification of the victim is parallelled in Triadism, where the Liberated-in-Life enjoys the exalted Tremendous State by virtue of his (real, not symbolic) identification with the Supreme Śiva.[5]

(3) The ancients in the Old Testament would burn the victim by God's command, and these victims thus consumed would emit an odor very agreeable to God as attested to by scripture.[6] Now this "special perfume" for God's enjoyment is spoken of by Abhi-

[1]Ibid., p. 56.
[2]Ibid., pp. 61, 63-64.
[3]Ibid., p. 56.
[4]Ibid., p. 57.
[5]*PS*, v. 73.
[6]Condren, p. 57.

nava in his *Essence of the Tantras*: in connection with sacrificial "offering of all things to the Supreme Lord," he says,

> the exterior use of delightful things (like offered *flowers and perfumes*) is recommended in view of the fact that all such things, through *their capacity to delight*, are able to enter consciousness spontaneously; the offering of these to the Supreme Lord is thus easy indeed.[1] (Italics mine.)

(4) The victims immolated by fire would cause God to enter into communion or participate with them—as though He were identified with the victims. Now actual identity or identification with God, as we have observed, is integral to Triadic metaphysics. But Catholicism, the theology of Difference (like the Hindu Dualist Vedānta) rejects this identity except in a representative sense. And we notice the use of the latter throughout the literary history of the Church, beginning with the first canonical writings of the New Testament.

Even in the Old Testament, we find this trend in the use of fire as a symbol or even "embodiment" of God. Condren stresses it in the relationship of Moses and his people to God when he says: "The God they adored was a devouring fire."[2] God appeared to them in the desert and on Mt. Sinai as a "column of fire." Thus they felt any offering to God was best given to the "consuming fire of God."

St. John of the Cross' theology will be the subject of the next archetype; but it is noteworthy to compare him here to Condren on the destructive fire of God, since he refers to the same quotation from Deuteronomy. St. John says God *could* be a destructive force but is not. "Moses," he claims, "says in Deuteronomy, our Lord God is a consuming fire—that is a fire of love."[3] Thus, for Condren, in the sacrificial sense, it appears that God *is* the consuming fire, but for St. John He is the "flame of love."

> Oh, the great glory of you souls that are worthy to attain to this

[1]Richard F. Cefalu, "*Shakti* in Abhinavagupta's Concept of *Mokṣa*," Ph.D. dissertation, Fordham University, 1973, p. 204.

[2]Condren, p. 57; cf. Deuteronomy 4:24.

[3]St. John of the Cross, *Living Flame of Love*, trans., ed., and introd. E. Allison Peers (New York: Image Books, 1962), p. 181.

> supreme fire, for, while it has infinite power to consume and annihilate you, it is certain that it consumes you not, but grants you a boundless consummation in glory![1]

Returning to Condren, God would be represented by this fire and would enter into communion with the Old Testament sacrifices. Unable to give their victims to God to be changed into Him, the ancients would give them to the fire, and they would be changed symbolically into a *representation* of God, who is fire—the purest and noblest of all the elements.[2]

The last three reasons for the inflammation of the victim given by Condren may be taken together, since they all refer to the three divine attributes intended to be recognized by that sacrificial act—(5) Sovereignty, (6) holiness and (7) plenitude. By destroying the life and being of the victim, God is affirmed the source of all life and of all being, in that He has absolute power over all creatures.

Moreover, Condren continues, in words so thoroughly Triadic:

> Sacrifice answers to all that God is, it recognizes Him as the Sovereign Being to Whom every being is owed in sacrifice. It regards Him in His own incomprehensible grandeur and perfection as Being Itself—beyond all invocation, all light, all thought, all name, and all term, beyond all representation, all love. In offering all to God, we profess that *He is All*: in destroying all, we affirm that He is in no way part of anything in the universe, and that nothing is in any way part of Him.[3] (Italics mine.)

Except perhaps for the words "nothing is in any way part of Him", Abhinava himself might have accepted this passage as a summary of Triadic metaphysics: Everything is Śiva-without-second; all the phenomenal universe has its source in Him, emanates from Him, and returns to Him. He is not "part" of anything, because He *is* everything. Abhinava's affirmation of God's sovere-

[1]Ibid., pp. 182-83.

[2]Condren, p. 58.

[3]Condren, p. 59. This passage is also found in Bremond, pp. 310-11; however, I feel that Montgomery's translation: "we declare that there is nought in all the universe that is not as nothing before Him," is a poor and inaccurate rendering of "nous protestons qu'il n'est rien de tout ce qui est dans l'univers, et que tout n'est rien de lui."

ignty is the most emphatic in Difference-in-Identity language, just as the French School's is the most emphatic in the language of Difference. The five pure categories attest to His absolute sovereignty over the entire universe. For Abhinava, all reality is a sacrifice to God in homage to His plenitude:

> ...sacrifice is the *offering of all things* to the Supreme Lord alone, with the purpose of strengthening the representation that *the sole ground of the existence of all things is none but this very Lord, and that nothing exists apart from him.*[1] (Italics mine.)

It must be noted, Condren adds, that every victim is being sacrificed in place of every other creature for which it is substituted and of which it is representative, and in some way, the entire universe is sacrificed in the victim.[2] In the same way it is said of Jesus in regard to all men.[3] Again, this has correspondence in Triadism, where each man is a microcosm of the universe.

Finally, Condren proclaims the plenitude or self-sufficiency of God by reaffirming, in terms perfectly accordant with Triadism, that

> Sacrifice testifies further that God is above all love, all adoration and all created things;...
> ...[He] is sovereignly honored by sacrifice, for when we offer Him something, we destroy it as useless to Him who possesses everything within Himself, and who has need only of Himself.[4]

(b) *Sacrifice in the New Law*

Condren completes this analysis of the mystical theology of sacrifice by relating it to the person of Jesus. He begins by remarking that the five parts of the sacrifice are not fully verified in the imperfect oblations of the Old Testament.[5] But they are in the New, in the perfect sacrifice of Jesus; there Christ—Himself both eternal priest and sacrifice, as the Pauline letter to the Hebrews

[1]Cefalu, p. 204.
[2]Condren, p. 60.
[3]Hebrews 2:9.
[4]Condren, p. 60.
[5]See pp. 130-31 above.

accentuates—has a specific and unmistakable role in each of these parts.[1]

Now the purpose of the unknown author of Hebrews was to contrast the eternal sacrifice of Jesus with the imperfect sacrifices of Israel, and the perfection and sufficiency of Jesus' sacrifice was the main point of the epistle. Condren and the French School adopted and developed this position. Therefore, this literary work is of extreme importance not only to the mystical theology of the French School, but also, more importantly, for the liturgical teaching of the Catholic Church. It is the only place in the New Testament where the redemptive act is interpreted as "sacrifice." Moreover, without the sacrificial theology of *Hebrews*, Catholics would be hard pressed to counter the argument that the Calvary event being a time and place happening, and as such, unrepeatable, the Eucharistic sacrifice is merely a symbolic ritual commemorating that completed historical event.

This is a question I will attempt to meet presently. However, it may be asked why there is need here of developing Condren's teaching on the sacrifice of Christ—an incarnate God, and a divine person united with a created nature—in a work on Triadism; for, according to the latter's metaphysics, the supreme deity is coterminous with reality, also lacks any incarnations or *avatāras*, and is not united to any nature that is not its own.

One answer is that the manifestations of Śiva, like the Incarnation of Christ, are communications of the divinity to finite individuals. In Triadism the individuals are identical with the communicating deity (as indeed they are in the Christian Trinity)—while in Catholicism the finite individual, Christ's human nature, is distinct from His divine nature and person. They are related not through identity, but through union—a "substantial" union, as Suárez describes it.[2] The intimacy of this union is a model for that of our own "accidental" union with Christ in the mystical body and with the Godhead in the Beatific Vision. Both unions, substantial and accidental, are describable in terms of figurative identity. It is in the context of this identity that an elaboration of Condren's teaching on Christ's sacrifice becomes pertinent, as some of its basic concepts, "emanation" and "absorption" are fundamental to Triadic thought.

[1]Condren, p. 68.
[2]Suárez, *De Ultimo Fine Hominis*, disp. 6, sect. 1, num. 6.

According to Condren, Christ's entire life, "since the first moment of the Incarnation throughout eternity is the true sacrifice."[1] As for the five parts of perfect sacrifice in relation to Jesus, Condren's development is as follows:

(1) The *sanctification* of Jesus as victim was accomplished in the Incarnation wherein the Son of God was consecrated by Divinity Itself as God's *Priest*,[2] and He renewed His consecration on Calvary.[3]

(2) The *oblation* was also accomplished at the moment of the Incarnation. The Son realizing that the Father's justice could not be satisfied by the imperfect, animal sacrifices of the old law, and knowing perfectly well the will of His Father, He offered Himself—*Victim* to the Father.[4] Thus, at the Incarnation, Jesus was at once both Priest and Victim. In these words of Jesus to His Father, "I have come to do Your will," we have an example, Condren says, of what was said at the outset of his treatise—the first duty of religion, as taught to us by the Son of God, is *sacrifice*. Only the Son could fulfil the will of the Father. For the centuries that preceded the Incarnation, man would have been powerless to express recognition to his Creator—his first obligation, if God had not chosen (sanctified) some animals as "representative" of His Son and was willing to have them offered to Him in this capacity; therefore, they had a "figurative" holiness.[5]

(3) The *Immolation* of Jesus occurred at Calvary on the altar of the cross.[6] Now the sacrifice of Jesus must not be seen as coterminous with His death (a common view); for, if it is so interpreted, the Eucharistic sacrifice, the quintessence of Catholic life, is merely symbolic.

The last two stages of Jesus' sacrifice, (4) the *Consummation* and (5) the *Communion*, because of their affinity belong to the risen life of Jesus. They are part, therefore, of His Resurrection and Ascension into Glory.

The communion and the consumption or consummation in the

1Ibid.
2John 10:36.
3Ibid., 17:19.
4Condren, p. 73; see also Hebrews 10:5-9.
5Ibid., pp. 74-75.
6Ibid., p. 77.

> sacrifice of Jesus Christ can be placed together since they differ only in their formal aspects. For the consumption and consummation of Jesus is the loss of His mortal life and the destruction of His bodily functions. It is His entry into the life of glory which is His due and His right as the Son of God. Now the communion is nothing more than the enjoyment of this same life in the bosom of His father.[1]

As Walsh points out, "This entire risen state of Jesus...is the actual return of the victim to God, the union of Jesus with His Father, and the consequent acceptance and ratification of His entire sacrifice."[2] For this reason, we can say with St. Paul, in the Incarnation, the Son of God was born Son of Man; in the Resurrection the Son of Man was born Son of God.[3]

To conclude Condren's treatise of Christ's sacrifice, I will paraphrase the brief, but excellent summary of Walsh, which, he says, represents "the central contemplation of the French School from which all their teaching and devotion flows easily and naturally."[4]

In His Incarnation, Walsh says, Jesus was essentially priest and victim since His work was that of religion and sacrifice. According to His Father's will, He took upon Himself human flesh—"emptying" Himself (figurative "self-annihilation") of His Divinity. He became, thereby, "Head" of all mankind and formed with them one mystical reality. He thus became mankind's only "perfect priest," *and with them and in them* offered Himself in sacrifice to the Father as the only perfect victim—Condren often uses this phrase "victim to His Father."[5]

Walsh continues in this Pauline language—and this is of the utmost importance if one is to draw any Catholic parallel to the Triadic concept of "absorption in the Divine"—with mankind and in mankind Jesus ascended back to heaven where He is consumed (absorbed) in the bosom of His Father:

> Granted the hypothetical necessity of the Incarnation, man's religious obligations demanded that Jesus be sent to earth as

[1]Ibid., pp. 81-82.
[2]Walsh, p. 53.
[3]Romans 1:3-4.
[4]Walsh, p. 20.
[5]Bremond, p. 299.

priest and victim.[1] The same inexorable logic demanded that He return to God *drawing with Him all mankind.* And there He remains forever victim, and forever the Head of His mystical body of which we are members. Christ, our head, our priest, our victim *is now in heaven* in the final glory of His priesthood, *as the source of all our life.*[2] (Initial italics mine.)

All this furnishes us with at least two new important areas of comparison between Catholic and Triadic theology.

(1) In the first archetype of this chapter, we looked at the Śaiva metaphysics of cosmic manifestation, but only insofar as the obscuring Mirific Power was concerned. Here, I will again search the same general area for comparisons. This time, however, the probe shall be more sweeping, covering a brief but broad overview, touching several concepts from "emanation" to "absorption" or compenetration in the divine, with greatest emphasis on the latter.

Now from earlier discussions we know that in Triadic theology both the phenomenal and noumenal worlds are emanations from Śiva or, in the gnostic sense, divine sparks that issue from, and eventually are "absorbed" in the Primordial Unity. Manifestation and absorption result from Śiva engaging in play or frolic—or motiveless activities, the three most prominent of them being creation, maintenance and destruction.[3] They occur in continuous and perpetual cycles, so that Śiva is ever creating, ever sustaining, and ever destroying. The Absolute, consequently, is both transcendent and immanent in His Śivahood and Energyhood, respectively. This is why we say "Śiva is All"—*omnia in omnibus.*

These concepts, in Catholicism, are translated into the language of representative identity. Bremond cites an interesting passage from Bérulle which treats the relationship of Jesus and Mary under the subtitle "Jesus in Mary"—where he not only uses the term "divine emanations" but also in a sense approaching the Triadic. Speaking of Mary's role as the mother of Jesus, he says:

1Here the author seems to imply that the Incarnation and sacrifice of Jesus was necessary if man was to fulfill his primary religious obligation to render homage to the awesome majesty of God. This is true, the French School would assert, irrespective of so-called Original Sin, or man's sinful nature in general, and the consequential need for redemption.

2Walsh, pp. 19-20.

3Pandey, pp. 83, 494; *VB* (Silburn), pp. 12-13; *MM* (Silburn), pp. 47-48.

> She is not, she lives not nor operates; in her is God, living and operating in her. And what is more, He is, He lives, He operates, to take upon Himself a new being, a new life, to bring about within the Virgin an operation like to that which through all eternity He has wrought in Himself, *approaching the most nearly that can ever be to the divine emanations.*[1] (Italics mine.)

Bérulle again uses the term "emanation," this time more figuratively; in addition, he alludes to the divine actions of creation and maintenance.

> Let us adore God, *ever creating*, *ever referring* the world to Himself, *governing* and renewing it by continual creation, so that the created being is *ever emanating* from God and has *subsistence* only in this continuous and *perpetual emanation*...let us reverence it.[2] (Italics mine.)

Naturally, we would not expect to find "annihilation" specifically mentioned among the powers listed in this Bérullian passage; however, in the Triadic sense annihilation *is* here—for, the "recreating" and "re-emanating" implied in this excerpt suggest the destruction which necessarily precedes a new creation in the never-ending cycle.

So also is the transcendence and immanence implicitly expressed by these words of Bérulle:

> God is All, He is everywhere, He does all...majestically, mightily, and graciously. He is alike in Himself and in His Works. As He is in Heaven, so He is on earth; acting on earth as in Heaven.[3]

For a parallel to the all-important concept of "absorption" in Triadism—the goal of all the Ways of Libreation, we will turn to St. Paul and the French School. In the Triadic theology of Difference-in-Identity, it has been pointed out several times, absorption is an actual reality. Since this cannot occur, factually, in Catholicism, we must look for absorption expressed figuratively. The theo-

[1]Bremond, p. 81.
[2]Ibid., pp. 108-9.
[3]Ibid., p. 79.

logy of St. Paul, Bérullian thought, and the sacrificial adoration of Condren give us this parallel.

The Pauline expression "in Christ Jesus", which occurs over a hundred times in Paul's letters, is perhaps the best New Testament example of figurative absorption. Although in some cases it means only that our lives are in harmony with the principles of Christianity,[1] in other places it is to be understood in the full sense—to be "in Christ Jesus" means to be intimately united with Him and to live His life.

By Baptism we have "clothed" ourselves in Jesus Christ; "all are one in Christ Jesus."[2] Our lives are "hidden now with Christ in God. When Christ our life appears, then [we] shall appear with him in glory."[3] So assumed are we in Christ, that the Apostle can say: "the life I live now is not my own; Christ is living in me."[4]

"Putting on the new man" is a Pauline expression that implies the receiving of "new life" by incorporation in Christ. "Our old self" made us "slaves to sin";[5] we must, therefore, put off the "old man" so that we might "put on that new man"[6] who was created through the death of Christ.[7]

In order for Christ to "live in us," Bérulle says, "we are obliged to surrender ourselves to the Son of God, to die in ourselves." He continues:

> We, ...are a 'capacity of God'; better still, we are nothing else, for 'there is more of nothingness than of being in our being'. ...God 'has rendered us capable...of living in another', which proves both the 'feebleness' of our natural life, and its nobility, for that 'other', if we desire it, will be God Himself.[8]

Now the above phrases from various letters of St. Paul "imply a transmission of Christ's life and do not in any way suggest a kind of pantheistical fading away of our personalities."[9] Therefore,

[1] I Corinthians 3:1; 2 Corinthians 12:2; Romans 16:19.
[2] Galatians 3:27-28.
[3] Colossians 3:3-4.
[4] Galatians 2:20.
[5] Romans 6:6.
[6] Ephesians 4:22-24.; Colossians 3:9-10.
[7] Ephesians 2:15-16.
[8] Bremond, p. 70.
[9] Amiot, p. 145.

we "annihilate ourselves in Christ" in a figurative sense, in that we "destroy" our imperfections and frailties by participating in Christ's mysteries, or in His various "states" to use Bérullian language.[1]

Furthermore, Bérulle tells us that God offers us Jesus—but, in a figurative sense; he uses Triadic language which is about as close as can be expected to the "self-recognition of our Śiva-nature" concept:

> He is life, and we must live in Him, by Him and for Him....As God, in giving us life, gives us this world and ourselves, so, in giving us Jesus for the true life, He again gives us to ourselves, for we were lost without this life. And, in His abundance He gives us a new world, that is to say, Himself.[2]

On the subject of self-annihilation consequent upon the Incarnation, and using a familiar simile of absorption in a compatible substance, Bérulle says that this "death" tends

> to draw us, unite us and make us lose ourselves in God. The first is done by His greatness, the second by His unity; the third by His fulness; for the greatness of God separates us from ourselves and all created things, drawing us to God; *His unity receives and unites us in Him*; *and His fulness possesses and absorbs us* in the immense ocean of His perfections, as the sea attracts and absorbs a drop of water.[3] (Italics mine.)

The last clause in this quote is one frequently found in variant forms in Hindu literature: "he is merged in Brahma, as water in water, as milk in milk;"[4] and, "absorbed (in contemplations) as salt is absorbed in water."[5]

Now we have already seen numerous Triadic examples of the Tremendous God's destructive force which is all-consuming. This is precisely what Condren says here in regard to God's relation to the creature:

[1]Walsh, pp. 6-7.
[2]Bremond, pp. 70-71.
[3]Ibid., p. 74.
[4]*PS* (Barnett), v. 51.
[5]Lallā, v. 29.

> Jesus Christ indeed offered Himself to the Father also *to be consummated in us*, that is to be *in us as another self*, to hold the place in us that we hold, there to perfect and fulfil His grace, spirit and mysteries: *to appropriate to Himself the creaturely attributes*, and at the same time to *absorb and fulfil them in the Divine attributes and perfections.*[1]

Therefore, through the Incarnation, we form one "mystic" reality (body) with Jesus as our "head," and so were mystically drawn with Him and in Him when, in His risen life Jesus returned to His Father.[2] In His exaltation before the throne of God, we are absorbed with Him into the bosom of His Father—not entitatively as in Triadism, but mystically or representatively as in Catholicism.

(2) As for the second comparison, we have already alluded to the Buddhist concept of *momentariness* or the belief in the single moment and its connection with the Interstitial Void[3]—a theory that Triadism had adopted, and consequently rejected the notion of temporal continuity. It was also stated, in a quote from Abhinava, that mystical experience can be realized when, putting an end to the past and future modalities of time, the yogī rests fully appeased in an *eternal present*. This perpetual "intersection" or "rupture" between these two modalities constituted the Interstitial Void, the "undifferentiated plenitude" or the fullness of the Tremendous State. In other words, the only true place of repose is the *eternal present*—the abode of Śiva.

It is in this notion of the *eternal present* that a parallel to Christ's sacrifice can be seen. In the sacrifice of Jesus, His Resurrection, Ascension, and consequent Exaltation in heaven is the ultimate act—when He entered the heavenly sanctuary to be consumed in the bosom of His Father, in recognition and ratification of His perfect, life-long sacrifice. Hence, that which was transitory forever passed away, and that which belongs to the realm of God forever remains. Because His sacrifice is brought to completion in a sphere where there is no past and no future, only an *eternal present*, the earthly events of this sacrifice, although historically completed, are given eternal reality and are, therefore, made eternally

[1]Bremond, p. 316.
[2]Walsh, pp. 19-20.
[3]See pp. 63-64 above.

present. Thus, the objection of a completed historical act cannot rightly be raised; indeed, through the Eucharist this eternal present is demanded. So Catholicism, like Triadism, has its one and only true place of repose, the *eternal present*—the abode of Jesus.

Before I pass on to the next archetype, I will mention the third major theologian of the French School, Jean-Jacques Olier (1608-57), who, like the other Oratorians was thoroughly Bérullian in his theology. He was also totally committed to Condren's essential doctrine of our duty of self-effacement, of sacrificing and annihilating the self, in order to give place to the Spirit of God. Olier's uniqueness lies in his almost Buddhistically profound sense of self-abandonment. The following examples express his extreme sentiments:

> The purity of love...is extreme. It places the soul into detachment and separation from all self-interest, and lifts it above the love of its own salvation; so that the soul is content with all that shall befall it, knowing well that whatever may happen to it, will be for the glory of God....The soul in this condition finds its peace in venerating and adoring God's Justice and Judgements,...to which it yields without return upon self.[1]

And from a prayer, in words even more severe, he says:

> 'Be content...with the loss of my life...and even with that of my soul; for if my damnation be to Thy pleasure, joy and glory, at this very hour rejoice Thou then in my loss. *I care not at all,* for I seek but Thy joy and satisfaction, and nought else. Meseems that hell itself would be desirable, did I see that it was for the satisfaction of God and for His honour'.[2]

C. *Archetype III: the Dark Night of Mystical Awakening*

There are two broad areas or pervasive themes in the mystical theology of St. John of the Cross (1542-91) from which Triadic parallels might be drawn. The first is in the concept of "living

[1]Bremond, p. 428.
[2]Ibid.

flame," or the Divine Light which consumes the mystic. The second is in the notion of "dark night," a period of spiritual "awakening" or "turning" (*metanoia*).

Included in the first area would be images and metaphors relating to luminosity—light, flame, fire, lamp, and candle. We have seen many instances of Triadism's preoccupation with luminosity in concepts like self-luminosity or the Light of Śiva.[1] The four-stanza poem of St. John entitled, *Living Flame of Love* could serve as comparison here—especially the third stanza:

> Oh, lamps of fire, In whose splendours the deep caverns of sense which were dark and blind
> With strange brightness Give heat and light together to their Beloved![2]

Not only the symbols of light and darkness, but also the concept of "deep caverns," employed here to describe the heart or soul of the mystic as the divine abode by St. John, is a fertile field for Triadic comparison.[3]

Ample source material for the second theme can be found in the Dark Night of Śiva, treated at length in the previous chapter, and in St. John's *Dark Night of the Soul.*[4]

Rather than treat both the concepts of "light" and "dark night," however, I have decided for the following reasons to explore only the latter theme for Catholic and Triadic comparisons. The notion of "divine light" is an integral part of the "dark night"; hence, no separate treatment of the former is necessary. Furthermore, com-

[1]See the following publications of Silburn which I have used throughout this work: *Bhakti*, pp. 13, 17-19, 23, 28-29, 33-34; 47, 57, 82, 86-87, 90; vv. 12, 34, 41, 51, 57-58, 61, 68, 80, 95, 113. *Hymnes*, pp. 25, 31-32, 34, 38, 57-58, 68-70, 79, 90, 92. *MM*, flame: pp. 18, 72, 93-96, 127; fire: pp. 80, 93-96, 144, 146, 148-50, 158, 160; illumination: pp. 50, 75, 138, 141; lamp: pp. 72, 90, 92-95, 107, 140, 146-48. *P.S.*, pp. 23, 35, 38, 40, 53; vv. 10-11, 12-13, 30, 35, 43-44, 55-56, 62, 64-66, 68, 76, 81, 87, 95. *VB*, pp. 13-14, 59; vv. 21, 29, 53, 61, 76, 85-87, 89, 110, 135, 149.

[2]St. John, *Living Flame*, pp. 81-137; 205-261.

[3]See especially, Lallā, q. 105 quoted above, p. 106; see also, *Bhakti*, pp. 28-29, 31, 45-47, 59, 64, 69, 80, 89; *Stav*, v. 12 (quoted above, p. 97), and 58; *VB*, v. 89 and com. p. 128 referred to above, p. 64, n. 5.

[4]St. John of the Cross, *Dark Night of the Soul*, 3rd rev. ed., trans. and ed., with intro. by E. Allison Peers (New York: Image Books, 1959).

parisons between the two "dark nights" will produce parallels greater in number and richer in detail than those that could be developed from the theme of "light." Finally, concentration on the second area of overlapping imagery will permit a greater emphasis on detail without redundancy than if both areas were treated separately.

1. The Meaning and Application of the Term: "Dark Night"

Quatrains 3 and 4 of the *Wise Sayings* of Lallā,[1] contain a general parallel to the first five stanzas of St. John of the Cross' *Dark Night of the Soul.*[2] It seems that a comparison of these stanzas is the most logical place to begin a study of Catholic and Triadic parallels to the notion of *dark night*. The main reason is that it will afford us an early opportunity to become acquainted with five of the eight stanzas (and for our purpose, the most important ones) of this mystical poem which forms the basis of my archetypal treatment of St. John. Thus, from a general comparison I can move on to more specific parallels between the two traditions regarding this concept.

It must be stressed that I am not writing a commentary, so I will not be treating the poem as a whole. My only interest is in St. John's theological development of the concept under discussion in order that it can serve as a basis for Triadic comparisons. Therefore, for this added reason, it is profitable to cite the major portion of the poem here as a sort of introduction to the treatment that is to follow.

The first poem offered shall be *Dark Night*, sts. 1-5, followed by Lallā's *Wise Sayings*, qs. 3-4. Raised alphabetical symbols, explained in the legend that follows, shall indicate parallel elements in the two poetic works. The words to the left of the parallel lines (//) are taken from *Dark Night*, and those to the right are from *Wise Sayings*:

Legend: Dark Night // Wise Sayings

[a]*dark night, darkness, happy night // darkness*. The term "darkness" is only used once in Lallā, at the end of q. 4, but it has the same connotation as in St. John—it is the soul, the abode of God or of Śiva, where the lamp of knowledge burns and disperses the

[1]Lallā, pp. 25-26.

[2]St. John, *Dark Night*, pp. 33-34.

darkness of ignorance: it is a contemplative darkness. Obviously the "day and night" of q. 3 is merely a synonym for "all the time," and, therefore, is not germane.

[b]*yearning || passionate longing*. Both terms are indicative of the anguish and desire of love in the soul seeking God.

[c]*happy || lucky*. These two adjectives convey the same thought —the good fortune of the soul who is privileged to be guided along on the journey toward God or Śiva.

[d]*went forth || go forth*. Again there is perfect parallel—the soul embarks on a spiritual quest.

[e]*house, place || house*. This is the soul of the mystic, wherein God is encountered at journey's end.

[f]*light (in the heart), guide || lamp (of knowledge), inner light*. This is the illuminating and divine light present within the soul of the mystic which guides the sojourner and disperses the darkness of ignorance. A contrast is made in St. John to other lights which do not guide the soul.

[g]*he, Beloved || learned man, him, true nature, truth*. All these terms refer to the ultimate goal of this search—God. In Lallā the Ultimate first takes the form of a *guru*; then she realizes the "tru-th"—the Supreme Self and her self are one and the same nature.

[h]*joined, transformed || laid hold; seize, hold tight*. The basic meaning amounts to the same thing in both these works—Divine union, by means of a transformation or representative identity in St. John, and an entitative identity, a compenetration in Lallā. However, different imagery is employed; in the former, union is more subdued than the vehement "grasping" or "clutching" of Śiva, so typically Triadic, as seen in the latter case.[1]

Dark Night of the Soul, stanzas 1-5:

1. On a dark night,[a] Kindled in love with yearnings[b]—oh, happy chance!—
   I went forth[d] without being observed, My house[e] being now at rest.
2. In darkness[a] and secure, By the secret ladder, disguised—oh, happy chance![c]—
   In darkness[a] and in concealment, My house[e] being now at rest.

[1]Cf. *Stav*, v. 68.

3. In the happy[c] night,[a] In secret, when none saw me,
Nor I beheld aught, Without light or guide, save that which burned in my heart.[f]

4. This light[f] guided me More surely than the light of noonday
To the place where he[g] (well I knew who) was awaiting me—
A place[e] where none appeared.

5. Oh, night[a] that guided[f] me, Oh, night[a] more lovely than the dawn,
Oh, night[a] that joined[h] Beloved[g] with lover, Lover transformed[h] in the Beloved![g]

Wise Sayings, quatrains 3-4:

3. With passionate longing[b] did I, Lallā, go forth.[d]
Seeking and searching[d] did I pass the day and night
Then, lo, saw I in mine own house[e] a learned man,[g]
And that was my lucky star[e] and my lucky moment[c] when I laid hold[h] of him.[g]

4. Slowly, slowly, did I stop my breath in the bellows-pipe (of my throat).
Thereby did the lamp (of knowledge)[f] blaze up within me, and then was my true nature[g] revealed unto me.
I winnowed forth abroad my inner light,[f]
So that, in the darkness[a] itself, I could seize[h] (the truth[g]) and hold it tight.[h]

According to St. John, the term "dark night" means "purgative contemplation, which causes passively in the soul the negation of itself and all things." It is a period of purification and progression which the mystic undergoes as he journeys on the spiritual road toward his goal—"the state of the perfect, which is that of Divine union of the soul with God."[1] The phrase, "the Dark Night of Śiva" is used in precisely the same sense by the mystic poets of Triadism;[2] for, in this Night of Undifferentiation, the soul progresses in the secret and silent darkness—stripped and annihilated of all doubt and dualism, and all that is not Śiva[3]—to the illumination of the Light of Love. So here too, we find that the Dark

[1]St. John, *Dark Night*, pp. 36-37.
[2]Cf. p. 96 above.
[3]Cf. p. 97 above.

Night is a spiritual *metanoia* the soul experiences as it strives for Divine union.

According to the mystical Doctor, the Dark Night consists of two stages: The *first* is the Active Night of the Sense, purifying the sensual part of the soul.;[1] it is designed for beginners who "meditate" on the spiritual road.[2] In this phase the soul is wont to spend its time in prayer, penances, fasts, the sacraments,[3] and in dying to its affections and to itself.[4] Here the soul, through these acts of mortification is "lulled to sleep...in the house of its sensuality," with respect to its passions and desires.[5] This means that the four passions of the soul—joy, grief, hope, and fear—are calmed through continonus mortifications. The natural desires in the sensual part of the soul have been quieted by means of habitual times of aridity.[6] The harmony of the senses and the interior faculties cause a suspension of labor and a cessation from meditation, and the soul remains quiet and at rest.[7] For, "in order that the interior motions and acts of the soul may come to be moved by God divinely, they must,"St. John insists, "first be darkned and put to sleep...until they have no more strength."[8]

As we have seen, this "lulling to sleep" and the "calming of the passions," is what Triadism refers to as the "vigilant or mystical sleep"—a state of continuous contemplation, when the agitation of the spirits are calmed, and the saint plunges himself into Śiva where he resides in the "quietude of Love."[9]

When this occurs, the soul can go forth on the road of the Spirit, in the *second* stage of the night, which is the Passive Night of the Spirit. The Active Night has prepared the senses and faculties —although not completely, since impurities still remain—"for the reception of Divine influences and illuminations in greater abundance than before."[10] Hence, "God draws them forth from the state

[1]St. John, *Dark Night*, p. 21.
[2]Ibid., p. 22.
[3]Ibid., p. 38.
[4]Ibid., p. 36.
[5]Ibid., p. 37.
[6]This term will be elaborated below.
[7]St. John, *Dark Night*, p. 87.
[8]Ibid., p. 153.
[9]Cf. p. 97 (and especially note 3) above; cf. also, Silburn, *La Bhakti*, p. 58, and note 4.
[10]St. John, *Dark Night*, p. 22.

of beginners—...and begins to set them in the state of progressives —which is that of those who are already contemplatives," to the end that they may be prepared for "the Divine union of perfect love."[1] This higher road is also known as "the spiritual night of infused contemplation, through which the soul journeys with no other guide or support," the saint says, "than the Divine love 'which burned in my heart'."[2] It is "infused" in the sense that Divine contemplation is implanted by the Light of Wisdom in the soul of the mystic "passively and secretly, without the knowledge of the senses and faculties."[3]

(a) *The Active Night of Sense*

God takes the beginners, with their sensual imperfections, and first leads them into the Dark Night of Sense, where they may see how desperately they need God to set them on the path of the proficients (contemplatives).[4] For, "however greatly the soul itself labours, it cannot purify itself so as to be in the least degree prepared for the Divine union of perfection of love, if God takes not its hand and purges it not in that dark fire."[5] He seeks to bring the traveler on this lower road to a higher degree of love for Himself; to free him from "the ignoble exercises of sense and meditation" that he has been practising so assiduously in his search for God; and to lead them on to spiritual exercises "wherein they can commune with Him more abundantly and are freed more completely from imperfections."

> For they have now had practice for some time in the way of virtue and have presevered in meditation and prayer, whereby, through the sweetness and pleasure that they have found therein, they have lost their love of the things of the world and have gained some degree of spiritual strength in God; this has enabled them to some extent to refrain from creature desires, so that for God's sake they are now able to suffer a little burden and a *little aridity* without turning back to a time which they found more pleasant.[6] (Italics mine.)

[1]Ibid.
[2]Ibid., p. 26.
[3]Ibid., p. 182.
[4]Ibid., p. 60.
[5]Ibid., p. 46.
[6]Ibid., p. 62.

(1) The Aridities

God cures imperfections, St. John tells us, "by means of temptations, aridities, and other trials, all of which are part of the dark night." For, he continues, "the perfection and worth of things consist not in the multitude and the pleasantness of one's actions, but in being able to deny oneself in them."[1] He uses this term, "aridity" throughout his treatise—he speaks of "a little aridity," as we have just seen, when he treats the Active Night, and "pure aridity," as I shall indicate shortly, when he describes the Passive Night. Hence, the traveler in both nights finds it a constant companion. The Night of Sense, which is common, and experienced by many (beginners) "is bitter and terrible to the sense." The Night of Spirit, on the other hand, is experienced by few (proficients) and "is horrible and awful to the spirit."[2]

It is obvious that the term means "dryness," but in what sense and for what purpose is it connected to the dark night?

Just when these souls are receiving their greatest pleasure and sweetness from the spiritual exercises and mortifications in the sensual night, "God turns all this light of theirs into darkness, and shuts against them the door and the source of the sweet spiritual water which they were tasting in God whensoever and for as long as they desired." Suddenly and without warning, "He leaves them so completely in the dark" that they do not hnow where to turn their spiritual exercises—"for they cannot advance a step in meditation." Now, St. John says, "they are left with such dryness that not only do they experience no pleasure and consolation in the spiritual things...they were wont to find their delights and pleasures, but instead, on the contrary, they find insipidity and bitterness in the said things."[3]

The poetess, Lallā expresses this pain and anguish with the imagery of a door—not only closed but also "bolted":

> I, Lallā, wearied myself seeking for Him and searching.
> I laboured and strove even beyond my strength.
> I began to look for Him, and lo, I saw that bolts were on His door,...[4]

[1]Ibid., pp. 57-58.
[2]Ibid., p. 61.
[3]Ibid., pp. 62-63.
[4]Lallā, q. 48.

Utpala also refers to "groping" and "disoriented" progression of the mystic who suddenly, and for reasons he does not hnow, finds himself oppressed with the feeling he is deprived of the Divine presence which causes "bitterness and aridity for the heart."[1]

The reason for these aridities, then, is that "God now sees that they (beginners) have grown a little, and are becoming strong enough to lay aside their swaddling clothes and be taken from the gentle breast, so He sets them down from His arms and teaches them to walk on their own feet."[2] So, it is by means of these aridities that the soul is purged of its impurities and is able to move forward spiritually.

So much for the "what happens" and the "why it happens" of the soul's aridity; but the actual cause, or the "how it happens," is described at length by St. John:

> For the cause of this aridity is that God transfers to the spirit the good things and the strength of the senses, which, since the soul's natural strength and senses are incapable of using them, remain barren, dry and empty. For the sensual part of a man has no capacity for that which is pure spirit, and thus, when it is the spirit that receives the pleasure, the flesh is left without savour and is too weak to perform any action. But the spirit, which all the time is being fed, goes forward in strength, and with more alertness and solicitude than before, in its anxiety not to fail God; and if it is not immediately conscious of spiritual sweetness and delight, but only of aridity and lack of sweetness, the reason for this is the strangeness of the exchange; for its palate has been accustomed to those other sensual pleasures upon which its eyes are still fixed, and, since the spiritual palate is not made ready or purged for such subtle pleasure, until it finds itself becoming prepared for it by means of this arid and dark night, it cannot experience spiritual pleasure and good, but only aridity and lack of sweetness, since it misses the pleasure which aforetime it enjoyed so readily.[3]

Therefore, God is now guiding the soul, according to St. John, along a path quite different from the one previously traveled—

[1]Cf. pp. 100-101 above.
[2]St. John, *Dark Night*, p. 63.
[3]Ibid., p. 65

that of infused contemplation. The first path is of meditation and reasoning but the second concerns neither of these. It is well for these souls, he says, "to take comfort, to persevere in patience and to be in no wise afflicted. Let them trust in God"; for, St. John assures us, they will not be abandoned by God but will receive all that is necessary for the road, "until He bring [sic] them into the clear and pure light of love."[1]

(b) *The Passive Night of Spirit*

Now ready for the second night of spirit, "the soul can no longer meditate nor reflect in the imaginative sphere of the sense... For God now begins to communicate Himself to it, no longer through the sense, ...but by pure spirit,...by an act of simple contemplation."[2] And so, it is by means of these "little aridities" that the soul is purged of its impurities and is able to continue its journey. The aridities, of course, do not stop, but intensify into "pure aridities" in the Passive Night of the Spirit, as the following words of St. John clearly specify:

> He weans them from the breasts of these sweetnesses and pleasures, gives them pure *aridities* and inward darkness, takes from them all these irrelevances and puerilities, and by very different means causes them to win the virtues.... passively by means of the purgation of the said night.[3] (Italics mine.)

(1) The Painfulness of the Contemplative Night

Just as aridities occur in both nights in increasing severity—so does pain:[4] "the purgation of sense becoming effective when that of the spirit has fairly begun."[5] In fact, St. John, continuing to compare the two nights, emphasizes why the Night of Spirit is more purgative and painful than the Night of Sense:

> The night which we have called that of the sense may and should be called a kind of correction and restraint of the desire rather

[1]Ibid., p. 70.
[2]Ibid., pp. 67-68.
[3]Ibid., p. 60.
[4]Ibid., p. 24; this parallels the Triadic experience of increased pain in the purifying phases of progression, cf. pp. 101-106 above.
[5]St. John, *Dark Night*, p. 96.

> than purgation. The reason is that all the imperfections and disorders of the sensual part have their strength and root in the spirit, where all habits, both good and bad, are brought into subjection, and thus, until these are purged, the rebellions and depravities of sense cannot be purged thoroughly.[1]

Therefore during the time when God is drawing the soul by means of purifying aridities from meditation to contemplation—"wherein it no longer has any power to work or to reason with its faculties concerning things of God"—the spiritual persons are greatly afflicted with severe trials. Their intense suffering lies, not so much in aridities as in fear of being lost on the path; they feel that God has abandoned them, and all spiritual blessings are in the past, "since they find no help or pleasure in good things."[2] Therefore, from the beginning of this night, the soul has been touched with the anguish and yearnings of love.[3]

Pain, then, is a constant companion of the soul throughout the Passive Night. There is a perfect parallel here to Triadism; for, the same sense of anguish and frustration spoken of by St. John is also expressed in virtually the same language by Lallā and Utpaladeva.[4]

(2) The Divine Light of Contemplation and the
Faculties of the Soul

This Dark Night of Infused Contemplation is an inflowing of God in the soul which purges it from its ignorances[5] and imperfections. "God secretly teaches the soul and instructs it in perfection of love, without its doing anything, or understanding of what manner is this infused contemplation."[6]

[1]Ibid.

[2]Ibid., p. 69.

[3]Ibid., p. 142.

[4]Cf. pp. 104-107 above.

[5]See *PS* (Barnett), v. 25: "From its association with the darkness of ignorance (the Self) conceives itself in manifold diversity as objects and subjects, whereas it is one and self-identical." On the "darkness of ignorance," see *Stav* vv. 12, 58; cf. also pp. 26-27 above concerning the three impurities or ignorances which are the cause of bondage for the soul.

[6]St. John, *Dark Night*, p. 100; also pp. 73, and 193. This blind-like desire to attain Śiva without clear reasoning or precise means in mind is exactly what Utpala speaks of above when commenting on the Dark Night of Annihilation, cf. p. 96 and n. 4

This, however, raises a question—"Why is the Divine light... called by the soul a dark night?" In answer, St. John gives two reasons why Divine Wisdom is not only night and darkness but also torment and affliction for the mystic. First, because it transcends the limited capacity of the soul; secondly, because the soul is wretched and impure compared to the majesty of God. Wisdom is pain and affliction to the soul.[1]

The Doctor of the Church explains this paradox of Light and darkness in the following manner:

> The clearer and more manifest are Divine things in themselves, the darker and more hidden are they to the soul naturally; just as, the clearer is the light, the more it blinds and darkens the pupil of the owl, and, the more directly we look at the sun, the greater is the darkness which it causes in our visual faculty, overcoming and overwhelming it through its own weakness.[2]

The Divine Light of contemplation acts upon the soul in the same way; it "assails the soul which is not yet wholly enlightened, it causes spiritual darkness in it"; its great supernatural light overcomes and overwhelms it, darkens and empties it of its natural intelligence (light). Hence, St. Dionysius, among others, aptly calls this infused contemplation "a ray of darkness" for the soul yet to be illuminated and purified.[3]

This purgative darkness must first overshadow the soul before the supernatural Light can illuminate it:

> And thus it is fitting that, if the understanding is to be united with that light and become Divine in the state of perfection, it should first of all be purged and annihilated as to its natural light, and, by means of this dark contemplation, be brought actually into darkness. This darkness should continue for as long as is needful in order to expel and annihilate the habit which the soul has long since formed in its manner of understanding, and the Divine light and illumination will then take its place.[4]

[1]St. John, *Dark Night*, p. 100.
[2]Ibid , pp. 100-101.
[3]Ibid., pp. 101, 117.
[4]Ibid., p. 121.

One can draw the same analogy here as in the treatment of the French School's doctrine of self-renunciation and adherence to God. At the same time that the self-emptying of the soul is occurring, it is being filled with God, just as the in-rushing air immediately replaces the water poured from a vial. Similarly, as the darkness dissipates the mind's natural light, the void is immediately filled with the Divine Light of understanding.

While God is accomplishing all this through dark contemplation, the soul is suffering great anguish because "it is unable to raise its affection or its mind to God, neither can it pray to Him, thinking, ...that God has set a cloud before it through which its prayer cannot pass."[1] However, God is purging the soul, annihilating it, emptying it, and consuming it in the Divine fire of this contemplation.[2]

This Divine light or fire acts upon the soul that is being purified (for perfect union with God) as the flames of a fire act upon a log of wood. We recognize this metaphor in Bhaṭṭa's expression, "Torch of Devotion," acting upon and "consuming the wood of all existences."[3] St. John developed his own metaphor as follows. Fire first dries the wood by extracting all moisture; it then makes the log dark and black, removing all its accidental imperfections "which are contrary to the nature of fire." Next, it begins to kindle it externally and give it heat. Finally, the flames dig deeply into its center, removing all internal perfections and converting the wood into flames so that only fire remains. It is to be noted that "the wood has neither passivity nor activity of its own, ...Thus it is dry and dries; it is hot and heats; it is bright and gives brightness; ...All these properties and effects are caused in it by the fire."[4]

The "Divine fire of contemplative love" acts analogously on the soul. First, by means of aridities, it purges the soul of all contrary accidents; it annihilates the soul, and makes it black and dark, so that it seems worse than before. These imperfections are made "visible to the soul because it is so brightly illumined by this dark

[1]Ibid., p. 115.

[2]Ibid., pp. 106-7. On self-annihilation or passionless detachment of the ascetic in Triadism, see section on *Śiva, the Archetypal Ascetic,* pp. 88-96 above.

[3]Cf. p. 107 above.

[4]St. John, *Dark Night,* pp. 127-28.

light of Divine contemplation." Even as the log was not immediately transformed into fire but was first made ready—so also the soul is made ready by great affliction. [1]"The fire of love once again attacks that which has yet to be consumed"—just as fire attacks wood more intensely and penetrates it more deeply, refining away the inner impurities. Therefore, it "acts with more force and vehemence in preparing its most inward part to possess it."[2]

And so, the Divine fire is first employed in drying up and making ready the "wood" of the soul, rather than affording it heat; but as time progresses, "the fire begins to give heat to the soul." The latter experiences "this enkindling and heat of love" until it is ablaze with the fire, enveloped in living flames which illumine the soul's faculties that were heretofore in darkness.[3]

The darkness which plagues the soul relates to its desires and faculties (memory, understanding, and will), "for all these are darkened in this night as to their natural light, so that, being purged in this respect, they may be illumined with respect to the supernatural." When darkness descends upon the soul, the spiritual and sensual desires are quieted and mortified—

> the affections of the soul are oppressed and constrained...the imagination is bound...memory is gone; the understanding is in darkness...and hence the will...is arid...void and useless; and in addition...a thick and heavy cloud is upon the soul, keeping it in affliction, and...far away from God.[4]

The fire of God, on the other hand, St. John says, counteracts the darkness by dispersing this cloud and dispelling the darkness in all directions,[5] and reversing the hold on the soul's faculties:

> This is naught else but His illumination of the *understanding* with supernatural light, so that it is no more a human under-

[1]Ibid., pp. 128-29.
[2]Ibid., p. 130.
[3]Ibid., p. 138.
[4]Ibid., p. 150.
[5]Cf. *Stav* v. 12 where the supreme Light penetrates the profound cavern of Śiva, dissipating the darkness of ignorance in every direction—see p. 97 and n. 5 above; this note refers to st. 3 of St. John's *Living Flame*, quoted above on p. 144, in which the author also speaks of the divine light which dissipates the darkness of ignorance and doubt.

standing but becomes Divine through union with the Divine. In the same way the *will* is informed with Divine love, so that it is a will that is now no less than Divine,...So too, it is with the *memory*; and likewise the affections and desires are all changed and converted divinely, according to God. And thus this soul will now be a soul of heaven, heavenly, and more Divine than human.[1] (Italics mine.)

There is an interesting parallel here to what was said in the previous chapter as to the faculties of the soul in the Dark Night of Śiva. At the beginning of that section,[2] it was stated that "this night spreads to the faculties." There the dark night took on several meanings, some of which relate to the faculties—becoming, in consequence, the Night of Will, and of Thought. *The Night of Will* enkindles the mystic with the "fire of love" prior to illumination. Here, also, in the Catholic parallel, the fire of God infuses the *will* with Divine love.

The *Night of Thought* causes a "new knowledge" to replace in the mystic "the differentiated and false knowledge of the senses and of the *understanding*." *Memory* would of necessity be included in this Divine conversion, since it too is part of the *Night of Thought*. It was further stated, in the prior section, that "the faculties are suspended" and "the prestige of the Mirific Power is erased."

Likewise, in St. John's treatise, Light illumines the *understanding* so that it is no longer a human understanding but a Divine one. "God will enlighten the soul, giving it knowledge, not only of its lowliness and wretchedness, ...but likewise of the greatness and excellence of God."[3] "*Memory* is also purged of...knowledge."[4] This means that a new knowledge—a "purgative and loving knowledge or Divine light"[5]—has replaced the old knowledge possessed prior to illumination. And finally, the "cloud of obscurity" is lifted from the soul by the all-penetrating Divine luminosity. This is the same as saying the prestige or authority of the Mirific Power is erased.

[1]St. John, *Dark Night*, p. 146.
[2]See p. 96 above.
[3]St. John, *Dark Night*, p. 79.
[4]Ibid., p. 116.
[5]Ibid., p. 127.

2. The Stages of Mystical Progression

Silburn identified eleven stages or cycles of Triadic mystical progression[1] which begin with uninterrupted meditation and end in a triumphant and Divine union; there are successive stages between these two which replace each other suddenly and unnoticeably.[2] St. John of the Cross treats what he calls "the ten steps of the mystic ladder of Divine love."[3] The initial step is the *self-annihilation* of the soul, a self-emptying of profane desires and worldly attachments. In the concluding step of *deification*—achieved only in the heavenly life—the soul becomes wholly assimilated to God: "all that it [the soul] is will become like to God,...and will be, God by participation."[4]

Now parallels can be drawn between these two schemes, for, both begin, more or less, with the meditative stage and conclude in Divine union in the next life, because even the true Śaiva mystic must wait for death to realize full participation.[5] However, it would be arduous to attempt to draw parallels between the intervening stages. The resulting comparisons would appear forced, artificial, and incomplete. Hence, I will compare mystical progression within the two traditions more generally, where correspondence is greater in evidence, according to the following scheme. The four Ways to Liberation, we will remember, were divided into two stages or paths—the Inferior and Superior Paths. The former consisted of the Individual and Energic Ways, which comprised ascending degrees; the latter concerned the Divine and Null Ways, which comprised no degrees.

Using this same general format, I will attempt to show that there are striking parallels between the major components of this classification and the twofold division of St. John's *Dark Night*—the Inferior Path corresponding to the Active Night of Sense, and the Superior Path, to the Passive Night of Spirit.

[1] *VB* (Silburn), pp. 173-94; see also Matus, pp. 160-64.

[2] Silburn, *La Bhakti*, p. 38, and n. 3.

[3] St. John, *Dark Night*, p. 167; for the process see pp. 167-75.

[4] Ibid., p. 175.

[5] Silburn, *La Bhakti*, p. 68, n. 1; see also *PS* (Barnett), p. 736, com. to v. 61: the Liberated-in-Life "thus redeemed lives on in the flesh, ...until his final redemption on death." Cf. *PS* (Silburn), p. 43: "...n'est qu'après la mort que l' âme s'identifiera au Seigneur.

(a) *The Inferior Stage*

It should be again noted that these mystical stages, whether Triadic or Catholic, overlap and differ in degree of common features as well as in kind of characteristic features.

Now, we recall, the adept who travels thc Triadic Inferior Path is absorbed in the various yogic exercises, including "meditation." This practice, present in all Ways of Liberation, begins as discursive thought and continues through the successive Ways until it finally becomes pure and undifferentiated. Furthermore, the climactic point of this Way is "appeasement of thought"—a self-absorption or "mystical quietude" in which the soul retreats within itself and remains at rest.[1]

We find an almost exact parallel here in St. John's beginning stage of the Active Night. This Night of Sense is the initial "meditative" phase whose aridities produce an appeased sense of inner quietude:

> When the aridities proceed from the ...purgation of sensual desire,...it gives the soul an inclination and desire to be alone and in quietness, without being able to think of any particular thing or having thedesire to do so...and troubled not about performing any kind of action, whether inward or outward.[2]

St. John continues, further on, to sketch out a simple plan of conduct for beginners who, at first find solace in meditative practices, but who now wish to climb to the higher rungs of the mystical ladder:

> The way in which they are to conduct themselves in this night of sense is to devote themselves not at all to reasoning and *meditation*, ...but...merely to leave the soul free and disencumbered and at rest from all knowledge and thought, troubling not themselves, in that state, about what they shall think or meditate upon, but contenting themselves with merely a peaceful and loving attentiveness toward God, and in being without anxiety, without the ability and without desire to have experience of Him or to perceive Him. For all these yearnings disquiet and distract

[1] Cf. pp. 40-41 above.

[2] St. John, *Dark Night*, p. 66.

the soul from the peaceful quiet and sweet ease of *contemplation* which is here granted to it.[1] (Italics mine.)

Continuing to the second "degree" stage of the Inferior Path of the Energic Way, we remember that its apogee was "mystical realization", which is also called "infused contemplation."[2] I stressed that "mystical realization" must not be confused with the concentration and meditation of the Individual Way.[3] I also observed that Abhinava uses the term in the sense of an "obscure tendency," as when a person undertakes a task even though "he does not have a clearnotion of his course of action."[4] It is the means of liberating the yogī from the discursive thought processes of the previous Way.[5] Finally, we saw that Imagination ("infused contemplation") served as a bridge between the conceptual thought (duality) of the Inferior Way and the inexpressible intuition(non-duality) of the Divine Way.[6]

However, although I treated "mystical realization" as the high point of the Energic Way, following Silburn's format, it must not be inferred that it is peculiar to this Way. It is, in fact, present in all the Ways, since "absorption" or "compenetration" (the one goal of "mystical realization") remains, in varying degrees, the object of all the Ways to Liberaion.[7]

(b) *The Superior Stage*

"Infused contemplation" or "mystical realization" is an important characteristic in the superior stages of Triadism—since the ultimate goal here is self-realization of one's Śiva nature. In the introduction to her translation of Abhinava's *Quintessence of Ultimate Truth*, Silburn says that "mystical realization," the essence of "an undisguised intensity, blinded by passion and constantly directed toward Śiva," also corresponds to the "dark contemp-

[1]Ibid., pp. 70-71.

[2]See pp. 48-49 above.

[3]See p. 50 above; cf. also *Stav*, v. 36 where meditation and contemplation are listed as separate and distinct, but successive stages in a precise gradation toward Śiva.

[4]See p. 49 above.

[5]See p. 50 above.

[6]See p. 61 above.

[7]See p. 50, n. 7 above.

lation" of Christians. "It extends," she says, "over the entire field of mystical life up to illumination and even beyond."[1] And again, in the same work she quotes Abhinava: "Thanks to mystical realization, he (the yogī) arrives at the state of identity with Śiva in the totality of categories."[2]

In the conclusion to her treatise on the eleven stages of mystical progression, Silburn has this to say of the gnostic and his "infused contemplation":

> The supreme Realization (*bhāvanā*) which he experiences again and again at the very interior of the highest undifferentiated and appeased Reality...is the uninterrupted self-awareness (*vimarśa*) of the Absolute 'I' reposing in the infinite Light of Consciousness (*prakāśa*) or the compenetration of divinized Energy and of Śiva.[3]

Kṣemarāja begins his commentary to the verse upon which the above statement is based by saying: "*Bhāvanā*—powerful and indeterminate inclination of the total person toward Śiva—reaches its culmination point in Self-Recognition."[4] Therefore, "mystical realization" finds its achievement in absorption in Śiva—the ultimate realization of one's true nature.

Now we can find a true parallel in St. John, for the superior path—the Night of Spirit—is called "infused contemplation," and this night is characterized by the same sense of inner divine guidance, which is beyond the mystics' understanding and is, as we have seen, an essential element in the Triadic parallel.

There is further correspondence between the Passive Night of Spirit and the two superior Ways of Triadism. In my treatment of the Divine Way, I said that the concept of "mystical fervor" constituted, in itself, a brief path to Śiva; it also signified an intense thrust (*élan*) or desire, an innate impetus or yearning for God.[5] We find this same "yearning" or "thirst of love" in St. John's contemplative night: "There grows within souls that experience

1*PS* (Silburn), p. 46, and n. 6.
2Ibid., v. 52.
3*VB* (Silburn) p. 193; reference is made here to v. 145.
4Ibid., com. to v. 145, p. 163.
5See p. 67 above.

this arid night concern for God and yearning to serve Him."[1] But, St. John says, when the spiritual night commences, "this enkindling of love is not felt, because this fire of love has not begun to take a hold."[2] Also contributing to the initial lack of any feeling of love or yearnings is the impurity of human nature and the fact that the soul has not understood its own state,...and has, therefore, given it no peaceful abiding-place within itself."[3] These last two reasons find their parallels in the Energic and Individual Ways, respectively.

St. John continues:

> Yet sometimes, nevertheless, there soon begins to make itself felt a certain yearning toward God; and the more this increases, the more is the soul affectioned and enkindled in love toward God, without knowing or understanding how and whence this love and affection came to it.[4]

This corresponds to the Triadic third Way of Liberation—the Divine Way of the incomprehensibly spontaneous *élan* of the heart.

Finally, there is a comparison to be seen between the Passive Night and Triadism's highest Way—the Null Way or No-Means of self-realization without Initiation. Although all the Triadic Ways lead to self-realization, only the Null Way does so directly, instantly, with a minimal use of means.[5] The essential attribute of this path is "freedom"—Triadism's chief characteristic.[6] And freedom is of the nature of the Light of Consciousness. The soul which attains this perfect freedom is a divinized being who realizes this impassible Tremendous State of the Liberated-in-Life.

All that which has been said of this Dark Night of Spirit "comes to pass in the soul passively, *without its doing or undoing anything of itself* with respect to it."[7] (Italics mine.) For, as the soul journeys, says St. John, "it is supported by no particular interior light of understanding, nor by any other exterior guide,...its love alone,

[1] St. John, *Dark Night*, p. 86.
[2] Ibid., p. 142.
[3] Ibid., p. 72.
[4] Ibid., pp. 72-73.
[5] See p. 68 above.
[6] See p. 69 above.
[7] St. John, *Dark Night*, p. 187.

...which now moves and guides it, and makes it soar upward to its God along the road of solitude, without its knowing how or in what manner."[1] Thus, "it now goes about the things of God with much greater freedom and satisfaction of the soul."[2]

Here, then, is a classic example of No-Means—"without light or guide, save that which burned in my heart."[3] It is for this reason that the Night of Infused Contemplation is also called the "Way of Illumination," "wherein God, Himself, feeds and refreshes the soul, without meditation, or the soul's active help....in order to pass to the Divine union of the love of God."[4]

God divinizes the soul as much as is possible in this life. Now "stripped and denuded of its former skin" and made "to die to all that is not naturally God," the soul is clothed with "new knowledge" —the realization of its true nature. This, as we saw above, "is naught else but His illumination of the *understanding* with supernatural light, so that it is no more a human understanding but becomes Divine through union with the Divine."[5]

D. *Archetype IV: The Impassible State of Deification*

I conclude this study with a brief treatment of the soul's deification through impassibility. For the Christian parallel to this Triadic state of Liberation-in-Life, I have chosen the *apatheia* of Clement of Alexandria[6]—second century theologian, first of the Greek Fathers, teacher of Origen, and founder of speculative theology.[7]

1. Impassibility

Clement's theology, like Triadic, is gnostic in character; it is in

[1]Ibid., p. 193.

[2]Ibid., p. 91.

[3]Ibid., st. 3, p. 34.

[4]Ibid., p. 88.

[5]Ibid., p. 146; for the fuller quote, see pp. 156-57 above.

[6]Clement wrote three major sequential works: *Exhortation to the Heathens* (*Protrepticus*), aimed at winning pagans to Christianity; *The Instructor* (*Paedagogos*), addressed to the newly converted Christians—those in the "lower life", and his most famous work, *The Miscellanies* (*Stromata*), meant specifically for the perfect Christian (true Gnostic) who travels the path of the "higher life."

[7]Johannes Quasten, *Patrology*, vol. 2: *The Ante-Nicene Literature after Irenaeus* (Westminster, Md.: The Newman Press, 1953), p. 7.

fact called Christian Gnosticism.[1] In its belief, the true gnostic assimilates to God by means of a "perfect pureness of mind."[2] As he increases in knowledge and perfect truth, so also does his purification, "for knowledge is quick in purifying."[3]

Moreover, Clement's doctrine, like Triadic Mysticism and St. John's Dark Night, professes two stages of Gnostic living: a lower life of preparatory training and purification, characterized by the moderation of passions (*metriopatheia*); and a higher life of Gnostic perfection distinguished by the total annihilation of passion, the state of impassibility or apathy (*apatheia*).[4]

The process of purification—as one would expect, having studied the mystical theologies thus far—results in a state of passionless detachment from the material world. This separation of the soul from the appetites of the flesh is essential if the true Gnostic is to assimilate to God. This idea is a major theme in Clement and examples abound in his works. As to the moderation of passions, he says:

> In all things...extremes are dangerous, and middle courses good. And to be in no want of necessaries is the medium. For the desires which are in accordance with nature are bounded with sufficiency.[5]

But it is clear that, for Clement, nothing less than complete remission of passion is the goal of the higher life:

> We must...rescue the gnostic and perfect man from all passions of the soul. For knowledge (*gnosis*) produces...impassibility, not moderation of passion. And the complete eradication of desire reaps as its fruit impassibility.[6]

[1]According to Clement, true *gnosis* is the Wisdom of God as revealed by His Son, *Stromata* (hereafter abbrev. *Strom.*) 6.7.494 (reference is to book, article, and page, respectively). All citations are from the works of Clement as found in *The Ante-Nicene Fathers: Translations of the Writings of the Fathers down to* A.D. 325, vol. 2, ed. A. Roberts and J. Donaldson (Grand Rapids: Wm. B. Eerdmans Pub. Co., 1962).

[2]Ibid., 4.22.435.

[3]Ibid., 7.10.539.

[4]Charles Bigg, *The Christian Platonists of Alexandria* (New York: Macmillan & Co., 1886), pp. 86-87.

[5]*Paedagogos*, 2.1.242.

[6]*Strom.*, 6.9.497.

So totally annihilated are the Gnostic's passions that he is never even tempted: "For he never exposes his soul to submission, or capture at the hands of Pleasure and Pain."[1] This state of the soul places the true Gnostic on a par with the angels:

> He, then, who has first moderated his passions and trained himself for impassibility, and developed to the beneficence of gnostic perfection, is here equal to the angels.[2]

Just as Śiva, for the Triadic mystic, is the impassible archetype of the Divine Ascetic, Christ, for the Gnostic Christian, is the model of divine impassibility: "God is impassible, free of anger, destitute of desire."[3] Consequently, Christ too is passionless and therefore perfect: "I know no one of men perfect in all things at once, while still human, ...except Him alone who for us clothed Himself with humanity."[4] In another section of the *Stromata*, Clement portrays this passionlessness; although he is unclear as to whether it is eternal or was progressive, he is nevertheless clear as to its being a genuine attribute of Jesus: "The Lord, who without beginning was impassible"; this suggests a preexistent *apatheia*. However, a few sentences further, he alludes to a developmental passivity when he states that Christ, "having assumed flesh, which by nature is susceptible of suffering, trained it to the condition of impassibility."[5]

2. Deification

It is through passionlessness, therefore, that the Christian Gnostic reaches the final stage of his quest, which, Clement says, is achieved "by being assimilated to God, and by becoming truly angelic." He also asserts, in this same passage: "ye have cast off the passions of the soul, in order to become assimilated, as far as possible, to the goodness of God's providence."[6]

The Greek Father insists that "it is possible for the Gnostic

[1] Ibid., 7.7.735.
[2] Ibid., 6.13.504.
[3] Ibid., 4.23.437.
[4] Ibid., 4.21.433.
[5] Ibid., 7.2.525.
[6] Ibid., 7.14.547.

already to have become God."[1] This assimilation produces a being not unlike the Liberated-in-Life of Triadism. Hence, we are told, a Gnostic is one who is "formed perfectly in the likeness of the teacher—made a god going about in flesh."[2] It is quite evident, nevertheless, that deification is reserved for the Gnostic soul only after death—again, in keeping with the Triadic and Catholic parallels already seen: "not even...will he be called perfect in the flesh beforehand, since it is the close of life which claims this appellation."[3]

S. Lilla, a modern student of Clement, develops this same theme in his study of the Greek Father's theology. According to him, there *are two stages to* Clement's *gnosis*. Initially it can be attained here on earth, but it reaches its climax after the death of the body, when the soul journeys back to its original abode. After becoming deified, it can enjoy, in complete and perpetual rest, the uninterrupted and insatiable contemplation of the highest divinity (Beatific Vision) together with the other *theoi* (heavenly bodies).[4]

There are many passages in the *Stromata* that deal with the subject of "contemplation"; in fact, since Clement identifies it with *gnosis*, it can be viewed as his major theme: "We," he says, "are those who are believers...and who are Gnostics...not describing actions by speech, but Gnostics in the exercise of contemplation."[5] And, in another part of this work, the identity of terms is even more clearly underscored: "Knowledge (*gnosis*) is essentially a contemplation of existences on the part of the soul, either of a certain thing or of certain things, and when perfected, of all together."[6] Again, he says: "Knowledge or wisdom ought to be exercised up to the eternal and unchangeable habit of contemplation."[7]

The Stromatist also makes the term "contemplation" stand for a variety of concepts, such as : divinization, divine discourse, Beatific Vision, rest in God, communion, and passionlessness.[8] This

[1]Ibid., 4.23.437.
[2]Ibid., 7.16.553.
[3]Ibid., 4.21.433.
[4]Salvatore Lilla, *Clement of Alexandria: A Study in Christian Platonism and Gnosticism* (London: Oxford University Press, 1971), p. 142.
[5]*Strom.*, 5.1.444.
[6]Ibid., 6.8.496.
[7]Ibid., 6.7.494.
[8]Ibid., 4.6.416, 6.9.497, 6.13.504, and 7.10.539.

contemplation (*gnosis*), which enables the perfect Christian to assimilate to God, seems to parallel the "infused contemplation" that deifies the Christian mystic in St. John's Dark Night. For, as Clement says: "He is the true Only-begotten, ...who impresses on the Gnostic the seal of the perfect contemplation, according to His own image."[1] Similarly, G. Maloney, another modern commentator on the works of the early Fathers, has this to say in discussing Clement and the stages of gnosis:

> The first level in the ascent to the *gnosis* is the purification that is brought about by... the practice of virtuous, mortifying actions. Such virtues developed *apatheia*, which prepared the ground for an infusion of deeper faith, leading the Christian to... contemplation, another name that Clement often uses for *gnosis*.[2]

The *Stromata* is also rich in references to Gnostic deification—as is seen from the following excerpts, which I believe best exemplify Clement's thought, as well as correspond to Triadic teaching on the subject. In the first excerpt, the impassible Gnostic enjoys the Beatific Vision:

> Man, when deified purely into the passionless state, becomes a unit...and through his own spotless purification beholds the holy God holily;...[and when]...contemplating...uninterruptedly, is as far as possible assimilated to God.[3]

Then—in what appears to be close to the Triadic notion of appropriating and identifying with a deity by contemplating his image—we have the Gnostic who

> devotes himself to contemplation, communing in purity with the divine,...enters more nearly into the state of impassible identity, so as no longer to...possess knowledge, but to be... knowledge.[4]

[1]Ibid., 7.3.527.

[2]George A. Maloney, S.J., *Man, the Divine Icon*: *The Patristic Doctrine of Man Made according to Image of God* (Pecos, N.M.: Dove Publications, 1973), p. 63.

[3]*Strom.*, 4.23.437.

[4]Ibid., 4.6.416; cf. p. 35 above.

Finally, the ultimate goal is reached—"indissoluble union":

> The Gnostic...[is]...like to God, ...assimilating as far as possible the moderation which, ...tends to impassibility, to Him who by nature possesses impassibility; and especially having uninterrupted converse and fellowship with the Lord. . . .each man who is [thus] admitted to holiness being illuminated in order to indissoluble union.[1]

[1]Ibid., 7.3.526.

CONCLUSION

We have seen how the Supreme Śiva, in order to realize one aspect of His infinite nature, the phenomenal and multifarious universe, sets aside His divinity and enters the spatio-temporal realm of the finite—the product of His own creation. He accomplishes this feat through His Mirific Power which masks His undifferentiated luminosity and, through myriad diverse manifestations, projects the cosmic world of phenomenal and noumenal reality. God becomes man. But this setting forth on the finite road of existence is only the first half of the divine journey; having satisfied the need to discover His cosmic reality, Śiva liberates Himself from the bonds of manifestation, and, through the same Mirific Power, returns to His unicity upon the very road previously traveled. Thus, according to Triadic theology, man's essential nature is divine; he attains liberation, even in this life, when he comes to realize his true Śiva-nature and, in consequence, returns to his original state of union with the undifferentiated Light.

This perennial quest of man to attain oneness or communion with transcendence or the deity is not, of course, peculiar to Śaivism alone, it is common to all religious persuasions. The universal goal is the same, but the specific "means' employed and the form of the deity differ vastly. Thus, although the three main schools of Triadism worship the same Supreme Śiva, each subscribes to a different means or Way to Liberation. These means are affected by divine grace which ranges from feeble to intense, corresponding to each of the four Ways: *absorption in the object*, through certain yogic practices (Individual Way of the Family School); *absorption in Energy*, principally through the awakening and rise of the Coiled Potency resting at the base of the mystical centers of the body (Energic Way of the Gradation School); *absorption in the Void*, in which self-realization is attained spontaneously by the yogī through a simple act of the will (Divine Way of the Family School); and lastly, *absorption in pure bliss*—the instantaneously realized, divinized Tremendous State of the Liberated-in-Life (Null Way of the Self-Awareness School).

Since knowledge or recognition of one's divine nature through self-awareness is the singular goal of these schools, the overall theological system is called Gnostic Triadism. However, in Triadic metaphysics, Śiva is at constant play or frolic with His Energy—the Goddess Śakti; from their union proceeds the human heart, "palpitant and emissional in its essence,"[1] linked to its parents through love. There is thus a devotional aspect to Śaivism, which underscores the inseparable love-union of the divine couple—and the yearning of the creature for its God. Devotional Triadism is evidenced in the love poems of the devotional poets of Kashmir.

Finally, Triadism (both Gnostic and Devotional) becomes more meaningful if we abstract the theological archetypes latent in its doctrinal elaboration, and compare their variants which are specifically Triadic with the specifically Catholic. Of the four archetypes we chose to examine, the Triadic variants were: the Breaking Through the Mirific Power and the Return to Light, Sacrificial Self-Annihilation, The Dark Night of Śiva and Impassibility. And the Catholic variants were: the Breaking Through the Obscuration of Faith, according to John of St. Thomas; the Sacrificial Self-Renunciation of the French School; the Dark Night of Mystical Awakening, as delineated by St. John of the Cross; and lastly, the Passionlessness of the Christian Gnosticism of Clement of Alexandria.

However, these parallels are mostly peripheral, in that they fail to attain what may be called Triadism's central message, in which perhaps the deepest level of its correspondence with Catholic doctrine lies. This level may be said, in Chatholic terms, to be formed of the theology of the Beatific Vision. The content of this transcendent experience is ineffable, but if any words can serve to describe it, those of Abhinavagupta can do as well as any other:

> All this is therefore one Reality—a Reality undivided by time, unconfined by space, unenfeebled by accidents, unconstrained by configurations, unexpressed by words and unmanifested by norms of knowledge. It is the cause, at Its own will and pleasure, of the attainment of the essences of these things, from time to norms. It is the sovereignly free Reality, the concentration of beatitude. And I am absolutely It—there, within me, is reflected the universe![2]

[1] *TS*, Opening Paeans, 1, quoted by Pereira, pp. 372-73.
[2] *TS*, ch. 2, as trans. by Pereira, p. 376.

Therefore, it may be claimed that on the issue of a beatific awareness of God, a fundamental insight is common to both traditions—the difference in doctrinal elaboration results mainly from a difference in the metaphysical model employed to formulate that insight in conceptual terms. As we have often remarked, Difference-in-Identity is the Triadic model, and Difference the Catholic. I will, therefore, conclude my study of Triadic theology with a Catholic reflection of what I consider to be this fundamental insight.

I base my reflection on the thought of the two most powerful luminaries of Baroque Scholasticism, Francisco Suárez (1548-1617) and John of St. Thomas (1589-1644),[1] whose treatment of the theology of the Beatific Vision is not only as brilliant and profound, to my knowledge, as any in Christian thought, but is also preoccupied with the same concepts that are basic to Triadic thought itself. What follows, therefore, mainly consists of passages from the works of these two Baroque theologians.

To begin with, the Beatific Vision is absolutely supernatural. It is the most perfect realization of God:

> It must be affirmed absolutely and simply that only God is the object of our essential beatitude, and that, in this manner, He is sufficient for our beatitude without the participation of the creature.[2]

The insight (or in Catholic terms, revelation) of God alone being the cause of our joy was, apparently, first given to the Hindus, for the great Upaniṣadic theologian of joy, Varuṇa says: "He is truly Savor itself. One who relishes this Savor is filled with joy. If this pervasive Being were not joy who could exhale, who inhale ? He alone is the cause of joy."[3] And, says the *Kaṭha Upaniṣad*, proclaiming the doctrine of grace of God attainable by man only through divine election: "This Self is not attained through teaching, not through sacrifice, and not through much learning. By him alone whom He elects is He attained. That Self of his then reveals His very own form."[4]

[1]I am indebted to Dr. José Pereira for his assistance in researching and translating from the Latin the various passages from the works of Suárez and John of St. Thomas contained in this section.

[2]Suárez, *De Ultimo Fine Hominis*, tractatus primus, disp. 5, sect. 2, num. 3.

[3]*Taittirīya Upaniṣad*, 2, 7, quoted by Pereira, p. 243.

[4]*Kaṭha Upaniṣad*, 1. 2. 23; also *Muṇḍaka Upaniṣad*, 3. 2. 3.

Our ultimate happiness or beatitude can be said to consist in intimacy with the divine transcendence and to comprise three elements. *First*, the attainability of this transcendence solely through its gratuitous self-communication, or grace (which Triadism calls the Energic Fulmination). The ideal metaphysical model to articulate this insight conceptually seems to be Difference, since transcendence, as such, cannot be identical with what is not transcendence. On this point there seems to be fundamental disagreement between Catholics and Triadists.

Second, that the exaltedness and intimacy of this experience is so overpowering, as to obliterate any sense of distinction between the participant and the object of the experience. The ideal metaphysical model seems to be Difference-in-Identity, if not Identity alone. On this point, some Catholic Theologians lean towards the Triadic viewpoint and others away from it.

Third, that this beatific experience, which by virtue of its being a luminous and vivid awareness may be called a Beatific Vision, is itself incomposite and undifferenced. Here again the ideal metaphysical model seems to be one for which Identity is reality's ultimate condition. On this point, the accord between Catholics and Triadists is almost complete.

Let us take these elements in turn. As to the *first*, while both the Catholic and Triadic systems are emphatic in affirming the gratuitousness of grace, they disagree on how that gratuitousness is to be justified, or how the nature of grace is explained. Catholic theology justifies this gratuitousness through the doctrine of creationism. The creature is intrinsically nothing, existent solely through its Creator's will and omnipotence: its very existence is gratuitous. But it is not entirely so; for assuming that God desires to create a human being, He owes that being a human *nature*, and all that is requisite for that being to function humanly. Thus grace properly belongs to a *supernature*; it comprises whatever God chooses to give that human nature—which is in no way owed to it—such as happiness through the attainment of Himself. As Suárez says: "Grace taken in its most precise sense presupposes a person, or a nature, on which it is conferred—and hence the first creation of man...is not, properly speaking, said to be grace, because it presupposes nothing, but confers the first being."[1]

[1]Suárez, *Gratia I*, Prolegominum 3, cap. 2, num. 4.

As for Triadism, it is difficult to see how the system's postulates can justify the gratuitousness it so unambiguously predicates of the Energic Fulmination, because both it and man to whom it is communicated are Śiva Himself, and hence necessarily existent. For, even in Triadism, God, supremely independent and free though He is, cannot will His own annihilation, and cannot not will Himself.

According to both systems, grace is a participation of the divine nature. This doctrine is easily explained in Triadism, because participation is interpreted—as the sense of the word itself suggests it should be—as entitative identity between God and man. But creationism bars the Catholic use of Identity language. Grace is a created quality inherent in an intellectual nature also existent through causality; while God is "Existence Itself through Essence." (*ipsum esse per essentiam*)—a concept which, as Suárez declares "cannot be abstracted from created and increate being—Therefore it cannot be formally participated by a created quality [like grace] ...It is impossible for a created quality to participate in the divine nature, insofar as the latter is imparticipated being."[1]

This is also true of independence and plenitude of being—which are God's highest attributes, both in Catholic theology and in Triadic. And independence, Suárez says,

> is also formally incommunicable and imparticapable, because it cannot, even in its formal concept, abstract from created and increate being—for, in the intrinsic concept of independent existence, increate being is included. It is a contradiction for created being to be independent, as is evident from the terms themselves, since dependence pertains to the intrinsic concept of creation. And also because the participation of independence through dependence is a contradiction in terms, as the creature participates in nothing except through dependence. Hence, in so far as it is a creature, it cannot participate in independence...
>
> One can finally demonstrate with almost the same reasons about the plenitude of being, in which is included the formal or virtual comprehension of being, or of all possible perfection. For so proper is this attribute to Existence Itself by Essence or to increate existence, that it is in no way possible to abstract, in

[1]Ibid., num. 28.

> that formal significance, a concept that is common to God and the creature. And neither is it understandable how it might be communicated to the creature, as it requires infinity, absolutely. For either the entire adequate reason conveyed by those words ["plenitude of being"] is communicated, and this conflicts with the limitation of the creature, or only a part of it is; and thus the plenitude of being is not communicated in so far as it is *plenitude*, but only something of it—in the manner in which it is also participated by all created being.[1]

In what sense, then, can Catholic theology—notwithstanding its creationist Difference—conceive of grace as a participation of the divine nature? Suárez answers by distinguishing a being's mode of existence from its mode of knowability:

> God's mode of being is of a higher order and significance than all the existence or mode of being of any possible creature;
> therefore God's intelligibility is of another significance and order than every mode of knowledge connatural to any possible creature;
> therefore it cannot be seen by any creature at all through the powers of its nature.
> The first antecedent is proved, because God in His being is the purest and most simple Act—while every creature has a certain composition, and, so to speak, materiality, if compared with the divine purity.
> The first consequence is proved, because the mode of knowing accords with the mode of being, and similarly, the knowledge and intelligibility of God is proportional to His perfection in the order of being; therefore, in so far as a thing has a higher mode of being in its existence, to that extent it is intelligible in a higher manner. On the other hand whatever has a lower mode of being is in fact knowlable and intelligible in a lower way. Therefore, from the different mode of being of the intelligible object and the intelligent nature, their improportion is rightly deduced, so that one may not be naturally known by the other as it is in itself.[2]

[1]Ibid, num. 28.
[2]Ibid., *De Deo Uno et Trino*, lib. 2, cap. 9, num. 7.

And God's mode of being is intellectual: "not in the manner of a principle or intellectual radix, but as subsistent intellection itself; but the intellection and knowledge of God are most formally identical; therefore actual knowledge through essence is as though it were the ultimate essential constituent of the divine nature."[1]

This Triadic conviction, of the ultimate being, by essence, Intelligence—that is, consciousness untouched by material limitations—seems to have been first expressed around the tenth century B.C. the Vedic sage Mahīdāsa, for whom God is "the pure intelligence, the eternally active self-conscious reason."[2] It was reaffirmed in by the eighth century B.C. by his illustrious successor, Yājñavalkya: "As a lump of salt thrown into water dissolves into the water itself, and cannot be taken out, for wherever one may draw that water it is nothing but salty—so also this great endless and unlimited Being is concentrated Intellection [or compact mass of wisdom, *vijñānaghana*]."[3]

Grace, then, makes it possible for us to participate in the intellectuality of this wisdom or Intellection. Says Suárez:

> as the divine nature is an intellectual nature of an order higher than any created intellectual substance is or can be, the grade of intellectuality found in the divine nature is participated by habitual grace in a certain divine and supernatural way, so thus it cannot indeed be participated in such a way by any created substance, either by itself or by a power connatural to itself. This is explained in terms of the primary object of the divine intellect ...For the divine essence, in so far as it is an intelligible object in itself, and as immediately terminated by an intuitive vision of God's very essence, is so much elevated by reason of Its purest actuality and immateriality, that It cannot be connaturally seen by any intellectual substance except Itself. But through grace and the supernatural gifts, created intellectual nature is in fact elevated to participate that grade of divine intellectuality, in which it can intuit the intelligible object of the divine essence in Itself.[4]

[1]Ibid., *Disputationes Metaphysicae*, disp. 30, sect. 15, num. 15.

[2]Benimadab Barua, *A History of Pre-Buddhistic Indian Philosophy* (Delhi: Motilal Banarsidass, 1970), p. 66.

[3]*Bṛhadāraṇyaka Upaniṣad*, 2. 4. 12.

[4]Suárez, *De Gratia III*, lib. 7, cap. 1, num. 30.

All these ideas are lucidly summarized by John of St. Thomas:

> Grace is consequently a certain similitude or flash ["fulmination"] of divine intellectuality, elevating the rational creature so that it may perceive God as the specifying object of that supernatural and gratuitous intellectuality [grace]. Because, as our [human] intellectuality has the sensible essence as its object, and the intellect of the angel the spiritual essence, so also the intellectuality of grace, which is a participation of God, regards the divine essence, and consequently the pure Act divine being as knowable in Itself...
>
> Also, grace is said to be an expression of the divine nature not as an intelligible representation, but as an intellectual potency, or as the principle of intuiting God in Himself. It thus formally conforms with God in a conformity of *object*, as exists between the knowing faculty and its specifying object; but it does not conform in a conformity of *entity*, as though the participant form belonged to the same entity as God.[1]

It is thus apparent that the disagreement between the two systems is mainly on the explanation of the nature of grace and not on the fact of its gratuitousness or of its being, which is in Triadic language—the Energic Fulmination of the Divine Consciousness, or, in the language of John of St. Thomas—a Fulmination of Divine Intellectuality (*fulgor divine intellectualitatis*).

Let us now examine our last two elements, where the Catholic-Triadic conflict grows progressively less. The *second* element concerns the intimacy of the human experience of divine transcendence. In Triadism, this causes no problem, because, with Śiva attained, the human knower and the divine known are not distinct, but undifferentiatedly identical, participating in the greatest possible kind of intimacy and connaturality—the *identity* of being and awareness. But Catholic theology, unable to use Identity language, has great difficulty in explaining how the experience of intimacy with a God so exalted in His transcendence can be connatural to a creature so abysmally inferior in its being, no matter how

[1]John of St. Thomas, *Cursus Theologicus, Tractatus de Gratia* (Paris: Vives Edition, 1883), disp. 22, art. 1, num. 12.

transfigured by grace and the Light of Glory. For a conscious being's experience of happpiness must be vital, interior, and thus connatural to itself, if it can be said to be that being's experience at all. In attempting to reconcile connaturality with intimacy, some Catholic theologians tend to emphasize creatureliness and connaturality, and thus moving away from Triadism and accentuating Difference; others, the intimacy and the transcendence, thus approaching Triadism in doctrine and focussing on Identity.

For Scholastic epistemology, knowledge arises when object is united to knowing faculty. The union is not however entitative but representational. Entitative union with the faculty does not render an object knowable, unless its existential form is, so to speak, translated into an intelligible one. This intelligible form is thus a vicarious substitute for the object when the latter is absent, and is also an instrument leading the faculty to produce the object's formal similitude or concept—thus rendering the object actually known. The vicarious substitute is known as the *species impressa* or presentative form, and the knowledge of the object the *species expressa* or concept. The production of the concept is a vital act of the intelligence, hence connatural to it and part of itself. A non-connatural experience is thus impossible.

Catholic theologians generally agree that the Beatific Vision can remain connatural to the human intelligence without the latter requiring that God be rendered intelligible and present through a created presentative form. For God is already more intelligible in His being than any presentative form of Him can ever be; also, His immensity renders Him more intimate to the creature than even the creature's awareness of itself. It is therefore "more connatural that God be intelligibly united" to the created intelligence "by His own self, than by a presentative form acting as His substitute."[1]

But is it not more natural, on God's part at least, to permit the creature to act in a wholly creaturely way, and thus to have a created presentative form too? John of St. Thomas responds to this question:

> It is more connatural for God to operate through created forms, when those forms function as powers operative of themselves, and proper to the created thing. Then it is indeed more conna-

[1]Ibid., Q. XII, Primae Partis, disp. 13, art. 2, num. 10.

tural of God to permit them to act, than to impede them, or to substitute Himself. But when those forms act as only representative and substitutes of something else, if that something is present and sufficiently actuating by itself, it is then rather superfluous and less connatural that the operation occur through the other [the created form] instead of through that [the increate presentative form]."[1]

Be that as it may, the sole function of the presentative form is to help the human intelligence to form its own concept or word (*verbum*). Here the disagreement among the two theologians begins. Suárez affirms that it is impossible, even *de potentia absoluta*, for created intelligence to experience the Beatific Vision, for else the connaturality of the experience would be destroyed. For, remarks the *Doctor Eximius:*

> I assume, first of all, that it is impossible, even through God's absolute power, for the created intellect to see God through an increate vision. It is, therefore, necessary that it see Him through a caused activity, in fact, even one elicited by the created intellect itself...But, even through God's absolute power, it is impossible that there be any activity without an object intrinsic to itself as the act of heating without heat...it is therefore impossible that the created activity of seeing God be without its appropriate object, and this object is the concept...or, in other words, it is impossible for the created intellect to be formally constituted as actually seeing God without a created form, whose formal effect is to constitute the intellect as actually knowing; but that form is essentially a concept...[2]

On the other hand John of St. Thomas, emphasizing the intimacy and sublimity of the Beatific Vision, leans more to the Triadic view, declaring that we cannot see God except through His own essence, for, he argues, it is impossible for a created concept to represent God in His essential transcendence. Such a concept is abysmally inadequate, in comparison with the divine essence, in its capacity to represent its transcendent Object; and "to belong

[1]Ibid., num. 12.
[2]Suárez, *De Deo Uno et Trino*, lib. 2, cap. 11, num. 9.

to an inferior order as concerns similitude...is the same—as being the similitude of an object belonging to an inferior order."[1] The order we are here concerned with is none but the divine order itself, and, says John of St. Thomas, the intelligibility intuited in the Beatific Vision cannot be different in quality from the intelligibility of the object of that Vision, God in Himself; "because, since all that exists entitatively in the object flashes back in the presentative form in a representative and intelligible manner, it is necessary that the intelligibility of the object and the presentative form not be of a different kind."[2]

John of St. Thomas, it is true, is arguing about the presentative form, not the concept; but, as he later claims,[3] the same arguments which prove a created presentative form of God to be impossible, prove a created intuitive concept of God to be impossible too. And he continues:

> if an intelligibility other than the divine were to exist in the presentative form, it would, by this very fact, be a created intelligibility, because there is no intermediary between the divine and the created. Consequently, it would, in virtue of this, fall from God infinitely and would hence be transformed into an intelligibility of another order. It would therefore not be possible, to equalize and proportion it immediately, in its intelligible being, to God, but to another object which would not be God but a creature—and it would be more remote from the representation of God than a corporeal being from the spirit.[4]

We come now to our *third* and last element, the undifferentiatedness of this transcendent experience. Here Triadic and Catholic theology have no basic disagreement. The Beatific Vision, says Suárez,

> is a simple cognition without any comparison or discourse. For it is a knowledge of a higher and divine order; hence, just as God, without composition, sees predicate in subject and their mutual union, effect in cause, or conclusion in principle—so

[1]John of St. Thomas, *Cursus Theologicus*, Q. XII, Primae Partis, disp. 13, art. 3, num. 10.

[2]Ibid., num. 18.

[3]Ibid., art. 5, num. 9.

[4]Ibid., art. 3, num. 18.

also the blessed creature, even more, perceives all that he knows through that knowledge in a simple intuition, which is indeed most true of that Vision, in so far as it terminates in God—for, as such, it is most simple even on part of the object [the divine essence], because in the latter it manifests the most simple Truth in which there is no composition at all. If, however, the Vision terminates in the creature, even so it is simple in itself, for it manifests all things in one most simple and eminent Presentative Form [the divine essence]. And lastly [this Vision of the creature in God] is the same most simple act as the Vision of God Himself.[1]

Therefore, as a Catholic theologian, I make bold to suggest that on the issue of the Beatific Vision, the Catholic and Triadic systems are recipients of the same divine revelation—a revelation recognizable as basically identical, even through the diverse metaphysical models in its conceptual articulation. This statement does, it is true, bring up an issue which has long engendered much theological debate; namely, can divine or supernatural revelation rightly be said to have inspired the doctrines of non-Christian religions, or are these insights the result of natural revelation. I will address my final comments to a brief assessment of this vital issue.

God's transcendence has a twofold aspect: being and intelligibility. Now God's transcendent being can never be attained by any creature, but His intelligibility can. This also is of two kinds: first, insofar as it is attainable by the creature's own *natural* powers through reflection on its relation to God—in His role as creator, sustainer, and provider. This constitutes the order of nature or *natural revelation.* But there is another dimension of God's intelligibility which is totally empty of all reference to the creature. This is the order of the supernatural, and insights are attained here by *supernatural revelation.*

Christian theology tells us that certain doctrines belong, without any doubt, to the supernatural order, since the limited powers of man's finite faculties could not have conceived them. The fact that God is one and three (Trinity), that He can identify and unite with human nature (Incarnation), and that He gratuitously communicates Himself with the creature (Grace) and makes Himself

[1]Suárez, *De Deo uno et Trino,* lib. 2, cap. 18, num. 7.

eternally present (Beatific Vision) are all examples of doctrines known to the Church through supernatural revelation.

Now if these and other doctrines of the same order can be found, at least suggested if not clearly defined, in other religions, can we not say this (similarity of doctrine) proves supernatural revelation outside the Judeo-Christian tradition, as far as we can humanly presume it?

There is ample proof, as Pereira points out, that these religions do, in fact, reflect our basic truths:

> Non-Christian faiths are impregnated with truths which Christians hold to be supernatural—infused prayer, the inspiration of scripture, religion with a universal message, forgiveness of sin, an eternal heaven and hell, the Last Judgment, good and evil spirits, the resurrection of the body, *creatio ex nihilo*, the divine maternity, the efficacy and necessity of grace andt he primacy of love in the attainment of salvation; God as our blessedness, and indeed in the absolute aspect of his being, or his intimate life; the Virgin Birth, the death and resurrection of the redeemer, vicarious suffering, the Divine Word or Logos, the Incarnation, and the Trinity.[1]

To this Heiler adds: "there is no religious concept, no dogmatic teaching, no ethical demand, no churchly institution, no cultic form and practice of piety in Christianity which does not have diverse parallels in the non-Christian religions."[2] Furthermore, Pereira points out, "these truths not only show no sign of Judaic origin but are seen to rise in [these] faiths suddenly and without antecedents, making plausible the belief that they were directly and newly revealed by God."[3] He again reaffirms this by saying that the "similarities of doctrine—particularly supernatural doctrine—leave us with no alternative but to posit a universal revelation."[4]

[1]José Pereira, "Epiphanies of Revelation," in *Thought*, 51:201 (June 1976), p. 190.

[2]Friedrich Heiler, "The History of Religions as a Preparation for the Co-operation of Religions," in Mircea Eliade and Joseph Kitagawa, *The History of Religions: Essays in Methodology* (Chicago and London: The University of Chicago Press, 1959), p. 139.

[3]Pereira, "Epiphanies," p. 190.

[4]Ibid., p. 197.

It would appear that Newman also adhered to the concept of a universal revelation from which our Christian truths emanated, as the following excerpt from one of his essays seems tos uggest. This guaranteed revelation, the Christian, he says, "is only the continuation and conclusion of what professes to be an earlier revelation which may be traced back into prehistoric times, ...as far as we know, there never was a time when that revelation was not—a revelation continuous and systematic with distinct representatives and an orderly succession."[1]

It thus seems not only possible but probable that in the vast amount of theological literature some divine revelations exist unrecognized, in messages "which have been revealed but not guaranteed—preservation from error being, as we believe, a privilege accorded only to the two Testaments."[2] However, it is for the Church's *Magisterium* to give us this guarantee. And there are numerous theologians today who would agree that the Church, since Vatican II's Declaration on the Relationship of the Church to Non-Christian Religions, is moving in this direction; so that one day, they believe, non-Christian insights will also enjoy the status of guaranteed revelation.

Thus Church, therefore, with this end in mind and until that time comes, should "consult" informed theologians when the latter exercise their role as *sensus or consensus fidelium*; for, in Newman's words, "the body of the faithful is one of the witnesses to the fact of the tradition of revealed doctrine, and because their *consensus* through Christendom is the voice of the Infallible Church."[3] Next, it is the obligation of theologians to make available to the Church, from the literature of non-Christian religions, all the evidence carefully gathered and analyzed, supporting claims for supernatural revelation.

[1]John Henry Newman, *An Essay in Aid of a Grammar of Assent*, pt. 2, ch. 10, sect. 2, subsect. 5; New Impression (London: Longmans Green and Co., 1910) p. 431.

[2]Pereira, "Epiphanies," p. 204.

[3]John Henry Newman, *On Consulting the Faithful in Matters of Doctrine*, edited with an introduction by John Coulson (New York: Sheed and Ward, 1961), p. 63.

GLOSSARY OF TRIADISM

The following sanskrit terms are listed according to the order of the Sanskrit alphabet. The page location for each lettered sub-division, therefore, is included (in parenthesis) for ready reference. Only those terms which are characteristic to Triadism are contained in this tabulation; the more common words are incorporated in the text where they first appear but are excluded from the glossary.

a	(183)	au	(187)	d	(191)	y	(197)
ā	(185)	k	(187)	dh	(191)	r	(198)
i	(186)	kh	(188)	n	(191)	l	(198)
ī	(186)	g	(189)	p	(192)	v	(198)
u	(186)	c	(189)	b	(194)	ś	(200)
ū	(187)	j	(190)	bh	(195)	s	(201)
e	(187)	t	(190)	m	(196)	h	(203)

akula — Non-Familial; Śiva unrelated to Energy; the first of the emanations of the Pure Way.

akhyāti — absence of discrimination regarding true identity; non-intuition in its true nature.

aṇu — individual soul (atomic) which through illusion has become "fragmented" or separated from Śiva; it has lost its omnipresence and has confined itself to its own egoism; see *jīva*, *nara* and *paśu*.

aṇḍa — cosmic sphere—literally "egg"; latent state of the universe; see *śivatattva*.

advaita — the All, the Unique, the One-without-second, non-duality; monist.

adhvan — Path—the sixfold path signifying the vibration of divine energy; it represents both a descent from, and a return to primordial unity.

anākhya — indefinable state, one of the five powers of the Ultimate, which, according to the

Gradation School, are as follows: Creation (*sṛṣṭi*), Conservation (*sthiti*), Destruction (*saṃhāra*), Indefinable (*anākhya*), and Splendor of Freedom (*bhāsā*); see *pañcakṛtya.*

anākhyacakra wheel of the indefinable state wherein the twelve Consuming Energies or *kālīs* to be worshipped are contained.

anāśritaśiva Śiva, without relation to the universe, absolute void. Positioned at the threshold of emanation, he is not yet part of the categories; see *śūnyātiśūnya.*

anāhata uninterrupted, inarticulated interior sound produced by the movement of breathing; Unbeaten, the fourth mystical center of the body; see *nāda.*

anugrahaśakti Energy of grace; see *śaktipāta.*

anuttara the unsurpassed, the highest Reality. There are many meanings associated with this word, some of which differ among the various Triadic schools.

anupāya the Null Way, the way to final emancipation or realization of the ultimate Reality—the characteristic feature of the Self-Awareness system; see *ānandopāya.*

anubhavitṛ universal conscious Subject; perceiving subject.

anubhavitṛtā conscious subjectivity.

anusvāra nasal sound (ṃ), incarnate essence of Śiva.

antaḥkaraṇa internal organ or Inner Faculty formed by the union of the three categories: Instinct, Egoism and Mind—the psychic faculties.

antarvimarśa interiorized self-awareness; see *bahirvimarśa.*

antarvyoman inner sky; interior space where breaths and duality are dissolved; cavity or vault of the heart, interior place of peace; applies also to the firmament.

anyāpoha elimination of "the other" in order to define a thing.

apara the inferior level on the journey to the Abso-

	lute; that belonging to the ordinary life of the individual; see *para* and *parāpara*.
apāna	inspired or descending breath; see *jīva*.
apohanaśakti	differentiating activity which consists in negation; the sense of a word being determined only by the negation of all that it is not.
abhimāna	personal infatuation, superestimation of self.
abhiṣeka	initiation by means of the consecration of the disciple by his guru.
abheda	nondifference; identity.
amṛta	nectar of immortality; ambrosia, mystical happiness.
amṛtabīja	germ or seed of immortality.
artha	ultimate sense, perfect comprehension of the Reality.
ardhacandra	half-moon; see *candrārdha*.
ardhendu	subtle energy of sound.
avikalpa	state of perfect indetermination or undifferentiatedness; undermined intuition, free from mental division; see *nirvikalpa*.
avidyā	ignorance.
aśūnya	non-void.
asāmya	inequality, harshness, unevenness; opposite of *samatā* and *samatva*.
asmitā	self-sentiment; "Ego"-ness, "I"-ness.
ahaṅkāra	factor of individuality, egoity, self-agent.
ahantā	"I"-ness, interiority, thatness or selfness; pure subjectivity; see *pūrṇāhantā* and *aham*.
aham	I supreme; it is the absolute "self"-ness or "that" -ness; equals *pūrṇāhantā*—eminent *mantra*; mystical formula.
ahaṃvimarśa	self-awareness; see *ātmabuddhi*.
āgama	divine word which forms the life or other means of knowledge; the internal activity of the Lord, pure Consciousness; a collection of self-awarenesses or beliefs expressed in words; revealed texts; Sacred Tradition.

ājñā — Command, the sixth mystical center of the body.

āṇavamala — "individual," "infinitesimal" or cogenital impurity, atomic, reducing the soul to the state of *aṇu* or infinitesimal being.

āṇavopāya — Individual Way; inferior way of the infinitesimal or ordinary soul which exericses varied activities (such as yoga) in order to attain Śiva.

ātmabuddhi — self-consciousness; see *ahaṃvimarśa*.

ādispanda — initial vibration.

ādyaspanda — initial shock or disturbance.

ānanda — joy, blessedness.

ānandacakra — wheel of joy.

ānandaśakti — Energy of Joy.

ānandopāya — Blissful or Joyful Means; see *anupāya*.

ābhāsa — reflection, appearance; all that we can perceive or conceive.

āmarśana — self-awareness; see *parāmarśa*.

āśaya — subconscious tendencies, predispositions, latent energies; see *saṃskāra* and *vāsanā*.

icchā — intention, will, desire.

icchāśakti — Energy of Will.

icchāspanda — vibration of the will.

idantā — object, objectivity, the "this-"ness.

īśvaratattva — Supreme Lord category.

uccāra — functioning of the breath; associated with the recitation of *bhairava*, of the mantras *HA*, of *AUM* (*OM*).

uttara — liberation from something, bondage from which freedom is attained; the use of expression. Like *anuttara*, the term has numerous and varied meanings.

udāna — ascending breath which is elevated until *brahmarandhra*; also called "central fire."

udyama, udyoga — enthusiasm, mystical fervor, act of illumination, awakening of the heart.

unmattabhairava — thoughtless (in a mystical sense); "The Demented Tremendous God."

unmanā — energy which transcends thought, supreme

	energy identical with *parāvāk*.
unmīlanasamādhi	ecstasy with eyes opened.
unmeṣa	supreme awakening; deployment of the universe, awakening.
upādhi	contingence, what is associated to a thing does not belong to it by essence and veils its true nature; incidental limiter.
upāya	means of liberation, Way of deliverance.
Umā	Energy, wife of Śiva.
Umāpati	Śiva, Lord of Umā.
ūrdhva	raised or structured *kuṇḍalinī* or Coiled Energy.
ekāgra	point, concentration of thought.
AUM, OM	mystical syllable.
aunmukhya	an intense attentiveness derived from turning oneself toward.
kañcuka	the five sheaths which enslave man: Aptitude (*kalā*), Knowledge (*vidyā*), Desire (*rāga*), Time (*kāla*), and Fate (*niyati*).
kaṇḍa	the inferior center; see *cakra*.
kapardin	ascetic whose hair is curled in the form of a conch shell.
kapālin	Śiva, bearer of the garland of skulls.
kartṛtā	free activity.
kalā	Aptitude, determining and limiting activity —one of the sheaths; pure energy, subtle energy; divine functions.
kalātattva	Aptitude category.
kalāśakti	Aptitude Energy; determinative energy at the source of fragmentation, fragmentary energy.
kāma	god of carnal love; desire.
kāmakalā	mystical triangle of the heart; same as *trikoṇa*.
kārmamala	impurity of action—its relation to the act.
kāla	time, one of the five sheaths.
kālatattva	Time category.
kālasaṃkarṣaṇī	Energy which destroys time by pressuring it.
kālī	divine energy which engenders time; see *Bhairavī*, Consuming Energy.

kuṇḍalinī, kuṇḍalī	Coiled Potency; divine energy of breath and of concentrated virility.
kumbhaka	retention of breath.
kula	Family; undifferentiated energy.
kulabindu	Family Nucleus.
kulamārga	Way of the Family, of energy and sexual practices; see *kaula*.
kulayoga	Familial mystical union.
kulācārya	powerful master, Master of the Family.
kulāveśa	absorption into pure sexual energy; ingress into the Family.
kuleśvara	Lord of the Family, Master of the universe.
kulopāya	Familial Way or Śiva Way.
kuhana	magical process or tickling the body.
kevala, kevalin, kaivalya	unique, absolute; isolated from transmigration, but not achieving identity with Śiva.
koṭi	point—initial, intermediary or final.
kaula	see *kulamārga*.
krama	temporal succession, gradation.
kramamudrā	mystical attitude of spontaneous equalization reconciling ecstasy and ordinary states.
kramacaryā	sexual Gradation (School) practice, rite.
kramasamatā	achieved harmony.
kramābhyāsa	practice in which interior happiness is experienced as an oscillation between the Self and the universe which is poured out to the exterior, afterwards returning to Self wholly impregnated by external joy.
kriyā	both ordinary and divine activity.
kriyāśakti	Śiva's Energy of Activity; energy utilizing the activity of the organs; equals *vimarśa*.
kṣaṇa	precise instant, catalyzer; see *koṭi*.
kṣetrapati	Master of the sanctuary; the Self.
kha, khe	hub of the universal wheel at the center of things.
khecarī	Sky-roaming Goddess; regal energy, one of the five currents of energy.
khecarīmudrā	determined mystical attitude; Sky-roaming

	Goddess Seal.
khecarīsāmya	smoothly attained equality; stands for both liberation in life, and final emancipation; Sky-roaming Goddess equality.
guṇa	one of the three Attributes or constitutive qualities of the Sāṅkhya category of Matter in nature (*prakṛti*); they are as follows: Brightness (*sattva*), Passion (*rajas*), and Darkness (*tamas*).
gocarī	one of the five currents or streams of energy; the "accessible" Goddess, inferior to *khecarī*.
grāhaka, grāhya	subject which apprehends; limited subject and object.
cakra	wheel, center; the centers are situated at different points of the vertebral column and of the brain; cosmic wheel; wheel of energies, of sounds, and of the three eyes; stage of rising of *kuṇḍalinī* or Coiled Potency.
cakravartin	Master of the wheel of energies.
camatkāra	cry of surprise, marvelling at self-awareness; ecstasy in art; enraptured seizure at the time of self-awareness.
candrārdha	energy of subtle sound; see *ardhacandra*.
cit	absolute consciousness.
citi	pure consciousness in its dynamism.
citikartṛtā	the act of the agent expresses consciousness by its same activity; therefore, both the act and the agent are not distinct.
citkriyā	conscious activity.
citta	divine thought; empirical consciousness; unstable human thought; Heart.
cittapralaya	disappearance of thought (Way of Śiva).
cittaviśrānti	quietude or appeasement of thought (Way of the Individual).
cittasambodha	awakening of thought (Way of Energy).
citprakāśa	Light of Consciousness.
citśakti (*cicchakti*)	Energy of Consciousness.
cidākāśa	ether of consciousness.

cidānanda	conscious bliss.
cidānandaghana	mass of consciousness and of happiness.
cidghana	indivisible mass of consciousness.
cetanā	introverted consciousness, intermediary between *citta* and *cit*.
caitanya	self-consciousness; absolute, ultimate consciousness.
jagadānanda	cosmic or universal bliss.
japa	recitation of a *mantra*, but this is different from an oration because all the efficiency of the word is contained within it.
jīva	individual soul or person; breath, see *apāna*; see also, *aṇu*, *nara* and *paśu*.
jīvanmukta	The Liberated-in-Life; the equal of *bhairava* because he enjoys divine energies.
jīvanmukti	Liberation-in-Life.
jñānavid	the gnostic, see *jñānin*.
jñānaśakti	cognitive energy, Śiva's Energy of Knowledge; eye of knowing.
jñānasiddha	inferior masters.
jñānin	he who enjoys or possesses gnosis or knowledge (*jñāna*); the gnostic or *jñānavid* is superior to the *yogī*.
jñānopāya	Way of Knowledge; see *śāktopāya*.
jyeṣṭhā	elevated energy.
tattva	ultimate Reality; principle of phase of emanation; category of reality.
tantra	religious treatise, dissertation; revealed works; sacred books.
tamas	one of the three *guṇas*, principle of inertia and the opaque; spiritual darkness.
tirodhānaśakti	Concealing Energy, which veils and obscures reality—cause of differentiation and limitation.
turīya	fourth state, illumination, ecstasy, unalterable essence of the soul, differentiated from *turyātīta*.
turyātīta	beyond the fourth—corresponds to *bhairava* state; permanent or definitive illumination beyond the fourth.

trika	Triadic system of Śaivism founded by Vasugupta; Triadism: Śiva, Energy and *nara* (man).
trikoṇa	see *kāmakalā*.
dikcarī	Quarter-roaming Goddess; one of the five streams of energy.
dīkṣā	initiation.
dūtī	messenger, female partner of a *yogī*, consort.
dūtīyajana	sexual rite; "Consort Sacrifice."
dvādaśagocara, dvādaśānta, dviṣaṭkānta	width of twelve fingers; exhaled breath; any one of the centers of the body; center above the interior of the skull; cosmic omnipresence. Also named *mūrdhānta* and *brahmarandhra*.
dvaita	duality.
dhāman	Śaiva domain; universal receptacle; the absolute; equivalent to brahman.
dhūrjaṭi	"Matted-Locks-Weighted," divine ascetic, Śiva.
dhvani	resonance, suggestion in art, vibration.
nara	individual; see *aṇu*, *paśu* and *jīva*.
navātma	formula (to be repeated ninefold).
nāḍī	One of innumerable channels or conduits that nourish the centers of consciousness in the body.
nāda	internal sound; symbol of energy; vibrating energy of sound; mystical sounds heard on leaving the awakening state.
nādabindu	Sound Nucleus; sound and light (or Śakti and Śiva).
nādānta	end of sound; subtle energy.
nikhila	the All, absolute, indivisible, without fault.
nibhālana	mystical intuition.
nimīlanasamādhi	ecstasy with eyes closed.
niyati	Fate; causal restriction, one of the five sheaths.
nirodhikā, nirodhinī	restraining (potency); subtle energy of sound.

nirvikalpa	see *avikalpa.*
nirvikalpapramātṛ	subject forever free from duality (*vikalpa*).
nirvikalpasamādhi	ecstasies without elements, do not admit subject-object distinction; profound absorption without thought; limpid mirror.
nirvikalpāvasthā	state of indifferentiation.
niveśana	penetration into the Absolute Self.
niṣkala	indivisible, spontaneous; see *bhairava.*
nistaraṅga	waveless; exempt from undulation.
pañcakṛtya	fivefold divine activity according to the Self-Awareness School: Creation (*sṛṣṭi*), Conservation (*sthiti*), Destruction (*saṁhāra*), Obscuration (*tirobhāva* or *tirodhāna*), and Grace (*anugraha*); cf. *anākhya.*
pañcaśakti	The Five Energies (Macrocosmic Consciousness) are as follows: Consciousness (*cicchakti*), Joy (*ānandaśakti*), Will (*icchāśakti*), Knowledge (*jñānaśakti*), and Action (*kriyāśakti*).
pati	Lord, master; the first of the three categories of Śaivism—the others are Beast (*paśu*) and Bond (*pāśa*).
para	supreme, transcendence.
parabīja	supreme source or principle, greatest of the *mantra.*
paramaśiva	The Supreme Śiva, the Absolute, the All.
paramārthasatya	ultimate reality, absolute truth; see *saṃvṛtisatya.*
parāpara	supreme-non-supreme; subtle level of transcendent-immanent.
parāmarśa	intuitive and global self-conscious awareness; a desire to act; affected conscious being; conscious reaction; procession of sounds.
parāvāk	transcendent and undifferentiated word (*nirvikalpa*)—always shines interiorly, it is pure consciousness (*citi*), free of connotation and of all sound; totally undifferentiated supreme Word. Equivalent to *unmanā.*

parispanda	trembling wave, subtle vibration.
Pārvatī	wife of Śiva.
paśu	Beast, the second of the three categories of Śaivism; man, enslaved being, slave of energies, head of the flock; see *aṇu*, *jīva* and *nara*.
paśupati	Śiva, guardian of the flock.
paśyantī	Visioning Speech, forming a trio with Interjacent and Displayed Speech; undifferentiated sound, deceptive energy of the word; see *prathamā tuṭī*.
pāta	flight over.
pāśa	Bond, the third of the three categories of Śaivism.
piṇḍanātha	eminent *mantra*.
puruṣa	soul—supreme entity of the spiritual order according to the Sāṅkhya—Cosmic Being of the *Ṛg Veda*; limited being, but not yet individualized.
pūrṇa, *pūrṇatā*, *pūrṇatva*	fullness.
pūrṇāhantā	fullness of subjectivity; interiority of consciousness; absolute subjectivity, I identified with the All.
prakāśa	Light; luminous and undifferentiated consciousness;light of consciousness; revealing (things).
prakāśacakra	wheel of light, right eye of Śiva; represents the means of knowledge; it is the union of *dikcarī* (powers of perception) and *gocarī* (organs of action).
prakṛti	Matter; nature; see *pradhāna*.
prakṛtyaṇḍa	sphere of Matter.
prajñā	intuition.
pratipatti	mystical realization.
pratibimba	reflection without object.
pratibhā	intuition of self, pure illumination which surges spontaneously.
pratīti	apperception (clear, conscious perception), perception from esthetic feeling.

pratyabhijñā	Self-Awareness system founded by Somānanda; Recognition of self as identical with Śiva.
pratyavamarśa	self-conscious awareness.
pratyāhāra	convention; contraction and fitting in.
prathamā tuṭī	trembling of the will (from the act of consciousness); see *paśyantī*, *koṭi* and *kṣaṇa*.
prathamaspanda	initial vibration.
prathamā koṭi	initial point, first instance; trembling of the act of consciousness.
pradhāna	primordial nature; see *prakṛti*.
pramāṇa	Norm of Knowledge; logical criteria—knowledge linked to dream; see *svapna*.
pramātṛ	conscious subject.
pramātṛtā	essence of conscious subject.
pramiti	pure consciousness of self and resulting knowledge.
prameya	object of knowledge; circle of objectivity.
praśānta	appeased, satisfied, amiable.
prājña	wisdom proper to profound sleep.
prāṇa	breath, life, vital force, vital air, expired breath.
prāṇana	the sixth breath animating the rest, infinite cosmic Life.
prāṇaśakti	vital energy, Energy of breath.
prāṇahaṃsa	"Breath Flamingo"; breath from the center.
prāthamikālocana	pre-perception.
preraṇa	divine incitation.
bahirvimarśa	conscious awareness (exteriorized).
bindu	Nucleus; luminous point appearing in the course of the meditation point or *ṃ*; symbol of Śiva; concentration of luminous energy; free act; energy of the word; point without dimension.
buddhi	Instinct, "mind," faculty of judgement, thought.
buddhitattva	Sāṅkhya category of Instinct.
bodha	supreme Consciousness, divine Intelligence—forms the substance of Śiva under the same title as *svātantrya*; illumination.

brahman	neuter: the absolute in *Vedānta*—it is pure *prakāśa*, divested of energy associated with illusion, masculine: God, organizer of the cosmos, the Creator.
brahmatattva, brahmasattā	existence of brahman, equanimity.
brahmanāḍī	central channel; equivalent to *madhyanāḍī* and *suṣumṇā*.
brahmarandhra	slit or crevice of brahman, superior center equivalent to *dvādaśānta* and *śikhānta*, see also *udāna* and *sahasrāra*.
brahmāṇḍa	sphere of the brahman: cosmic egg, universe.
brahmānanda	Brahman Joy.
bhakti	ardent devotion, divine love.
bhava	Universal Being or existence; phenomenal existence repeated; evolution, equivalent to "becoming" (*saṃsāra*).
bhāva	supreme modality, modality of the future, universal reality revealed by *bhāvanā*.
bhāvanā	mystical realization, infused contemplation, intense creative imagination, evocation, conviction.
bhāsā	Splendor, Ultimate Reality of the *krama* system.
bhūta	the elements of fire, earth, water, and air.
bheda	Difference.
bhedābheda	Difference-in-Identity.
bhairava	The Tremendous God Śiva, the dreadful, who swallows diversity; his relationship to the universe; *bhairva* state (theopathetic state); the Absolute, undifferentiated Śiva; see *niṣkala* and *sakala*.
bhairavamudrā, bhairvavīmudrā	Seal of the Tremendous God/Goddess, mystical attitude; fixation of the glance and all the senses.
bhairavayāmala	intimate union of Śiva and energy; see *or rudrayāmala*.
bhairavaśāsana	Dispensation of the Tremendous God;

Triadism.

bhairavī — The Tremendous Goddess; consciousness figured as divine energy which swallows all diversity; Śakti, Energy of *bhairava*.

bhrūmadhya — center situated between the eyebrows, its opening and contraction.

maṇipura — Jewel City, the third mystical center of the body.

madhyanāḍī — central channel; see *nāḍī* and *suṣumṇā*.

madhyamaprāṇa — central breath.

madhyamapada — state of the environment.

madhyamāvāk — Interjacent Speech, forming a trio with Visioning and Displayed Speech; intermediary word, subtle.

madhyaśakti — energy of the center.

manas — empirical thought, common sense (experiential), naturally unstabled thought; heart.

mantra — mystic formula; see *aham* and *mahā*.

mantravīrya — efficacy of the formula, of the "I".

mantrasiddha — formula which possesses mystical intuition; concerning the heart.

manthānabhairava — Śiva who churns the universe.

mala — pollution, defilement, three in number.

mahā — great, mystical formula of absorption of the cosmos into *bhairava*.

mahākāla — The Great Time Destroyer.

mahāguhā, *mahāguhya* — the great enigma, profound abyss, cavern.

mahāpuruṣa — the great Person, the Unique, refuge of all persons, God.

mahāmelāpa — great Union.

mahārtha — great meaning, absolute sense.

mahāvyāpti — great fusion, omnipenetration.

mahāśūnya — great void.

mahāsattā — great existence; existence in Self, transcendent Reality, ultimate Reality.

māyā — cosmic illusion—objective manifestations as separated from conscious light. It is *svātantrya*, free activity of Śiva; Mirific

	power.
māyāṇḍa	sphere of illusion.
māyāpramātṛ	conscious subject, the prey of illusion.
māyāvin, māyin	magician, Śiva.
māyāśakti	The Mirific Energy, source of illusion inasmuch as it refers to the autonomy of divine consciousness in its objective manifestations.
māyīyamala	impurity of illusion—cause of cosmic differentiation.
mukti	liberation, it is revelation of self-essence; equivalent to *mokṣa.*
mudrā	mystical movement or attitude; seal of unity sign of the cosmic dancer; see *bhairava/bhairavīmudrā* and *kramamudrā.*
mūrdhānta	see *dvādaśānta.*
mūlādhāra	Root Support, the first mystical center of the body.
melāpa	union.
melāpasiddha	given over to union.
yantra	machine, here the cosmic wheel of energy.
yama	god of death, restrictor, equivalent to *vikalpa.*
yāmala	union of the couple (Śiva and Śakti), inseparables.
yugapat	simultaneously, concentration bearing upon the moment.
yoga	mystical union, discipline—combined ascetic practices of the eight members.
yoganidrā	mystical sleep.
yogī, yogin	he who is advanced on the path of deliverance; utilizes the *mantra*; gives homage to Śiva in acts, prayers and religious duty; he who is absorbed in Śiva.
yoginī	divinized energies of the Tremendous State, the liberated one; initiated female practicing yoga; the initiator appearing in a dream.
yoginīmelaka	banquets and secret rites where the *yoginīs* take part, divinized energies.

yoginīmelana, yoginīmelāpa	see *yoginīmelaka.*
yogīndra	master yogī, he who travels the path of Śiva; king of the yogīs who frequent the Supreme Path.
rajas	Passion, one of the three Sāṅkhya Attributes which engenders suffering; see *guṇa.*
rasa	delight in art, esthetic and mystic savor, quintessence, esthetic sentiment—eight or nine in number.
rāga	desire or attachment, one of the five sheaths.
Rudra	Śiva the Terrifying.
rudra	spirit (soul) possessing divine powers, which direct the movement of the cosmos.
rudrayāmala	intimate union of Rudra and Energy.
rudraśakti	Energy of the Terrifying; eminent grace.
lelihānīmudrā	attitude (posture) called gourmand or suction.
vapu	beauty of The Tremendous God, cosmic essence, rarely the body of The Tremendous God, marvelous reality.
varṇa	phoneme, subtle energy of the word.
vaikharī	Displayed Speech, forming a trio with Visioning and Interjacent Speech; ordinary articulated speech.
vāk	speech, word, Word.
vāmā	energy which projects the outside world.
vāsanā	conceptual latencies, unconscious tendencies, results (residues) of past acts—their role in esthetics and in the creation of the universe; equivalent to *saṃskāra.*
vikalpa	conceptual dualization which always differentiates one thing from that which it is not, it is the source of the subject-object duality; alternative, dichotomy.
vikalpakriyā	bipolar activity.
vikāsa	expansion of energy; see *saṅkoca.*
vijñāna	discriminating knowledge—surpasses all others because it is self-awareness; ultimate self-consciousness; knowledge—both

ordinary and supreme.

vidyā knowledge, discriminating but limited; one of the Five Sheaths; pure knowledge.

vidyātattva category of (limited) Knowledge.

vimarśa self-awareness, free act of consciousness appearing as a shock; see *svātantrya*; conscious awareness, rapport with *prakāśa* (Light); free act of consciousness, interiorized and exteriorized; free energy of consciousness.

vimarśopāya Way of Conscious Awareness; See *anupāya*.

viyat aerial space between heaven and earth, symbol of infinite expansion of spatial void.

virāṭ Luminous cosmic body according to the *Vedas*.

virūpākṣa "having deformed eyes"; Śiva of the third eye.

viśuddha Immaculate, the fifth mystical center of the body.

viśrānti mystic repose, appeasement in art.

viśrāntisthāna locus of mystical repose.

viśva the all in its dispersion, the awakening.

viśvamoha wandering from the cosmic order; universal delusion.

viṣa poison or omnipenetration.

viṣuvat equinox, equilibrium between breaths.

visarga Emission; energy of breath—its two points; pure energy of emergence, and projection from duality.

vīrya vital and virile efficiency; mystic efficiency.

vṛtti agitation.

vṛndacakra wheel of totality.

vaiṣamya roughness, disequilibrium resulting from duality.

vyaṅgyārtha, vyañjana suggestion in art.

vyañjanā penetration of suggested sense.

vyāna Pervasive Breath, forming a quintet with the Ascendant, Descendant, Equilibrant, and Vertical Breaths; cosmic life.

vyāpinī	energy which replenishes the universe; omnipenetrating energy.
vyāpti	omnipenetration, fusion in all, triple penetration.
vyoman	vault of heaven, unlimited or infinite firmament of consciousness; dynamic space engendering the void where all comes to be swallowed up.
vyomavyāpti	pervasion of cosmic ether.
vyomavāmeśvarī	The Lovely Sovereign Lady of Heaven; sovereign energy equal to supreme Word.
vyutthāna	dispersion proper to daily activity; daily activity opposed to *samādhi*; state of sleepless consciousness.
śakti	Divine Energy, identical to Śiva; stage in the *kuṇḍalinī* process; phase of self-energy.
śaktikṣobha	effervescence or stirring of Energy.
śakticakra	wheel of Energies.
śaktitattva	Energy, the second category or emanation of the Pure Way.
śaktipāta	Energic Fulmination, "fall of energy"; see *anugrahaśakti.*
śaktivikāsa	expansion or blossoming of energy.
śaktivisarga	Emission of Energy.
śaktisaṃkoca	contraction of Energy; opposed to *śaktivikāsa.*
śaktyaṇḍa	sphere of energy.
śabdabrahman	sonic brahman; absolute sound.
śabdabhāvanā	an obscure tendency toward verbal expression.
śabdabhairava	Sonic Tremendous God.
śabdarāśi	totality of sounds.
śambhu	blessed, it is applied to Śiva-the-Beneficent.
śarva	Śiva-the-Destroyer.
śāktasiddha	Master of Energy.
śāktopāya	Energic Way of deliverance through the intermediary of pure energy; Way of Energy proper to the Gradation system.
śāmbhavopāya	The Divine or Śiva Way, the superior Way of access to Śiva, the best of ways in order

	to approach Śiva.
śikhānta	equivalent to *brahmarandhra* (superior center of the body); "flame top."
śivatattva	the highest of categories, supreme category, the first emanation of the Pure Way.
śivarātri	Night of Śiva, Śiva the Mystical Night.
śivavyāpti	reabsorption of the universe in Śiva.
śuddhavidyā, sadvidyā tattva	Pure Wisdom, fifth and last emanation of the Pure Way category of pure manifestation; pure science or knowledge.
śūnya	Empty, void; consciousness under a limited form.
śūnyatā	Emptiness, void, vacuity.
śūnyātiśūnya	absolute void, beyond the void.
śūlin	bearer of the trident, Śiva endowed with three Energies.
saṃrambha	trembling of consciousness; initiative.
saṃvitti, saṃvid	consciousness, universal consciousness.
saṃvṛtisatya	relative "obfuscating" or common-sensible truth, opposed to *paramārthasatya.*
saṃsāra	the world of transmigration, of perpetual becoming; impetuous continuance of the world.
saṃskāra	conceptual latencies, predispositions, latent energies; equivalent to *āśaya* and *vāsanā.*
sakala	man provided with a body—the state of Beast (*paśu*); all, composite nature.
saṅkalpa	synthetic function of thought (*manas*); it is consciousness which limits empirical thought and an object which lacks clarity; imagination.
saṅkoca	contraction of energy, relinquishing of energy; means of penetrating the heart; see *vikāsa.*
saṅghaṭṭa	vibrant union of Śiva and Energy, and of the sacred.
satyasaṅkalpa	realized intentions.
sadākhya	pure category; equivalent to *sadāśiva tattva.*
sadāśiva	The Ever Beneficent, the third emanation of

	the Pure Way; eternal Śiva, category inferior to that of Energy, the second emanation.
sadāśiva tattva	The Ever Beneficent Category; equivalent to *sadākhya*.
sadvidyā tattva	pure category of true science (knowledge); equivalent to *śuddhavidyā*.
samatā, samatva	achieved harmony, equality of spirit; homogeneity; opposed to *asāmya*.
samanā	displays sonic energy, uniform, equal; pure energy.
samādhi	concentration, peaceful meditation, contemplation (eyes closed and eyes opened), ecstasy.
samāna	equilibrated breath.
samāviś–, samāveśa	burial in Śiva or in His Energy—compenetration of the soul and Śiva; to be totally absorbed.
sarvamudrā	universal Imprint of the Lord.
sahaja	connate, spontaneous, innate.
sahasrāra	Thousand-Spoked, the seventh mystical center of the body.
sahṛdaya	sympathizing in art, "heart endowed."
sāṃsiddhika	master of perfect spiritual realization.
siddha	beings endowed with certain powers; spiritual master; faculty of a yogin; wizard or sorcerer.
siddhi	perfection, efficient and supernatural power; supreme accomplishment.
suṣupti	profound sleep, without dream associated with the knowing subject (*pramātṛ*).
suṣumṇā (*nāḍī*)	central canal linked to the seat of *kuṇḍalinī*; "Middle Way" connecting the seven mystical centers of the body; see *madhyanāḍī*.
sthiti	abode, continuance, spiritual station; conservation of the universe; permanence, stability.
spanda	Vibrancy, vibration of the breath—pure act in its initial (primordial) trembling vib-

	ration from which all becoming proceeds; vibrant spontaneous energy; see *ādispanda*, *parispanda* and *prathamaspanda*.
spandaśakti	vibrant energy.
sphuraṇa, *sphurattā*	vibrant and bursting conscious awareness.
svatantratva	liberty, same as *svātantrya*.
svapna	dream linked to knowledge (*pramāṇa*).
svasthā, *svasthiti*	abode, sojourn, continuance in itself.
svātantrya	divine liberty, taking the aspect of the Mirific Power; equivalent to *caitanya* and *vimarśa*; free spontaneity, absolute liberty.
svātantryaśakti	Energy of Freedom.
svādhiṣṭhāna	Own Place, the second mystical center of the body.
haṃsa	flamingo, swan, or Śiva; mystic formula; central ascending breath, spontaneous formula; Center, intermediary point.
haṃsī	female flamingo or swan, divine energy.
Hara	the Ravisher, name of Śiva.
hṛdaya	Heart, mystical center.

LIST OF ABBREVIATIONS

CHI	*The Cultural Heritage of India*, vol. 4.
IPV	*Īśvarapratyabhijñā Vimarśinī* of Abhinavagupta (Examination of the Supreme Lord's Self-Awareness).
IPVV	*Īśvarapratyabhijñā Vivṛti Vimarśinī* of Abhinavagupta (Examination of the Gloss of the Supreme Lord's Self-Awareness).
MM	*Mahārthamañjarī of Maheśvarānanda* (The Banquet of Great Meaning).
MVV	*Mālinīvijaya Vārtika Tantra* (Tantra on the Triumph of the Engarlanded Goddess).
PHṛ	*Pratyabhijñāhṛdayam of Kṣemarāja* (The Heart of Self Awareness).
PS	*Paramārthasāra of Abhinavagupta* (The Quintessence of the Ultimate Truth).
PT	*Parātriṃśikā-Tantra* (Tantra on the Trigesimal on the Supreme Goddess).
q(s)	quatrain(s) (poetic style of Lallā).
SA	*Śivastotrāvalī* of Utpaladeva (The Series of Hymns to Śiva).
SD	*Śivadṛṣṭi of Somānanda* (The Vision of Śiva).
st(s)	stanza(s).
Stav	*Stavacintāmaṇi* of Bhaṭṭṭa Nārāyaṇa (The Wishing Jewel of Praise).
TA	*Tantrāloka* of Abhinavagupta (Light on the Tantras).
TS	*Tantrasāra* of Abhinavagupta (Essence of the Tantras).
VB	*Vijñāna Bhairava Tantra* (The Tantra on the Tremendous Wisdom God).
VS	*Vātūlanātha Sūtra* (Aphorisms on the Mad Lord).
YS	*Yoga Sūtras* of Patañjali (Aphorisms on Yoga).

BIBLIOGRAPHY

I. *Translations and Commentaries of Original Works*

Abhinavagupta. *Hymnes de Abhinavagupta.* Traduits et commentés par Lilian Silburn. Institut de Civilisation Indienne. Fasc. 31. Paris: Boccard, 1970.

———. *Le Paramārthasāra.* Texts Sanskrit édité et traduit par Liliane Silburn. Institut de Civilisation Indienne. Fasc. 5. Paris: Boccard, 1957.

———. "The Paramarthasara of Abhinava-Gupta." Translated by L.D. Barnett. London: *Journal of the Royal Asiatic Society of Great Britain and Ireland,* 1910, pp. 707-47.

———. *Parātriṃśikā Vivaraṇa* 1, 3-7. Translated by Raniero Gnoli in *Luce della sacre Scritture (Tantrāloka) di Abhinavagupta.* Turino: Unione Tipografico-Editrice Torinese, 1972, pp. 839-56.

———. *Tantrāloka.* Translated by Raniero Gnoli. *Luce delle Sacre Scritture (Tantrāloka) di Abhinavagupta.* Turino: Unione Tipografico-Editrice Torinese, 1972.

———. *Tantrasāra.* Translated by Raniero Gnoli. *Abhinavagupta: Essenza dei Tantra* (tantrasāra). Turino: Boringhieri, 1960. Chapters 1-3 translated by José Pereira. *Hindu Theology: A Reader.* New York: Doubleday Image Book, 1976, pp. 372-78. Chapter 4 translated by Richard F. Cefalu, "*Shakti* in Abhinavagupta's Concept of *Moksha.*" Ph.D. dissertation, Fordham University, 1973, pp. 201-9.

Al-Gazzālī. *Al-Gazzālī's Mishkāt-al-Anwār* ("*The Niche for Lights*"). A translation with introduction by W.H.T. Gairdner. London: Royal Asiatic Society Monographs. Vol. 19, 1924.

Aquinas, Saint Thomas. *Basic Writings of Saint Thomas Aquinas.* Edited by Anton C. Pegis. 2 vols. New York: Random House, 1944. Vol. 2: *Summa Theologica,* 1-2.

Bādarāyaṇa. *The Vedānta Sūtras of Bādarāyaṇa: With the Commentary by Śaṅkara.* 2 Parts. Translated by George Thibaut. New York: Dover Publications, 1962.

Bhaṭṭanārāyaṇa. *Stavacintāmaṇi.* Translation and commentary by Lilian Silburn, *La Bhakti: Le Stavacintāmaṇi de Bhaṭṭanārāyaṇa.* Institut de Civilisation Indienne. Fasc. 19. Paris: Boccard, 1964.

Braille, John; Mc Neill, John T; and Van Dusen, Henry P. eds. *The Library of Christian Classics.* 26 vols. Philadelphia: The Westminster Press, 1953-66. Vol. 2: *Alexandrian Christianity: Selected Translations of Clement and Origen.* Introduction and notes by John Ernest Leonard Oulton, and Henry, Chadwick, 1954.

Bremond, Henri. *Histoire litteraire du sentiment religieux en France: depuis la fin des guerres de religion jusqu'a nos jours.* XI tomes. Paris: Libraire Armand Colin, 1967. Tome III (2 vols.): *La Conquête mystique: L'École française.*

———. *A Literary History of Religious Thought in France: From the Wars of Religion Down to Our Own Times.* 11 vols. New York: The Macmillan Company, 1928-36, Vol. 3: *The Triumph of Mysticism: The French School.* Translated by K. L. Montgomery, 1936.

Clement of Alexandria. *The Stromata or Miscellanies* in *The Ante-Nicene Fathers.* 10 vols. Revised by A. C. Coxe. Grand Rapids: Wm. B. Eerdmans Publishing Co., 1962. Vol. 2: *The Fathers of the Second Century.*

de Condren, Le P.R. *Le 'idée du sacerdoce et du sacrifice de Jésus-Christ.* Vitry-le-François: E. Hurault, 1849.

Deferrari, Roy Joseph. gen. ed. *The Fathers of the Church.* New York: Fathers of the Church, Inc. 1954. Vol. 23: *Clement of Alexandria: Christ the Educator.* Translation of Books 1-3 by Simon P. Wood, C.P.

Hakuin. *The Zen Master Hakuin: Selected Writings.* Translated by Philip B. Yampolsky. New York and London: Columbia University Press, 1971.

John of the Cross, Saint, *Dark Night of the Soul.* 3rd rev. ed. Translated and ed. with intro. by E. Allison Peers. Garden City, N.Y.: Doubleday Image Books, 1959.

———. *Living Flame of Love.* Translated and ed. with intro by E. Allison Peers. Garden City, N.Y.: Doubleday Image Books, 1962.

———. *Spiritual Canticle.* 3rd rev. ed. Translated and ed. with intro. by E. Allison Peers. Garden City, N.Y.: Doubleday Image Books, 1961.

John of St. Thomas. *Cursus Theologicus, Tractatus de Gratia.* Paris: Vives Edition, 1883.

———. *The Gifts of the Holy Ghost.* Translated from the Latin by Dominic Hughes, O.P. New York: Sheed & Ward, 1951.

Kṣemarāja. *Pratyabhijñāhṛdayam.* Samskṛta text with English translation and notes by Jaideva Singh. Motilal Banarsidass, 1963.

———. *The Secret of Recognition* (*Pratyabhijñāhṛdayam*): *A Reviving Doctrine of Salvation Medieval India.* English translation with notes by Kurt F. Leidecker. Madras: Adyar Library, 1938.

———. *Spandanirṇaya: Commentary on Vasugupta's Spandakārikās.* English translation by M.S. Kaul in Kashmir Series of Texts and Studies, no. 42 (1925).

Lallā. *Lallā-Vākyāni, or The Wise Sayings of Lal Dēd: A Mystic Poetess of Ancient Kashmir.* Edited with translation, notes, and a vocabulary by Sir George Grierson and Lionel D. Barnett. London: Royal Asiatic Society Monographs, vol. 17, 1920.

Maheśvarānanda. *Le Mahārthamañjarī de Maheśvarānanda: avec des extraits du Parimala.* Traduction et introduction par Lilian Silburn. Institut de Civilisation Indienne. Fasc. 29. Paris: Boccard, 1968. Also translated by José Pereira. *Hindu Theology : A Reader.* New York: Doubleday Image Books, 1976, pp. 381-88.

New American Bible. Paterson, N.J.: St. Anthony Guild Press, 1970.

Newman, John Henry. *An Essay in Aid of a Grammar of Assent.* New Impression. London: Longmans Green and Co., 1910.

———. *On Consulting the Faithful in Matters of Doctrine.* Edited with an introduction by John Coulson. New York: Sheed and Ward, 1961.

Patañjali. *Yoga Sūtras.* Translated by James Haughton Woods in *The Yoga System of Patañjali.* Commentaries by Vyasa and Vachaspatimishra, 1914. Reprint Delhi : Motilal Banarsidass, 1972. Chapter 1 translated by José Pereira. *Hindu Theology : A Reader.* New York: Doubleday Image Books, 1976, pp. 78-81.

Quasten, Johannes, *Patrology*. 3 vols. Westminster, Md.: The Newman Press, 1950-60. Vol. 2: *The Ante-Nicene Literature After Irenaeus*, 1953.

Radhakrishnan, S., ed. and trans. *The Principal Upaniṣads*. London: George Allen & Unwin Ltd.; New York: Humanities Press. Inc., 1953.

Roberts, A., and Donaldson, J., ed. *The Ante-Nicene Fathers: Translations of the Writings of the Fathers Down to A.D. 325*. American reprint of the Edinburgh edition edited by A.C. Coxe. 10 vols. Grand Rapids, Mich.: Wm. B. Eerdmans, 1962. Vol. 2: *The Fathers of the Second Century*.

The Roman Missal: The Sacramentary. New York: The Catholic Book Publishing Co., 1974.

Rūmī, Jalāl al-Dīn. *Mystical Poems of Rūmī: First Selection, Poems* 1-200. Translated from the Persian by A.J. Arberry. Chicago: The University of Chicago Press, 1968.

Sharma, B.N.K. *Śrī Madhva's Teachings in His Own Words*. Bombay: Bharatiya Vidya Bhavan, 1961.

Somānanda. *Śivadṛṣṭi*. ed. M.S. Kaul, with Utpala's *Vṛtti*, in Kashmir Series of Texts and Studies, no. 54 (1934), pp. 1-35. Translated into English by Raniero Gnoli in *East and West*, 8 (1957).

Suárez, Francisco. *Opera Omnia*. 26 vols. Paris: Vives Edition, 1856. Vol. 1: *De Deo Uno et Trino*, (*tractatus*) *De Sanctissimo Trinitatis Mysterio*. Vol. 4: *De Ultimo Fine Hominis*. Vols. 7-9: *De Gratia I-III* Vol. 26: *Disputationes Metaphysicae*.

Utpaladevācārya. *Śivastotrāvalī*. Commentary by Kṣemarāja. Benares: Chowkhambā Sanskrit Series Office, 1902. Chapter 13 has been translated into English by Durgaprasad Kachru. *Utpala, the Mystic Saint of Kashmir*. Poona, 1945.

Vasubandhu. *L'Abhidharmakośa de Vasubandhu*. Traduction et annotation par Louis de la Vallee-Poussin. Nouvelle édition anastatique presentée par Etienne Lamotte. Bruxelles: Institut Belge des Hautes Etudes Chinoises. 1971.

Vasugupta. *Śivasūtrāṇi*, ed. with Kṣemarāja's *Vimarśinī* by J.C. Chatterji in KST 1, Srinagar, 1911. Translated in

Indian Thought, vols. 3 and 4.

Vātūlanātha Sūtra: Avec le commentaire d'Anantaśaktipāda. Traduction par Lilian Silburn. Institut de Civilisation Indienne. Fasc. 8. Paris: Boccard, 1959.

Vijñānabhairava Tantra. Texte traduit et commenté par Lilian Silburn in *Le Vijñāna Bhairava.* Institut de Civilisation Indienne. Fasc. 15. Paris: Boccard, 1961.

———. Translation under the title of : *Aum Shri Vijnana Bhairava.* In the possession of the Kundalini Research Foundation, New York, N.Y. n.p.; n.d. pp. 1-42. (Mimeographed).

II. *Critical Works*

Amiot, François. *The Key Concepts of St. Paul.* New York: Herder and Herder, 1962.

Bamzai, P.N.K. *A History of Kashmir: Political, Social, Cultural.* 2nd ed. New Delhi: Metropolitan Book Co., 1973.

Barua, Benimadab. *A History of Pre-Buddhistic Indian Philosophy.* Delhi: Motilal Banarsidass, 1970.

Basu, Arabinda. "Kashmir Śaivism." *The Cultural Heritage of India.* 4. vols. Calcutta: The Ramakrishna Mission Institute of Culture, 1937-56. Vol. 4: *The Religions*, pp. 79-97.

Bharati, Agehananda. *The Tantric Tradition.* Garden City, N.Y.: Doubleday Anchor Books, 1970.

Biemer, Günther. *Newman on Tradition.* Translated and edited by Kevin Smyth. New York: Herder and Herder, 1967.

Bigg, Charles. *The Christian Platonists of Alexandria.* New York: Macmillan & Co., 1886.

Cefalu, Richard F. "*Shakti* in Abhinavagupta's Concept of *Moksha.*" Ph.D. dissertation, Fordham University, 1973.

Das Gupta, Shashi Bhusan. "Some Later Yogic Schools." *The Cultural Heritage of India.* 4 vols. Calcutta: The Ramakrishna Mission Institute of Culture, 1937-56. Vol. 4: *The Religions*, pp. 291-99.

de Bary, William Theodore, ed. *The Buddhist Tradition in India, China and Japan.* New York: The Modern Library, 1969.

Eliade, Mircea. *Cosmos and History: The Myth of the Eternal Return.* Translated from the French by Willard R. Trask. New York: Harper Torchbooks, 1959.

———. *Yoga: Immortality and Freedom.* 2nd ed. Translated by

Willard R. Trask. Bollingen Series 56. Princeton: Princeton University Press, 1969.

Ghosh, Atal Behari. "The Spirit and Culture of the Tantras." *The Cultural Heritage of India.* 4 vols. Calcutta: The Ramakrishna Mission Institute of Culture, 1937-56. Vol. 4: *The Religions*, pp. 241-51.

Haldar, Hiralal. "Realistic Idealism," in S. Radhakrishnan, and J.H. Muirhead, ed. *Contemporary Indian Philosophy*, 2nd ed. London: George Allen & Unwin, Ltd., 1952.

Heiler, Friedrich. "The History of Religions as a Preparation for the Co-operation of Religions." Mircea Eliade and Joseph Kitagawa. *The History of Religions: Essays in Methodology*. Chicago: The University of Chicago Press, 1959, pp. 132-60.

Hopkins, Thomas J. *The Religious Life of Man: The Hindu Religious Tradition.* Encino, and Belmont, Cal. : Dickenson Publishing Company, Inc., 1971.

Knowles, M.D. *The Nature of Mysticism.* New York: Hawthorne Books, Inc., 1966.

Koul [Kaul], Amand. "The Life Sketch of Laleshwari: A Great Hermitess of Kashmir." *Indian Antiquary* 50 (October and November 1921): 203-12.

——— . "Some additions to the Lallā Vākyāni: The Wise Sayings of Lal Dēd." *Indian Antiquary* 59 (June and July 1930): 108-11, 127-30.

Long, Charles H. *Alpha: The Myths of Creation.* New York: Collier Books, 1963.

Lilla, Salvatore R.C. *Clement of Alexandria: A Study in Christian Platonism and Gnosticism.* London: Oxford University Press, 1971.

Majumdar, R.C. "Evolution of Religio-Philosophic Culture in India," *The Cultural Heritage of India.* 4 vols. Calcutta: The Ramakrishna Mission Institute of Culture, 1937-56. Vol. 4: The Religions, pp. 31-62.

Maloney, George A., S.J. *Man, The Divine Icon: The Patristic Doctrine of Man Made according to the Image of God.* Pecos, N.M.: Dove Publications, 1973.

Matus, Thomas. "The Christian Use of Yoga: A Theoretical Study Based on a Comparison of the Mystical Experience of Symeon the New Theologian with Some Tantric Sources".

Ph.D. dissertation, Fordham University, 1977.

Monier-Williams, M. *A Sanskrit-English Dictionary*. Oxford University Press, 1899. Reprint Delhi: Motilal Banarsidass, 1970.

Pagliaro, Antonino, and Bausani, Alessandro. *Storia della Letterature Persiana*. "La Quartina," pp. 527-78. Milano: Nuova Accademia Editrice, 1960.

Pandey, Kanti Chandra. *Abhinavagupta: An Historical and Philosophical Study*. 2nd rev. ed. Varanasi: Chowkhamba Sanskrit Series Office, vol. 1, 1963.

Pereira, José. "Epiphanies of Revelation." *Thought* 51:201 (June 1976), pp. 185-204.

———. *Hindu Theology: A Reader*. Edited with an Introduction and Notes by José Pereira. Garden City, N.Y.: Doubleday Image Books, 1976.

Pratyagatmananda, Swami. "Tantra as a Way of Realization." *The Cultural Heritage of India*. 4 vols. Calcutta: The Ramakrishna Mission Institute of Culture, 1937-56. Vol. 4: *The Religions*, pp. 227-40.

Rangacharya, V. "Historical Evolution of *Śrī-Vaiṣṇavism* in South India." 4 vols. Calcutta: the Ramakrishna Mission Institute of Culture, 1937-56. Vol. 4: *The Religions*, pp. 163-85.

Rudrappa, J. *Kashmir Śaivism*. Prasaranga, Mysore: University of Mysore, 1969.

Sastri, K.A. Nilakanta. "An Historical Sketch of Śaivism." *The Cultural Heritage of India*. 4 vols. Calcutta: The Ramakrishna Mission Institute of Culture, 1937-56. Vol. 4: *The Religions*, pp. 63-78.

Shah, Idries. *The Sufis*. Introduction by Robert Graves. New York: Anchor Books, 1971.

Sharma, Lakshmi Nidhi. *Kashmir Śaivism*. Varanasi: Bharatiya Vidya Prakashan, 1972.

Silburn, Lilian. *La Bhakti: Le Stavacintāmaṇi de Bhaṭṭanārāyaṇa*. Texte traduit et commenté par Lilian Silburn. Institut de Civilisation Indienne. Fasc. 19. Paris: Boccard, 1964.

Sinha, Jadunath. "Bhagavata Religion: The Cult of Bhakti." *The Cultural Heritage of India*. 4 vols. Calcutta: The Ramakrishna Mission Institute of Culture, 1937-56. Vol. 4: The Religions, pp. 146-59.

Temple, Richard Carnac, Sir. *The Word of Lallā the Prophetess.* Cambridge, England: the University Press, 1924.

Tikku, Girdhari L. "Mysticism in Kashmir: In the Fourteenth and Fifteenth Centuries." *The Muslim World* 53:3 (July 1963): 226-33.

———. *Persian Poetry in Kashmir,* 1339-1846: *An Introduction.* Berkeley, Los Angeles, London: University of California Press, 1971.

Tollington, R.B. *Clement of Alexandria.* 2 vols. London: Williams and Norgate, 1914. Vols. 2: *Clemens, Titus Flavins, Alexandrinus.*

Walsh, Eugene Aloysius, Reverend. *The Priesthood in the Writings of the French School*: Bérulle, de Condren, Olier. Washington, D.C.: The Catholic University of America Press, 1949.

Walter, Howard Arnold. "Islam in Kashmir." *The Muslim World* 4:4 (October 1914): 340-52.

Wolfson, Harry Austryn. *The Philosophy of the Church Fathers.* Vol. 1. Third rev. ed., Cambridge: Harvard University Press, 1970.

Woodroffe, John, Sir. [Avalon, Arthur] *The Serpent Power: Being the Ṣaṭ-Cakra-Nirūpaṇa and Pādukā-Pañcaka.* 7th ed. Two works on Laya-Yoga translated from the Sanskrit, with introduction and commentary by Sir John Woodroffe (Arthur Avalon). Madras: Ganesh & Co., 1964.

Zaehner, R.C. *Hindu and Muslim Mysticism.* New York: Schocken Books, 1969.

INDEX OF NAMES

Note: In order to render these indices less cumbersome and to minimize confusion, the following procedure is followed. All entries are delineated according to the English alphabet; subject listings are to be interpreted in a mystical or theological sense unless otherwise noted; the letter *n* following a page reference indicates a content footnote in which information is supplied other than or in addition to the specific citation (s).

Abhinavagupta,
  ancestors of, 2-3, 12
  life and influence of, viii-ix, 3, 9-12, 13n-14n, 15, 80-81, 83
  teachers of, 6n, 7-8, 9n
  theological views on
    Beatific Vision, 170
    Devotionalism, 80, 83, 85n, 96, 98
    Mirific Power, 113
    sacrifice, 125, 128, 130n, 131-34
    Ways to Liberation,
      Divine Way, 31n, 63n-64n, 65, 142n
      Energic Way, 31n, 49, 51, 52n-53n, 54-60, 160n, 161
      Individual Way, 31n-32n, 33, 36n-37n, 38, 40-41
      Null Way, 68, 69n, 70-71, 72n-74n, 75-76
  writings of, viii, 4-5, 6n, 7-8, 9n, 12, 13n-14n, 15, 23n, 41n, 42

Al-Ghazzālī, Abū Ḥāmid, 81-82, 90
Al-Ghazzālī, Ahmed, 82
Amardaka, 2
Amiot, François, 123n, 140
Amelote, Denis, 120, 124-25
Ānandavardhana, 14
Aquinas, St. Thomas, 80, 113
Arberry, A.J., 82
Ardha Tryambaka, 5
Aśoka, 3
Atrigupta, 2-3, 12
Avalon, Arthur, 35n, 45n-48n

Bamzai, P.N.K., 83
Barnett, Lionel D., 26n, 29, 33, 45, 65, 74-76, 88, 141, 153n, 158n
Barua, Benimadab, 175
Basava, 16
Bausani, Alessandro, 86
Bernard of Clairvaux, St., 117
Bharata, 14
Bharati, Agehananda, 51, 56n, 58n-59n
Bigg, Charles, 164
Bourgoing, François, 120, 124,
Bremond, Henri, 118n-19n, 120, 122-25, 127, 133n, 137-43
Buddha, 3
Bulbul Shāh, Sharaf ud-Dīn, 83

Cefalu, Richard F., 132, 134
Clement of Alexandria, x, 163n-64n, 165-68
Cukhulaka (Narasiṁhagupta), 12

Das Gupta, Shashi Bhusan, 34, 45
de Bary, William Theodore, 62n
de Bérulle, Pierre, ix, 118-20, 122-24, 126, 138-41, 143
de Condren, Charles du Bois, ix, 118, 119n-20n, 124-28, 130-32, 133n, 134-37, 138n, 141-43
Dēd (Lallā), 85
Dionysius, St., 154
Dīpikānātha, 6n
Donaldson, J., 164n
Duns Scotus, John, 80

Eliade, Mircea, 36-38, 39n-40n, 45, 46n-47n, 58
Eraka, 7
Eudes, St., Jean, 120, 122

Gairdner, W.H.T., 81
Ghaṭakarpara, 13n
Ghosh, Atal Behari, 48, 56n
Gnoli, Raniero, 36n
Gorakṣa (Maheśvarānanda), 10-11, 60n, 63, 68-69
Grierson, George, 45

Hakuin, 72
Hamadānī, Mīr Sayyid 'Alī, 83, 85
Harṣa, 2-3
Heiler, Friedrich, 181

INDEX OF SUBJECTS

Reality, 91
Śambhu, 87, 105
Self-luminosity, 112
-without-second, 91
self-obscuration, 20-22
Śiva-the-Ascetic, 88
-the-Beneficent, 87
-union,f93, 100, 103-7, 161
-without-second, 133
Śivahood, 138
Supreme, 100, 102, 169
Ascetic, 88
Consciousness, 86
Light, 97, 156n
Lord, 87, 128
Person, 88
Self, 95
Śiva, vii, 15, 86
Spirit, see also *Bhairava*, *Lord*, 121
Three Triads or Powers, 4
Tranquilizer, 87
Transcendent Beyond the Categories, vii, 138
Trans-universal, 20, 112
Tremendous God, see *Tremendous God*; *Tremendous State*
Truth, 105
Ultimate, 7, 146
Being, 175
Principle, vii, 5
Reality, viii, 7, 21, 29-30, 86, 128, 172
Undifferentiated, 17, 20, 25, 41, 96
Consciousness, vii, 43, 76, 98, 111
Light, 169
Reality, or Unity, 15, 25, 113
Unicity, 113, 169
Unmanifested Absolute, x
Skull, 88
Sky, 100
Slave, see *Servant*
Sleep, mystical and vigilant, 97n, 108
Son of God, see also *Jesus Christ*, 122n
mysteries of, 120
Soul of the mystic,
Catholic, 111-12, 114-20, 122-25, 143-51, 152n-53n, 154-66
Hindu, 120-21
Islamic, 95-96
Triadic, 96-97, 103-5, 106n, 111-12, 117-18, 145-48, 150, 152n-53n, 155n-58, 159, 162-63, 166
Sovereignty of God, see *God*
Spanda, see *Vibration School*
Spirit, of the God of
Christianity, 143
of the Triadic mystic, 97
Spirits, good and evil, 181
Spiritual, awakening of the soul, see also *Dark Night*; *Metanoia*, 144
darkness, 96-100, 107-8, 111, 113-16, 118, 129, 145-50, 152, 153n, 154-55, 156n, 160-61
death, 105, 108, 124-25
desire, 104-6
exercises, 149-50
suffering, 101-2, 105, 181
Sport of bondage and release, 75
Stages of mystical life, 104-5
States of Consciousness, 42-43
Stromata, see *Clement of Alexandria*
Ṣūfīsm (Muslim mysticism), ix, 79-86, 93, 95n, 103n, 113
Sun, 96, 100
Supernatural Gifts of God, 175-76
Symbolism, see *Imagery*

Tantra, 2n, 5, 10, 12, 13n, 14
Tantric Formulas, 37-38
Tantrism, Buddhist, 59n
Hindu, 3n, 45-47, 56n, 59n
Temple of the divinized soul, see also *Ways to Liberation: Null Way*, 76
Temptations, 150
Theocentrism of the French School, 119-20, 122-25
Thought, 60, 99, 159-60
Thrust of the heart toward Śiva, 89n
Tomb, 98
Torch, of Illumination, 107
of Unity, 98
Tranquility, 111
Transcendence, of the divine, see *Divine Transcendence*; *God*; *Śiva*, 139, 178-81
of the mystic, 91, 110-12, 172
Transmigration, 91, 107
Tremendous, Consciousness, 89, 108
God, 25-26, 56-60, 62, 68, 75-76, 86-89, 95, 111, 118, 129, 141
Goddess, 58-59
State, see also *Bhairava*, *State of*; *Liberated-in-Life*, 42-44, 56-58, 64, 70-73, 88-89, 131, 142, 162, 169
Triadic, language, 141, 176
mystic, 117, 165
mysticism, see also *Mysticism*, vii, 76, 164
philosophy, 86
Śaivism, see *Triadism*
theology, 64-65, 70, 111, 123, 138-39, 163-64, 169-72
thought, 79, 138-39, 171, 178
Triadism
History of, see also *Abhinavagupta*
Devotionalism, 80-81, 84-88
early propagators of, 4-11